Here Lilwall sets off on ano
This cracking story is the perfe
library of adventure books.
Compass Magazine

The book serves as an engrossing window into the nascent
colossus that is China . . . where much that's written about
the country is concerned with the big picture, this
worm's-eye view is fascinating.
The Metro

It chronicles comedic run-ins, police interrogations, partying
with nomads, encounters with cave dwellers and casual
brushes with villagers in China.
Time Out HK

An honest, and often heart-warming, meditation on the
physical and mental hardships of extreme endurance, and
the rapidly changing landscapes of rural China.
Time Out Bejing

It should dispel at least a few stereotypes for most
people . . . readable, interesting and funny.
Adventure Travel

I can honestly say Rob's book has inspired me . . . time
to fire up Google, look at some maps and get
the notebook out.
Halfway Hike

Also by Rob Lilwall

Cycling Home From Siberia

Rob Lilwall

Walking Home From Mongolia

Ten million steps through China
from the Gobi Desert to the South China Sea

HODDER

First published in Great Britain in 2013 by Hodder & Stoughton
An Hachette UK company

This paperback edition first published in 2014

A CIP catalogue record for this title is
available from the British Library

ISBN 978 1 444 74530 6
eBook ISBN 978 1 444 74529 0

Typeset in Sabon MT by
Palimpsest Book Production Ltd, Falkirk, Stirlingshire

Printed and bound in the UK by CPI Group (UK) Ltd, Croydon CR0 4YY

Hodder & Stoughton policy is to use papers that are natural, renewable
and recyclable products and made from wood grown in sustainable
forests. The logging and manufacturing processes are expected to
conform to the environmental regulations of the country of origin.

Hodder & Stoughton Ltd
338 Euston Road
London NW1 3BH

www.hodder.co.uk

Contents

千里之行，始于足下

A journey of a thousand miles begins with a single step.

For Mum and Dad
Thank you for the home you gave me.

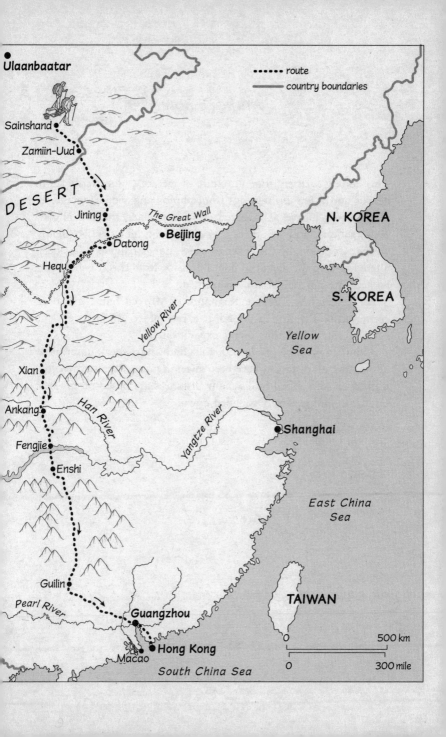

Author's note

This book is written from a mixture of memory, notes scribbled in diaries and a few promptings from photos and video footage. In some places I have abbreviated or reconstructed the wording of conversations, and in others I have probably got details slightly wrong. Occasionally the order in which things happened has been altered to help the narrative flow. But aside from this, I believe it is an accurate portrait of what happened.

For prices, the Chinese Renminbi (RMB) currency has been converted to the British pound at a rate of 10 RMB to £1 (the rounded rate at the time of the expedition).

Although most people in Mongolia and China speak in terms of kilometres, all distances have been given in miles. Because we often walked on unmapped trails, many distances are based on my best estimates, and generally rounded down.

Preface: The danger of atlases

Winter was at hand and the Siberian snows were beginning to scatter their way south into Mongolia when Leon McCarron and I set out to walk from the Gobi Desert to Hong Kong. Initially, we had intended to start in late summer, or at least early autumn, but preparations had spiralled out of control and we ended up taking our first steps into the desert in mid-November.

This was my second major expedition, and in many ways it was connected to the first. That journey had begun seven years previously when, aged twenty-seven, I packed in my job as a geography teacher in order to ride across the world on my bicycle. Rather than starting from England, I had flown just about as far away from home as I could think of – to northeast Russia – and then spent the next three years cycling back again. I called the trip 'Cycling Home From Siberia', and it became a rite-of-passage adventure, taking me through countries as far-flung as Japan and Papua New Guinea, Australia and Afghanistan. Before I got back to London, I had been robbed at gunpoint, struck down by malaria and knocked over by cars. However, it was the positive experiences that deeply affected me, especially the hospitable people from dozens of cultures whom I met as I travelled. And, best of all, while I was stuck in Hong Kong trying to hitch a boat ride across the South China Sea, I got to know a beautiful Chinese girl called Christine.

When I eventually got home I found my life would not continue where I left off. Rather than returning to teaching as I had planned, I ended up writing a book and giving lectures about the trip, and a TV network picked up my self-filmed video footage and made a series. Christine, meanwhile, was now working in London. Eighteen months after my return home, I proposed to her over a game of Scrabble in Kew Gardens.

Once we were married, we decided to move to Hong Kong, the city where we had first met – Christine's home, and now my new home. We settled into a flat on a leafy outlying island, a half-hour ferry ride from the skyscrapers. We had volunteered to set up a fundraising office for a children's charity we really believed in called Viva, and I continued to pay the bills through freelance speaking and writing work.

Life was going well. Yet, at the same time, I was getting itchy feet once more. A feeling deep inside was urging me to embark on a new expedition, something long and tough, that would test me to my limits all over again. I started casually browsing maps and atlases – always a dangerous activity – and before long I became fixated on the idea of a big trip through Mainland China.* I had loved the stretches of my bike ride that passed through the eastern and southern parts of the country. Now I was dreaming of exploring China's interior, with its lonely deserts, wild mountains and magnificent rivers. And there is much more to China than just its physical geography. It is the oldest continuous civilisation in history with the Great Wall and multitudes of other extraordinary historical sites. In recent decades, China has risen to prominence on the world stage, and now pundits proclaim that it will not be long before China rules the world. To top it off, my wife is Chinese. I wanted to get to know her, and Hong Kong's, motherland better.

But if I was going to explore China, how should I do it? After being asked at almost every dinner party since the cycling trip, 'How many punctures did you get?', I felt it was time to try a new, more challenging mode of transport. And so the idea of a walk started to ferment in my mind. Walking would be much slower, and

* Hong Kong is a part of China, but distinct from the mainland, culturally, economically and politically. It has its own currency, its own border crossings, and is known as a Special Administrative Region because it is governed under different rules.

physically harder, especially because I would have to carry all my heavy gear. But travelling on one's own two feet was also the most ancient means of transport – the way that the majority of people through history had encountered their world.

I mulled on possible routes, and began to think that traversing China on its vertical axis would be more interesting than going across its horizontal one: it would take in greater historical and scenic diversity. I also wanted to stay away from China's booming coastline, and instead journey inland, far from where most foreigners visited. I would pass through its core, at ground level, and see how China changed from top to bottom.

Then, as I lay in bed one night, the whole shebang came together in a single thought: 'Walking Home From Mongolia'. I was suddenly wide awake. I would start in the Gobi, and walk back to Hong Kong. It would be a long way – roughly the equivalent to walking from London to Kazakhstan, or from Los Angeles to New York. My mind started to fill with images of striding across windy deserts, climbing over misty hillsides, and camping in jade-green terraced fields; of braving epic storms, jumping in tranquil rivers, and meeting smiling people. The expedition took a hold of my mind. And, once that had happened, I could not shake it off.

I broached the idea with Christine during a walk up our local mountain. She listened quietly and, when I finished, we stopped walking and looked out across the bay. A ferry was chugging in towards the terminal, and tropical clouds filled the sky above the South China Sea.

'How long would it take?' she said, following my gaze, then glancing up at my face.

'Three to four months, I think.' I hoped. 'But I will only do it if you agree.' While cycling home from Siberia I'd been footloose and fancy-free, accountable to no one, and able to choose my route, my timing, my style. But I was no longer young and unmarried. This time I would need Christine's blessing.

'Hopefully, building on the profile from the last trip,' I continued, 'I can also get a TV network and sponsors to back it.' I knew I could not justify such a long trip purely for the fun of it. So I also had aspirations to film the expedition and do some freelance writing as I went. This would help cover the costs, and give it a professional rationale too.

Christine was quiet. 'I guess I am open to it,' she said eventually. She knew that I loved going on these crazy expeditions, yet as her eyes held mine for a moment, I saw she was frightened. We knew that she would not want to come with me because, although she liked a challenge (two years previously she had left a promising legal career to work in the charity sector), she enjoyed neither pain nor going for days without a shower, both of which would make up the bread and butter of the journey.

'We can use it to raise money for Viva,' I added. 'I think it will be a great platform for the charity.' I also hoped she could fly out to meet me two or three times, when I was taking some days off. We would thus not be entirely apart.

Christine looked vulnerable, bracing herself for the storms to come. It would be hard for both of us. 'OK,' she said, 'if this is what you really want to do.'

I've seen grown men reduced to little boys as their wives dismiss their deepest dreams as immature nonsense, but here was my wife giving me her permission, knowing the sacrifice. My mind swirled with gratitude and excitement. I could not believe that I was going to try and walk, quite literally, the length of China.

Part One

Into the Gobi

Хүний эрхээр зовохоор өөрийн эрхээр жарга

Better to suffer in liberty than delight in captivity.

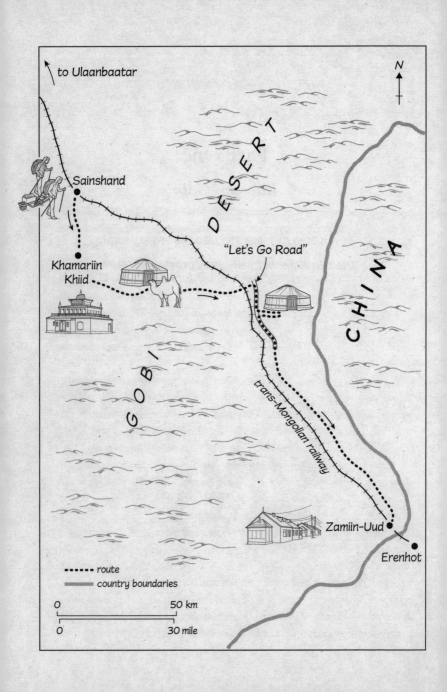

I

Start line in the emptiness

Distance to home: 3,000 miles

14 NOVEMBER

Standing outside the rundown hotel under a crisp blue sky, I fumble to attach the four ropes and carabiners to my rucksack. Then I hoist it onto my back, pick up my brand new walking poles and hurriedly put my gloves on. The air is cold, and the world is silent. Taking my first step, the ropes jerk taut and the steel trailer to which I am attached starts to roll along behind me. The wheels start to squeak. Molly Brown is loaded with 100 kilograms' worth of camping gear, camera equipment, food and water supplies. The harness lines tug at my waist and I step off the pavement, onto the road, and the wheels bump down behind me.

I look round. My expedition partner and cameraman, Leon, walks past, also wearing a rucksack, but without a trailer. We will be taking turns to pull Molly Brown, and I am going first. Leon holds a camera in his right hand and I let him stride ahead for a few metres until he stops and turns to film. I start moving again.

We are on the main street of Sainshand, a small town in Southern Mongolia in the middle of the Gobi Desert. This little town is our starting point, and my home in Hong Kong is over 3,000 miles' walk away to our south. Today is day one.

Like most towns in Mongolia, Sainshand bears the marks of a nation that was a Soviet puppet for much of the twentieth century. Both sides of the street are lined with unimaginative apartment blocks. They have now been repainted in garish colours, yet the uniform, communist windows still stare out at us, bitter and disinterested. A large grey chimney spouts black smoke into the dry, frozen air. The cracks of land between every building are filled with brown Gobi dust. We still cannot see the open desert because Sainshand is surrounded by a small ridge, and the first hour of the expedition will be spent walking to get beyond it.

A handful of Mongolians wrapped in thick coats and scarves walk past. Their rugged, serious faces break into bemused smiles as they look at me pulling Molly. Cars slow a little to chug alongside us, with their drivers and passengers also staring. I feel strangely detached from the world. I cannot believe that we are finally setting off. I have no idea of what lies ahead – what places we will see, what people we will meet, what adventures we will have.

Reaching a red traffic light, I stop and wait beside the line of cars. A couple of middle-aged ladies start crossing the road and, when I look up at them, they giggle. I smile back, sheepishly. I feel like a pantomime horse-drawn carriage, with me as the horse. As the lights turn green, most of the cars go straight on. But Leon and I turn left, south, out of town, towards the emptiness.

The road surface, still asphalt, curves through a gentle depression before climbing to an opening in the ridge. We pass a few wooden shacks and walled compounds on the outskirts of town. I am getting into my stride and, as I lean into the harness, Molly rolls forward and lurches back again with each step. My boots feel comfortable yet unfamiliar, and I hope I have worn them in enough. The cold sun is blazing above us, and the only sounds are the continued squeaking of Molly's wheels, and the clink, clink, clink of my poles on the tarmac.

As the road starts to tilt gently uphill, I gasp at the effort of pulling Molly. The frozen air cuts my lungs. It is only 14 November, hardly deepest winter, yet it is −10°C. This is warm compared to what we are expecting in the months to come.

Leon, who has been hanging back to do some extra filming, catches up, and a few minutes later we reach the gap in the ridge. We stop together and look out onto the Gobi Desert. It is a titanic plain of brown dust and gravel, as wide and long as an ocean, rumbling brazenly away from us in all directions. I can just make out a faint line of hills and ridges running along the horizon, beyond which the whole world melts into nothingness.

I shake my head. 'Crumbs, that looks big. Do you feel like walking across it?'

'We might as well, now we're here,' Leon says in his Northern Irish accent, smiling. He has floppy brown hair and a youthful, freshly shaven face. At twenty-five, he is nine years younger than me. He puts his poles down, and starts to set up the tripod.

I find it hard to grasp how far this land stretches and how long it will take us to walk across it. A week ago, on our flight to the Mongolian capital of Ulaanbaatar, I had looked down on the ruffled plains and worked out that for every minute it was taking us to cross the desert in a plane, it would take us half a day of marching.

I see, however, that in the foreground it is not entirely empty. The asphalt road continues southwest, but now we will be bearing away from it, southeast, on one of the dusty jeep tracks that scythes across the plain. I hold up my compass and confirm that the most prominent jeep track is heading in roughly the right direction. I also see that half a mile down this track there is a white felt tent – a nomad's ger.* It stands alone, defiant, as if it were the final outpost of civilisation.

Leon is still stooped over his camera. I wait until he has finished shooting a wide panning shot.

'Shall we go?' I say.

'I'm going to do some more filming, you go ahead.'

Silence hangs in the air for a moment. So this is it, our start line in the emptiness. After the months of hectic planning, there is nothing else to say, no more waiting, no more preparing. I take a deep breath and lean forward in the harness. Molly's wheels start rolling. We bump off the asphalt and onto the brown earth. The journey of ten million steps has begun.

---

* Known as a yurt in Central Asia.

2
The ger

Distance to home: 2,997 miles

14 NOVEMBER

Molly's wheels scratched the gravel behind me as I took my first slow paces into the desert. Although the Gobi was a bleak and hostile environment, I now saw that its floor was covered in patchy clumps of dry grass, and in the distance I caught sight of some large brown animals. Perhaps they belonged to the lone *ger* up ahead.

As I drew slowly nearer, a man emerged from inside, climbed on a motorbike and started to bounce through the dust in my direction. He crunched to a halt beside me. He was about thirty, with a faint beard, and a face that, to my unaccustomed eye, reminded me of Genghis Khan.* He was wearing a long green robe tied with an orange sash around his waist, and on his head he wore a red baseball cap, on top of which was perched a lopsided yellow builder's hat.

I smiled, and nodded my head. 'Hi,' I said.

He squinted at Molly, and looked me up and down. I was wearing a synthetic windproof coat and trousers from Hong Kong, a cheap pair of sunglasses, and a Mongolian rabbit fur hat from a market in Ulaanbaatar.

'*Ger, ger*,' he shouted above the noise of his engine. Then pointing to the *ger*, '*Jid, jid.*'

I concluded that he was inviting me to his *ger*, though I was not entirely sure.

'Thank you, I'll come in just a few minutes,' I said in English, gesturing to Molly.

---

* Chinggis Khan is more phonetically accurate, but throughout this book the more familiar Genghis will be used.

The man grunted and flicked his head, before revving his bike and driving towards Leon, who was walking two hundred metres behind me. Just before I reached the *ger*, the bike overtook me again. I saw the man waving at me to hurry up before disappearing through the *ger*'s low doorway.

'I think this guy is inviting us for a cup of tea,' I said, as Leon caught up.

'Yeah, that's what I thought too. I know we were hoping for some Gobi hospitality, but I wasn't expecting it so soon.'

I unclipped myself from Molly and lowered her to the ground. The greyish-white tent was perfectly round, two and a half metres high, and six metres wide. It did not seem to have ropes holding it up, but the whole structure must have been very stable – the Gobi is famed for powerful storms that, according to old travellers' tales, can rip a tent to pieces. A small crowd of white chickens pecked the earth around the entrance as Leon and I ducked inside.

We found ourselves in a warm, cosy, circular space, which smelled faintly of sweet milk. I pushed my sunglasses onto my head and my eyes adjusted to the light. Cluttered around the edges were several beds, tables and chests, all painted with colourful, angular shapes. Wooden staves weaved in zigzags up the walls and met in the middle of the roof, where the chimney, running up from the central stove, exited. Beside the stove sat a bucket of dry dung. A middle-aged couple were sitting to one side, watching a Mongolian soap opera on an old colour television.

The motorbike man gestured us to a bench, and as we sat down he slopped two cups of lukewarm tea on the table.

He sat down beside us. 'My name is Sahana,' he said, pointing to himself. He pointed at us and said, 'My name is?'

'My name is Rob,' 'My name is Leon,' we said.

'Rob . . . Leon,' repeated Sahana. Then he said, 'Hourse, hourse.'

'Yes, horses,' I said, assuming the animals I had spotted in the distance were Sahana's horses. 'How many do you have?' I started counting on my fingers.

Sahana did not understand, but said 'Yes, yes, hourse,' and pointed to the floor.

Perhaps he was saying that this *ger* was his house? Making conversation over our cups of tea was proving a little tricky. As the majority of the journey before us would be in China, we had concentrated on learning Mandarin beforehand. The only Mongolian word we knew was *biacla* (thank you). But we did have a letter translated into Mongolian that explained our journey. I had often used such letters on previous expeditions – I called them my 'magic letters', because once people understood what I was doing, they usually became less suspicious and more likely to help.

I dug out the letter and handed it to Sahana. He snatched it, looked at it briefly, and set it on the table. Perhaps he could not read, or perhaps he preferred talking. I pulled out a photocopy of a map and tried again to explain our plan.

'We are walking to Zamiin-Uud,' I said, wiggling my index and middle fingers in a walking movement. Zamiin-Uud was the border town with China, about 150 miles, or two weeks' walk south from here. I tried to indicate it on the map.

'Zamiin-Uud, ummh.' Sahana nodded. He looked across at Leon, who was pointing the camera at us.

'Is it OK to film you?' Leon asked.

'No, no,' Sahana said, shaking his head and waving for Leon to put the camera away. Leon lowered the camera. The lady who had been sitting watching us stood up and changed the TV channel.

We looked at the map again, and with my finger I traced the route we planned to take. After the Mongolian border we would be crossing into China, but this did not mean the end of the Gobi, for the desert continued south into Chinese territory for almost another month of walking. Eventually, we would breach the Great Wall and definitively enter what has sometimes been referred to as 'the core' of China – the heartland of its ancient civilisation. Then we would veer west, along the Great Wall for a while, before turning south once more and following the heavy torrent of the Yellow River towards the old capital of Xian. From here, we were heading due south all the way – through Southern China's uncountable lines of mountains, valleys, cities, forests and fields – until we reached the sea and Hong Kong. I was now expecting the journey to take us about five months.

This was a bit of a mouthful, so I simply said, 'Through China.'

'China!' Sahana scowled and shook his head. He seemed agitated, and started to make a throat slitting gesture.

'Throat slitting,' I said, turning to Leon. 'Is that what this guy would like to do to the Chinese, or what he thinks the Chinese will do to us?'

'I'm not sure,' said Leon, 'perhaps both?'

Sahana, seeing I did not fully understand, suddenly leaned across the table and grabbed my neck, his strong fingers tightening around my throat. I spluttered and nodded in a panic, 'Yes, OK, you do not like China.'

The rugged Mongol nomads of the grassy steppe* and arid desert differed deeply from the settled agriculturalists of China, the Middle Kingdom, and had been enemies down through the ages. Both disdained the other's way of life. The silk- and poetry-loving Chinese had viewed the nomads as uncivilised, illiterate barbarians, half-men, half-beasts, who wrestled, drank fermented mares' milk and sang throatily. The nomads had considered the Chinese to be rich, oppressive tax collectors and used their swift, superior skills in horsemanship to raid and pillage their enemies' land on a regular basis, sometimes with astounding success. However, in the 1600s, China had annexed Mongolia as its own territory for several centuries, and perhaps it was about this that Sahana was still bitter.

As if reading my mind, Sahana suddenly said, 'Genghis,' with his thumbs up. Then he said 'China' and leaned towards my throat once more.

From the moment we had landed in Ulaanbaatar the previous week, we realised that Genghis Khan, the greatest pillager of all, was something of a national hero. The capital's airport was named after him and there was a grand statue of him against the Parliament building. Vodka brands and banknotes alike bore his image.

'Ah, I see,' I said, nodding and pulling back. 'You like Genghis, and you like the way he went and conquered China.'

---

* Steppe is the name given to an eco-region of grassy plains found across Central and Northern Asia.

Although Sahana had been kind to invite us into his *ger*, the more time we spent with him, the more he seemed to resemble Genghis: he looked like Genghis, he liked Genghis, and grabbing me by the throat was just the sort of thing Genghis might have done. Genetic studies have shown that 0.2 per cent of the world's population, and 10 per cent of Mongolians are Genghis's living descendants. Perhaps it was a reasonable hypothesis that friendly but gruff Sahana, who kept grabbing my throat, was one of them.

Sahana's behaviour was becoming increasingly erratic the more we talked, and I started to wonder if he had been drinking. He growled at me, staring intensely. Then he started making a howling noise, followed by more throat-slitting gestures.

'Ah, wolves!' I said. 'Well, we have our poles.' I gestured that we would fight them off. I knew that although there were a few wolves, and even snow leopards and bears in the Gobi, the chances of seeing any of these creatures, let alone being eaten by them, were distinctly remote.

Sahana was unimpressed, and shook his head at me again with a mutter. It felt like time to leave.

'We should get going,' I said to Leon.

He nodded.

We said '*biacla*', grabbed the magic letter and stood up. Sahana followed us outside. As I reattached myself to Molly, he pointed south.

'Khamariin Khiid,' he said, emphasising the kh sound like a cough, his face relaxing slightly.

Khamariin Khiid was a Buddhist monastery in the middle of the desert. We were hoping to reach it in about three days' time to fill up our water bottles. Sahana's pointing seemed to confirm that the jeep tracks we had chosen were going in the right direction. By this, at least, we were reassured.

We shook Sahana's hand, said '*biacla*' a few more times and started walking away. He stood watching us leave, until a few minutes later I looked over my shoulder and his *ger* was just a small white shape, blurring into the vast expanse that had now become our home.

3
The first night

Distance to home: 2,996 miles

14 NOVEMBER

It was already mid-afternoon, and the white sun had started its trajectory towards the western horizon.

'What did you make of that?' said Leon. He was walking alongside me, planting his poles firmly in the gravel with each pace. He looked determined but relaxed.

'I'm not quite sure,' I said. 'It was a bit of a shock when he kept grabbing my throat.' We laughed nervously.

In my past travels, I had been fortunate enough to be invited in for tea by strangers all over the world. But if I was honest, Sahana's fierce manner had alarmed me. In Hong Kong I had met up with a man who had driven through Mongolia the previous year. While he was in the desert outside Sainshand taking photos, two drunk Mongolians on a motorbike had tried to mug him with a knife, though luckily he had been able to escape unharmed. I recounted this to Leon, and suddenly we were suffering from first-day jitters.

'I think it might be a good idea to keep out of sight when we camp tonight,' I said. 'The whole of Sainshand must have seen us leaving town, and we might be a bit of a tempting target with our big cameras.

At that moment, we saw a motorbike streaking along a parallel dusty track. We breathed a sigh of relief when it passed without stopping.

'We should try and make it to that next ridge,' said Leon. 'We'll be less conspicuous there.' Up ahead, the second small ridge was slowly becoming more defined and we could just make out where our jeep track cut through it.

We had been walking for two hours since leaving the town centre, and it was Leon's turn with Molly. I unshackled my rucksack, he shackled on his, and the three of us rolled off again. A column of telegraph poles ran through the desert ahead of us, and a few jeeps blazed across the skyline.

The sun disappeared in a flare of orange as we reached the ridge, and I got behind Molly and helped push her up the steep incline. By the time we reached the top it was dark, so we turned on our head torches as we skirted sideways until we found a clear patch of land. The temperature, meanwhile, had dropped into the minus teens. We threw on some extra clothes and stamped our feet to warm up, then pulled out our two little tents and pitched our first camp. I climbed into my tent and sleeping bag, and leaned outside to light the petrol stove – I was taking first turn with cooking duty. The flame burst upwards for a moment before stabilising. I put on our single pot to heat, and poured in water, instant noodles and tinned beef. Twenty minutes later, with the concoction boiling, I slopped half into the lid of the pan, which acted as our second bowl, and passed it across to Leon's tent. 'Dinner is served,' I said.

'Thank you,' said Leon, though his face betrayed a slight concern when he shone his head torch on the resultant mush. Leon was usually a vegetarian, but forced himself to eat meat when on expeditions. 'What is this stuff?' he said as he started eating.

'It's supposed to be beef, but I think it might actually be dog food,' I said.

'Better than dog meat, I guess.'

'Dog doesn't taste bad actually. It's certainly nicer than this.'

There was a brief but noticeable silence from Leon's tent before he continued eating.

I sat hunched in my sleeping bag, eating with my spoon. The feeling of being out here under the stars seemed strangely familiar, though it had been a good year and a half since I had last camped in the wild. At the same time, I felt exhausted, even though it was just 7 p.m., and we had only covered ten miles today – about 0.3 per cent of the way home. After I finished eating, I pulled out my diary and started to scribble.

Well, we have set off. Finally. Me pulling Molly. It's quite hard work – I think we are in for some sore muscles. This is going to be such a hard expedition – mainly because it is in winter. It is so far, so very far, to get home.

I found it hard to believe that just a few days ago we had been running between last-minute meetings like headless chickens in balmy Hong Kong. In fact, it felt as though I had been running around like a headless chicken for the past four months.

Almost a year previously, after getting the go-ahead from Christine, I had waded into the intimidating world of TV networks, and started trying to persuade someone to back the trip. There was some interest, but I was naïve in my approach, and the negotiations became both protracted and complicated. It was eight months before a network said yes, by which time it was almost July. With this green light, Leon and I could at last launch into serious preparations, which would take another four months. But the amount of time it had taken to get to this point also meant that we had to abandon the initial idea of a summer–autumn journey. Instead, we set ourselves a start date of 1 November – the absolute latest if we were to stay ahead of the winter.

Leon was based in London and I was in Hong Kong, so we worked remotely on our numerous preparations: getting fit, learning Mandarin, building a website, finding sponsors for our gear, sorting out visas and flights, researching the route and, importantly, doing a practice trip.

The months passed quickly with a deluge of emails and meetings. Gradually some things came together, but at the same time, others began to unravel. During our fitness training, Leon struggled with a shoulder injury and I got sore knees; we built a website, but it kept malfunctioning, so we had to build another one; some companies generously came forward with sponsored gear but, at the eleventh hour, a couple of the key ones backed out. There were also delays with finalising the TV contract, and as the network outlined their strict filming requirements, we began to think that we might have bitten off more than we could chew.

In the end it had been two weeks after our 'absolute latest start date' that flustered, exhausted, and having had no time to do a practice expedition, we finally boarded a plane bound for Mongolia.

I put down my diary and rummaged around for my toothpaste. The tube was partially frozen, but I managed to squeeze some out; after brushing my teeth, I unzipped the tent door to spit. The moon was casting a pale glow over the desert, and I could see a few lights on the ridge of Sainshand, twinkling in the distance. Sitting alone in my tent, the Gobi wind blowing in my face, with the manic, stressful months of preparation now behind me, I had a long overdue moment of peace and quiet. The scale of what lay before us began to dawn on me. It was one thing to dream up fun trips from the comfort of home, another to actually embark on them. We were about to walk across one of the coldest deserts on earth, and then trek the length of the world's fourth biggest country. We were fairly fit, but we were not Ironman triathletes. We were supposed to film the walk for a major TV network. We did not have a support crew or back-up if something went wrong. We could easily get lost, injured, or in trouble with the Chinese police.

I shivered. I'd camped in the extreme cold before, but tonight's relatively warm −15°C felt colder than I remembered it. The infamous Gobi winter was already setting in. We were going to have to move fast to stay ahead of its plummeting temperatures.

4
Leon

Distance to home: 2,986 miles

15–16 NOVEMBER

'So which way do you think to Khamariin Khiid?' asked Leon.

It was the morning of day two, and we were standing at a jumble of jeep tracks that headed in almost every direction across the wide Gobi plain before us.

'I have no idea,' I said. 'How does it look on the maps?'

For navigation, we had bought some topographical maps in Ulaanbaatar, but these showed only a handful of the many jeep tracks. We had also cached some Google Maps satellite images on our iPhone, but these showed all the jeep tracks and it was impossible to figure out which was which, now we were here on the ground. There were several more prominent tracks, but many jeep drivers had evidently grasped the liberating idea that there was nothing to stop them blazing their own new trails, like ships at sea. We debated the matter for several minutes, nervous about the possibility of getting lost so soon. The white exhaust of a jet cut silently through the sky far above. I felt very small, standing alone with Leon in the middle of this vastness.

Thankfully, a moment later, a jeep appeared in a cloud of dust behind us. We waved it down, and Leon ran over to speak to the driver. The driver knew Khamariin Khiid and pointed confidently to the broad, right track. The jeep roared away, and we walked onwards. I had taken first turn with Molly again this morning, though it felt harder work than yesterday. This was partly because the novelty and adrenaline of day one were gone, and partly because the jeep tracks were often corrugated and bumpy, which made Molly and her heavy load rattle and jolt.

While preparing for the trip, some veteran explorers had impressed on us the need to take only the minimal gear, ten kilograms or less. However, this turned out to be an impossible aspiration, because firstly we needed a lot of warm camping gear and clothes for the winter, and secondly we had a whole load of camera and technology gear for the filming. Moreover, on the initial desert stage of the expedition, we would have to carry plenty of food and water. In the twelve days it would take to walk to the border town, we were hoping to partially resupply at the Khamariin Khiid monastery, as well as a hamlet we had spotted on the map, and possibly also at a few nomad camps. However, we did not know how often we might encounter the camps. We initially planned to carry five days' worth of supplies, but in the end decided to take eight:

- Instant noodles x 30 (4 packs a night)
- Tins of meat x 8 (1 tin a night)
- Tins of peas x 4 (1 tin every other night)
- Bags of biscuits x 8 (1 pack a day)
- Slabs of chocolate x 24 (3 bars a day)
- 1.5-litre bottles of water x 36 (7 litres a day, including cooking)
- Loo roll x 2 (one each)

Together with a few luxury items to keep our morale up (an iPod, Kindle and diary each), we had well over 100 kilograms of stuff, making this leg of the journey equivalent to dragging a very large human corpse across the desert, slowly eating it as we went.

This was too much weight to carry on our backs. During our preparations, therefore, we had considered ways of pushing or pulling the load on wheels. My first idea had been to buy a couple of rugged baby buggies.* Leon, on the other hand, had sought advice from the great desert explorer Ripley Davenport. As it happened, Ripley had walked across the Gobi the previous year,

---

* While cycling across the Nullarbor Plain in Australia, I had met a cheerful Japanese gap-year student employing this very method, his buggy loaded up with biscuits and water as he walked across the country.

dragging a trailer. He had named the trailer Molly Brown after the *Titanic* survivor Margaret Brown, who had urged her lifeboat to go back to look for more passengers still in the water. He had finished his expedition in Sainshand and left Molly behind when he flew home. 'Assuming you can find her,' Ripley had said to Leon, 'you can have her.'

Our train had arrived in Sainshand at night, and Ripley's friend, Nassa, had been on the platform waiting to meet us. Nassa had taken us back to her little house by taxi, and we had walked through the darkness to a shed at the bottom of her yard. And there, beneath a couple of old mattresses and a bicycle, Molly sat waiting for us. She was made from welded steel, with four solid wheels, and she seemed relieved to have been rescued from premature retirement. When we loaded her up, our heaviest items were our bottles of water. We stored these inside pairs of woollen tights, which in turn were packed into cardboard boxes, in the hope of stopping the water from freezing too quickly. We piled these boxes, plus the other bags of food and gear, onto her chassis and strapped them down with ropes. Molly would be a difficult companion to haul across the Gobi, but we needed her.

The chain of events that had led me to invite my other expedition companion, Leon, had begun two years previously, under very different circumstances. Christine and I had been in New York and, although I was not a regular Twitter sort of guy, I had posted a short tweet about how this was 'a city that actually makes me want to get up early'.

It happened that Leon was in town, working as a camera intern for a well-known documentary maker. He was planning to set off on his own bicycle ride across the world and, since meeting me briefly at an event in London, he had been following my irregular tweets. When he saw I was in New York, he emailed asking if we could meet for a coffee.

It did not take long to spot young Leon in the café on Park Avenue. As we sat down, he explained the route he hoped to ride through America, Australia and Southeast Asia, finishing in Hong

Kong a year later. Christine and I had recently decided to move back to Hong Kong, and as Leon seemed like a nice guy, we invited him to come and stay with us when he arrived.

A year later, in Hong Kong, I was beginning to talk with TV networks about making a programme based on my Mongolia trip. On my cycling expedition, I had simply filmed myself, but this time I wanted higher-quality footage. However, I still wanted a self-sufficient expedition, without a support crew driving along with me. So I needed someone who was good with a camera and able to walk 3,000 miles. Initially I asked my oldest adventuring friend, Al Humphreys. Although Al said yes at first, a few months later, just as the TV network started to get interested, he emailed to say that he could not come after all. I was rather stumped. I did not know anyone else who fitted the bill.

That very weekend, Leon arrived in Hong Kong, and Christine and I went to meet him on our village waterfront. In contrast to the fresh-faced youngster we had met in Manhattan, he now sported a magnificent Crusoe-esque beard, and straddled a bike loaded with panniers and 10,000-miles' worth of stories. He had made it, and from here he would fly home.

Sitting on our sofa drinking beer that night, I asked Leon why he had done his cycling adventure – a question I had been asked a thousand times myself, and had never been good at answering.

'When I left university,' he said, swigging from his bottle, 'I realised that I liked adventure, and I liked camerawork. So I decided to go cycling and film it along the way too. I thought it would be a great start to a career as an adventure cameraman.'

My ears pricked up.

'I've enjoyed this trip so much, and I really want to do something in China again soon. I'd also love to go to Mongolia – that place looks really cool.'

I had at this point not even mentioned the walk to Leon. But as I got to know him better in the next few days, I realised that behind his beard he was clearly intelligent (he had received a first-class degree in film studies), and he was good expedition material (his recent bicycle trip proved that). We also seemed to share a reasonably laid-back temperament. I felt we would get on well.

So the day before Leon had left Hong Kong, I had asked him to come on the walk with me as cameraman. I was not sure Leon would accept my proposition, but after he had flown home and discussed the idea with his long-suffering girlfriend Clare, he had emailed me to say he was in.

For the next two days we moved onwards across the plain at our maximum speed of two miles per hour and another ridge came slowly into sight. Just before we reached it, mounds of dung appeared on the track. They looked fresh, and a few hundred metres later, we spotted the owners: Bactrian camels. These huge brown beasts, with their single humps and implausible faces, were gathered around some kind of well. As we drew closer, one of them, presumably the chief, turned to face us. He was ten feet tall.

We stopped and Leon set up the tripod to film. 'Did you know that George Lucas actually based the planet Tatooinne on Mongolia,' he said. 'I keep thinking about it when I look out across the desert, and think of the *gers*, which look like Luke Skywalker's house. And look at these camels, they're just like aliens.'

'Yes, they do look quite alien-ish,' I said, squinting at the chief camel. He stared back at me. 'Shall we walk through them, it might make some nice filming.'

'I don't think that would be a good idea.'

At that moment, the chief started to stomp forwards, his huge shoulders hunched like a gladiator's. These camels were not completely wild, but they were untended, and it would not be an amusing experience to have them butt us to the ground and stamp on our heads. The other camels raised their necks and turned to see if we dared take on their lead fighter. We did not, and instead veered sharply around them. I tried not to look nervous as I talked to Leon's lens about the approaching beast before we hurriedly walked away from his turf.

An hour later, with Leon in the harness, we began to climb the next ridge. The terrain grew soft and steep, and we wound into a series of hillocks, surrounded by wave-like rocks streaked with reds and browns. Ascending onto a broader hill, we saw two short, wide pillars made from stone and concrete. A string of blue prayer flags fluttered in the wind between them. A dog trotted past with a dead bird in its mouth – our eyes followed it down a track until, suddenly, from amid the rounded hill tops, we saw a huge white dome and golden stupa rising out of the earth. Behind it were a small scattering of huts and several dozen *gers* lined up in rows. We had reached the desert monastery of Khamariin Khiid.

5
The desert monastery of Khamariin Khiid

Distance to home: 2,957 miles

16–17 NOVEMBER

> Is there wine? Then drink!
> Is there a song? Then sing!
> Are there thoughts? Then talk!
> Is there brandy? Then drink!

So wrote Danzan Ravjaa, the eccentric Mongol Buddhist saint of the Gobi almost two centuries ago. The day before the expedition started, we had seen his statue in Sainshand – a grey figure levitating in the lotus position, with a submissive scorpion perched on his shoulder. His middle-aged and beardless face looked serene, and he wore a large pointy hat with a small skull at its tip. It was he who had made the site of Khamariin Khiid one of the most important spiritual centres in the country.

We rolled down into the monastery encampment. After two days in the emptiness, we found ourselves staring, wide-eyed, at the huge white dome with its golden stupa. We were elated to have made it here, because we needed to fill up our water bottles, and we were also excited by the thought of spending a night in one of the cosy pilgrim *gers* that we had heard were available for rent. It was almost evening, so we decided to postpone our look around the monastery until the following morning.

A middle-aged couple appeared and, after a bit of haggling, showed us to a *ger*. We spread our stuff on the four empty beds, and waited for the camel-dung stove to heat up. We felt a strong sense of relief to be back in the warm. There were also some electrical sockets, so Leon plugged in the camera batteries to charge and took out the laptop. Besides filming, walking and carrying half our gear, Leon was also responsible for technical administration, which included backing up and checking the footage we had taken. I leaned back on my bed, and reflected that Leon had a much harder job than me. Something else that had not made his life any easier was that he had had very little time to get to know the filming equipment before we set off. After waiting many months for some promised cameras from a key sponsor, they had pulled out at the last minute. We had therefore had to scramble to buy our own just a few days before we left.

We ate our noodles and dog food with our eyes glued to the little laptop screen, while it played back what we had filmed so far. We were reasonably happy with what we had shot, though I did sometimes look tense on camera, and Leon spotted some dust on the lens that he would need to clean off the following morning.

We finished eating, and Leon pulled out a small silver hip-flask.

'We've made the first landmark. I think we deserve our first swig,' he said.

He held the flask to his nose for a moment, closed his eyes, and tipped it back for a split second.

'Time for you to become a real man, Rob.' He handed it to me.

Leon's one luxury on expeditions, it turned out, was his hip-flask of whisky. I had never been much of a whisky man, but as Leon expounded how the dark, ambrosial liquid had spent decades maturing in oak sherry barrels in the Scottish Highlands, I followed his example, and tipped the flask back.

'Only one swig?' I said, coughing a little as the liquid burned pleasantly down.

'Yes, one for minor celebrations. We need to save the double swigs for major celebrations, and for when things get really bad.'

'Fair point,' I said, handing it back.

However, despite the hard liquor to wash down my dinner, my stomach did not feel great. Our diet thus far – noodles, beef, chocolate and biscuits – contained little fibre. My guts were not working very smoothly. Before bed I took a laxative pill, hoping that it would not kick in until the morning – the temperature was down to the low minus teens outside.

I woke just after 5 a.m. with a gurgling stomach and stumbled hurriedly out into the dawn. Scrambling onto the other side of a frozen ridge, I squatted down and enjoyed the sunrise in total privacy as a loud, satisfying explosion resounded across the emptiness. When I got back to the *ger*, Leon was up and cooking breakfast. He noticed the relieved expression on my face, and requested a laxative tablet for himself.

We walked back up to the monastery for a proper look, now noticing numerous golden statues of the Buddha, dotted on the hillsides and shimmering in the morning sun. Mongolia had been a predominantly Buddhist land for centuries, and followed Tibet's distinctive lama strand of Buddhism. Lama Buddhism includes the belief that its deities are regularly reincarnated in human form as lamas – as, for example, the famous Tibetan line of Dalai Lamas. In Mongolia, the best known are the Noyon Lamas, said to embody a powerful Indian tantric deity. Danzan Ravjaa, the Mongol saint whose statute we had seen in Sainshand, and who had made Khamariin Khiid such an important place, had been the fifth reincarnation of the Noyon Lama.

Leon and I reached the dome-shaped building and, entering through a large doorway, found ourselves in a huge white cavern, spotlessly clean, and pristinely decorated with Buddhist paintings and shiny artefacts. It felt strange to have suddenly moved from the wild Gobi into such a tame and serene sanctuary, and we whispered to each other, feeling out of place in our dusty expedition clothing. Before we had a chance to look around properly, and as if to confirm our sense of not belonging, a middle-aged female caretaker appeared and told us to leave.

Back outside, we climbed a wide set of stairs onto the roof. A group of local children, weather-beaten but smiling, had gathered. A couple of them had skateboards, and they darted around us, laughing and shinning down the steep parapets as if this was a playground, happily oblivious of the ten-metre drop if they slipped.

Danzan Ravjaa had himself spent his early childhood in poverty in the Gobi. But the local monks had recognised the little boy's divine attributes; he was soon hailed as the next Noyon Lama and sent to a monastery for training. As he grew up he displayed both wit and mischief, traits that grew with age, and in adulthood quickly gained a reputation – not so much for discipline and devotion as for being a brilliant playwright and poet, a heavy-drinking woman-iser, and a somewhat bizarre miracle worker.

Though these may seem strange qualities for a saint, he was widely loved, and in many respects a man ahead of his time, advocating more equality for women and education for children. Amid the rocky hollows around the monastery lay the remains of a three-storey theatre that he had built, and to which thousands of nomads used to flock to watch his plays. The performances were not for entertainment only, but were also filled with political satire against the oppressive forces at work in the nation. It was during a play that Ravjaa was said to have performed one of his more eccentric miracles: making his pee levitate in mid air as he stood on top of a hut. It was enough to make the raucous crowd behave itself. On his darker side, like many tortured artistic souls, he had a quick temper, and his disinclination to show self-restraint earned him enemies. Accounts of the final years of his life give the impression of a rather pitiful alcoholic with deteriorating health. It is thought that he eventually died after being poisoned, possibly by a spurned lover.

After his death in the mid-1800s, his disciples continued to dwell in Khamariin Khiid, until in the 1920s and 1930s Stalin's puppet government purged Buddhism across the country – hundreds of monasteries were destroyed, and tens of thousands of monks were executed or sent to labour camps. However, just hours before the army arrived to tear Khamariin Khiid to pieces, some loyal monks managed to bury over fifty chests full of Ravjaa's artefacts and works.

The decades passed and, with all evidence of Rajvaa gone, some began to say that the merry-making lama of the Gobi was only a legend. But knowledge of the whereabouts of the chests was passed down from father to son. With the collapse of the Soviet Union in the early 1990s, Mongolia regained full independence, and the latently practised Buddhism began to resurface. A man named Atangerel, a descendant of the original chest burier, now faithfully dug up the old chests, thus bringing to light Ravjaa's poems, plays, clothing and furniture. Not long after, Khamariin Khiid was rebuilt, becoming a popular destination once more for devout pilgrims, and for foreign tourists too.

As Leon and I stood looking out on Ravjaa's old stomping ground, a convoy of four jeeps roared up beside the dome and half a dozen Mongolian tourists piled out. They were wearing flashy clothes and were abuzz with mobile phones and cameras. A monk appeared and led them inside. A few minutes later they re-emerged, and started taking photos of almost everything in sight before leaping back into their vehicles and disappearing in another cloud of dust. It had probably taken them about an hour to drive here from Sainshand, twenty minutes for the photos, and it would take an hour to drive back again. A whole pilgrimage in less than two and a half hours – not bad.

Molly, Leon and I marched back into the wilderness, and the stupa and domes of the monastery gradually disappeared into the grit behind us, as if they had only ever existed in our imaginations. I thought more about the jeep-borne pilgrims we had briefly met. I wondered what they had been hoping to gain from their visit. Perhaps it was just a fun excuse for a jaunt through the desert, or perhaps they were in search of something more.

The concept of pilgrimage was a hard one to define, and even dictionary definitions are decidedly vague. Maybe the word has been devalued in recent decades, as planes and luxury tours have made travelling effortless. I preferred to think of pilgrimage as something that has a meaningful end-point, whether that be religious or personal, but also as something that tests the pilgrim and their commitment to reach that place. In this sense, it was a helpful framework for me to understand my own, often opaque, motivations for adventures.

On this expedition, I was trying to get home – a meaningful place, for sure. En route to this meaningful place, I hoped to have some fun, learn about the places I went through, and also to catch glimpses of the beauty and holiness that suffuse the world. But I realised now that wanting to face the tests of the road was also a strange – but significant – part of my motivation.

Undoubtedly, I would face physical tests – with ten million heavy footsteps to be taken; and there would be professional tests – with a TV programme to be shot. But there would also be tests of character and heart: who I was deep down, and who I was becoming. If the expedition failed, it would be a huge disappointment and a financial catastrophe, but not the end of the world. If, however, when I found myself in the thick of hard times, I let my heart become embittered and turned to stone, that really would be a failure. A big source of strength in my life, and something that gives my life meaning, is my Christian faith, which I had grown into as a child. I hoped that this would help me in these tests of heart and character. I sometimes liked to think of the whole of my life as a kind of pilgrimage, in search of the mysterious Christian God, whether I was on a literal journey or not.

And so as I walked, I prayed, with the pilgrims of old, that the king with his scarred hands and feet would walk with me, and keep my heart soft, and stop the expedition from becoming mere vanity. As the Celts used to say:

To go to Rome
is much trouble, little profit
The king thou seekest there
Thou wilt not find
Unless he travels with thee

My spiritual musings were rudely interrupted, by the sort of thing I imagined those of many pilgrims through the ages have been, when Leon and Molly stopped abruptly up ahead.

'Are you OK?' I called out to my brother pilgrim.

Leon was frantically disentangling himself from his rucksack and rummaging around in it. Suddenly triumphant, he pulled out some loo roll.

'I think the laxative is kicking in,' he shouted over his shoulder as he ran into the desert. 'Keep going, I'll catch you up.'

6

Winter cometh

Distance to home: 2,942 miles

18 NOVEMBER

We emerged from our tents the next morning to see a blanket of grey cloud had rolled across the sky. The temperature was now pushing towards −20°C, and by the time we set off it had started to snow. A white layer quickly dusted the floor and the visibility dropped to a few hundred metres. The sun glowed through only as a pale halo of white, and to the south I could see the dark shadow of a mountain looming through the snowfall. I pulled my scarf tightly round me to stop the snowflakes going down my neck, and we moved as fast as we could to keep warm.

In mid-morning the sound of an engine drifted through the semi-whiteout behind us – a motorbike. It was driven by a man in a bright red jumpsuit and he stopped when he reached us.

'Hello,' he shouted with a smile.

'Hello,' we shouted back. He had a young, clean-shaven face, and his outfit stood out like blood against the white landscape.

'My name is Tagwar,' he said in English. 'What is your name?'

'Rob and Leon,' we introduced ourselves. 'Nice to meet you.'

'What?'

'Nice to meet you.'

'What?'

'Err, never mind. We are going to Zamiin-Uud. Is this the right way?' I pointed along the road. We were heading east and hoped soon to intercept the main track heading south to the border town.

'Yes, yes, yes. Next?' said Tagwar.

'What?'

'Next?'

'Oh, err, Erlian.' The first town across the border in China.

'Next?'

'China.'

'Next?'

'Hong Kong.'

'OK, OK, OK,' he said, smiling and pointing to confirm we were going the right way. He started to wave his hands enthusiastically in a flat motion and exclaimed, 'ROAD, ROAD . . . LET'S GO . . . LET'S GO . . . LET'S GO ROAD!'

'Ah, a "Let's Go Road",' we nodded. Leon said that perhaps he meant an asphalt road – someone in Ulaanbaatar had told us of a rumour that one was being built down this way, though it must have been very new as it was not visible on the one-year-old Google satellite images.

Tagwar patted the back seat of his motorbike, offering me a lift.

'Err, sorry, we are not allowed to take lifts,' I said, 'and I will probably fall off as I am attached to Molly.'

'OK, OK,' shouted Tagwar, before letting out a final cheerful, 'Let's go!' and roaring away, at probably twenty times our walking speed.

Shortly afterwards, a *ger* appeared out of the whiteness. Outside it stood half a dozen camels, a flock of goats, a truck and Tagwar's motorbike. We could hear some dogs starting to bark and we hoped our poles would be enough of a deterrent. But as we drew closer, Tagwar and an older man emerged, subdued the dogs, and welcomed us inside with broad smiles.

Entering a *ger* during a Gobi blizzard was like stepping through a magical doorway. The land of bitter wind and swirling snow was suddenly replaced by an enchanted world of colour and shelter. I sat down next to Tagwar on one of the beds and took in my surroundings. The layout of the *ger* was similar to Sahana's, and a patter of snowflakes fell gently through a section in the roof where the felt had been folded back for ventilation. Two little girls, aged about two and six, sat on the patterned floor, staring at us with open mouths. A lady in her thirties with a pink scarf wrapped around her head smiled, stoked the stove and spoke to the older man in gentle, staccato tones. The man poured some milky tea into small china bowls and handed them to us.

'Camel milk,' said Tagwar.

'Thank you,' we said, beaming and gulping down the hot liquid. The lady offered us a bowl of fresh, deep-fried dough cakes, and I felt the warmth returning to my cold bones. Tagwar explained that these people were his friends, and he was on his way to Urgan, a town near Sainshand.

'Me,' he said, pointing to himself, 'wrestling teacher.'

He took out his mobile phone, and showed us a photo of him, or at least we assumed it was him, in a contorted, semi-inverted position on a wrestling mat, holding someone in a headlock. Since pre-Genghis days, there had been three main sports in Mongolia – archery, horse racing and wrestling. An early source recounts a wrestling match between two key champions, at the end of which Genghis demanded the victor break the back of the defeated champion. Today, although archery and horse racing are still practised at the annual summer games in Ulaanbaatar, it is wrestling that is the Mongols' greatest talent. Wrestling competitions sometimes attract over 6,000 contestants. Mongols have even branched into Japanese sumo wrestling, and in recent years have frequently become world champions.

The two girls continued to stare at us, and the older one produced an exercise book and proudly showed us neatly written lines of English handwriting. Somehow, they were getting an education out here, quite literally in the middle of nowhere. Leon had the camera out, and he flipped the LCD screen round. The girls were mesmerised by the images of themselves. The six-year-old posed excitedly with a victory sign. The two-year-old looked intently at herself and said 'Mama', before suddenly getting a shock and bursting into tears. Her big sister grabbed her and gave her a hug. We produced a bag of sweets and the older girl shyly took one. Her little sister was unable to decide on a sweet and instead took the whole bag and carried it off to her mother, who laughed gently.

'Sunglasses?' said Tagwar, indicating mine. He looked very proud as he tried them on; I guessed he was thinking how perfect they would be for keeping the snow out of his eyes while riding his motorbike. I had a spare pair, so I said he could keep them.

After about an hour, the warmth had started to make us feel drowsy and content. But we had to keep going, there was a winter on our tails, and it was not going to make life any easier if we started taking long tea breaks. Back in the cold, the older man beckoned us over to a Bactrian camel and invited me to climb on. I swung a leg over its back, and felt its muscles strain with immense power as it stood up, back legs first. Ten feet off the ground, for the next few moments I felt like a king – this would surely be the way to cross the desert in style.

We said our farewells and, as we got moving again, we saw a little blue coat bobbing up and down amid the huge herd of goats. It seemed that as well as practising her handwriting and looking after her sister inside the *ger*, the six-year-old girl also had the job of looking after 200 goats in a Gobi winter.

Plodding onwards through the whiteness, Molly and I drifted behind Leon; I tried to keep sight of him, despite the low visibility. Sometimes I saw his footprints in the snow ahead of me. At 5 p.m. the sky started to darken and the temperature dropped fast – even while pacing hard with Molly, I was still feeling cold. I saw the silhouette of Leon up ahead, standing beside a small embankment, stamping his feet. Suddenly, from nowhere, a truck hurtled into view, flew along the top of the embankment and disappeared into the sea of hills to the south.

'Well, here's the Let's Go Road,' shouted Leon, 'and it's definitely asphalt.'

7

The Let's Go Road

Distance to home: 2,927 miles

19 NOVEMBER

'How did you sleep?' Leon asked, as we set out fast down the Let's Go Road the next morning. The clouds had gone and the sky was a deep, cold blue.

'Not bad, but not great,' I said. 'The side of my body lying against the air mat kept going numb.'

'Sorry about that. It actually took me weeks to get them from the sponsor.'

We had camped the previous night in the lee of the Let's Go Road; for the first time, the temperature had dropped into the −20°Cs. Half the knack of camping comfortably in the extreme cold is to have a decent insulated mat to protect one's body from the frozen ground. We had somehow overlooked this in our preparations, and now were stuck with a couple of weedy air mats. In my desperation the previous evening, I had ripped up one of our disintegrating cardboard boxes to use as a bed.

And the cold was not just affecting our sleep. When cooking the previous night, I had found that our tins of so-called beef were frozen solid. I had to put the whole tin into the pot of brewing noodles to defrost before I could get the tin opener into it. Then, overnight, my breath had condensed into ice crystals on the inner tent, and when I sat up in the morning I was greeted by a shower of icicles down the back of my neck. As I got out of the tent, my feet were numb before I had my boots on, and as we packed we noticed that the water in our remaining bottles was three-quarters frozen. It was only our sixth day, and winter had well and truly arrived.

The Let's Go Road – with its jet-black ribbon of tarmac – unfurled before us, cutting a sharp line across the bright, snowy land. Its smooth surface allowed us to move considerably faster than normal, perhaps even at three miles per hour. But it was not only us moving faster – cars and trucks sped past sporadically, all seemingly out of control. Until very recently, Mongolians had been used to the bumpy desert tracks that acted as a natural speed check. This new road, combined with a bit of ice, and perhaps a drop or two of Genghis Khan vodka, seemed a perfect recipe for terrible crashes.

The white expanse around us, meanwhile, now looked more like tundra than desert. Tufts of grass broke through the thin carpet of snow, and in mid-morning we spotted several groups of camels, cows and beautiful black horses grazing on the hillsides. Although they were free to roam, these animals were all owned by nomads, whose *gers* were either invisible in the whiteness, or tucked away just over a neighbouring hillside.

During a short break, we stuffed biscuits into our mouths and gulped at our half-frozen water. 'If we find one, let's try and stay in a *ger* tonight.' We agreed, shivering.

As evening approached, we were relieved to spot two *gers* half a mile off the road. We walked across and met a pair of middle-aged goat herders herding their goats into a pen. They spoke no English, but we showed them our magic letter, and they immediately said we could stay in their spare *ger*. The stove was lit, and after Leon and I had brought in our frozen water bottles to melt, we sat down in a daze of relief and removed our boots. Desert hospitality was a wonderful thing.

An hour later we were beckoned through to the main *ger*, and treated to an amazing feast of hot, fatty stew with goat meat and tagliatelle-like pasta. It was a welcome change from our usual diet, though interestingly there were still no vegetables in sight. We grinned across at the two men, with their weather-beaten faces. As we ate, I wondered how they coped without laxative tablets. They grinned back. No, it did not look like they were in need of laxatives.

On a more serious note, this was the third nomad *ger* that we had visited, and I felt frustrated that we could not communicate better. I wondered what their lives were like. How often did they move camp? What did they make of the outside world? What had they seen during their lives out here in the desert? It was easy to romanticise the nomadic way, but it was probably a very tough life.

Traditionally, a nomad's livestock would have provided almost everything they needed to survive: meat, dairy products, chair coverings, clothing and transport. Only supplies of staple wheat or rice, and wood for building structures such as the *ger* frame, would need to be bought or bartered for. However, there was evidence that life was changing. Even right out here, in this *ger*, there was a TV on the table, and a couple of mobile phones tucked under the wooden stays in the roof. Outside we had spotted solar panels and a rudimentary satellite dish. However, tonight the TV was not working, and the older of the two men seemed to be missing his favourite show, as he was continually fiddling with the controls, and heading out to adjust the dish.

Although there are still tens of thousands of nomads using the desert as a low-grade common for their flocks, the nomadic life is increasingly under threat. Mongolia's population has increased six-fold in the past century, leading to serious concerns about over-grazing. Hundreds of thousands of nomads have moved to Ulaanbaatar, partly to look for more settled work, and partly because extreme winters have decimated livestock in recent years.

Leon and I had seen the consequent 'ger' city – tens of thousands of *gers* – around the outskirts. The migrants' practice of fuelling their stoves with garbage and cheap coal (rather than camel dung) is creating some of the worst urban air pollution on earth. But although there is extensive poverty and pollution, Ulaanbaatar's city centre is starting to boast more and more flashy designer shops, shiny offices and new apartment blocks.

We had come to a country on the cusp of monumental change. The colossal Oyu Tolgoi mine, just a few hundred miles from where we were walking, was due to begin production shortly. It is thought to be the biggest unexploited reserve for copper, silver and gold in the world, and is forecast to add up to 30 per cent to the country's

GDP, and bring in US$8 billion a year for the next fifty years. As a result of this and other resources, foreign investment was soaring. Mongolia's economy had recently become the fastest-growing in the world.

'This country is so rich in resources, and the population is so small,'* an expat had told us, 'that in a decade or two this place could become the next Dubai.'

And now, here in the Gobi, was the new 'Let's Go Road'. When finished, it would link Mongolia with China, the ancient enemy, but now the keenest customer for millions of tonnes of raw materials. Sitting in that warm, hospitable *ger*, as the temperature dropped into the low −20°Cs again outside, I thought of the two little girls we had met the day before. It was strange to imagine how much their lives might differ from those of their parents.

* With only three million people in the world's nineteenth largest country, Mongolia's population density is the lowest in the world.

8

The incident of the fallen poles

20 NOVEMBER

The two nomads fed us a beautiful hot breakfast of tagliatelle stew, but adamantly refused the money we offered them. 'We've got a lot to learn from guys like that,' Leon and I said to each other as we walked through the bitterly cold morning and back to the Let's Go Road. Just before we reached it, Leon decided to stay back and film a long-distance shot. I strode onwards. Half an hour later, I heard someone shouting and turned to see the lone figure of Leon waving against the bleak white backdrop. I stopped, and when he reached me he did not look happy.

'Why didn't you wait?' he said. 'I can't walk with the tripod, it's too awkward.'

'Sorry, I thought you would easily catch up.'

Leon looked down at Molly. 'Where are my poles?' He had balanced them on all the bags when he sent me ahead, but they were no longer there.

'They must have fallen off, didn't you see them when you came down to the road?'

'No, I cut the corner to the road.'

We stood squaring off for a moment, and then Leon huffed and said he would go back and look for them. He put down his pack and the camera by the roadside and marched back, retreating over our hard-won ground. I started pacing to keep warm, fuming in my head about Leon – the accusatory tone that he had just used had particularly grated on me. I grabbed the camera and filmed a video diary entry reflecting on what had just happened.

Although we were getting on well most of the time, it should not have been a surprise that we were beginning to annoy each other. From the moment it starts, an expedition combines frequent difficult decisions with long, intense periods of exhaustion, fear, stress, pain and boredom. Throw into the mix the fact that adventurers are usually strong-willed and stubborn, with over-inflated egos, and you have a great scenario for relationship meltdown. For this reason, the godfather of modern expeditions, Ranulph Fiennes, describes how vital it is 'to do a huge amount of careful preparation and selecting when recruiting the team for an expedition. People need to be physically strong, but you also have to test them mentally and test their character very carefully.'

However, in contrast to such careful tests of ability and character, I had recruited Leon on the basis of intuition, having known him for just a few days. During our four intensive months of preparation, we had communicated only by Skype. We had hoped to go on a two-day expedition in Hong Kong to practise working as a team and getting used to our gear, but as tasks spun out of control, we simply did not have time.

Half an hour later, Leon reappeared with poles in hand. We started walking again, side by side, in silence. At first the silence felt awkward, but it was good that we had both had some time to calm down. As we continued onwards, I realised we had to talk. We could not afford to let annoyances like this go unresolved, or else they would fester into resentment, and a downward spiral from there. It was not so much that we were about to have a massive punch-up or walk off our separate ways – though, given how long the trip was, we should not discount that as a risk. Rather, on this expedition, we were not merely trying to complete it together, but to film it together. And to film it well, we needed to remain friends – a cameraman filming or a presenter presenting before someone they disliked was hardly likely to produce good material.

Suddenly, before I had said anything, Leon spoke up.

'Rob, I'm sorry that I shouted at you. It was really hard to catch up with you when I was carrying the tripod.'

I was impressed that Leon had initiated the conversation and been the first to apologise. I felt slightly ashamed. Wasn't I supposed to be the older, more mature one?

'Yes, sorry I kept walking,' I said. 'I just thought you were doing some extra filming, and that you could put the tripod away in your pack.'

We talked on through the 'incident of the falling poles', sharing our perspectives, and acknowledging that we both had reasons to be annoyed and that, in this case, it basically came down to bad communication. We had to stop making assumptions that the other person had the same understanding as we did, and instead we needed to overcommunicate. If Leon wanted me to wait and keep an eye on his poles, he needed to tell me. If I wanted Leon to put away his tripod and catch up with me while I made headway with Molly, I needed to tell him. We talked about how we were bound to annoy each other on a regular basis. 'Clearing the air' conversations like this were going to be vital.

We were starting to run low on food, because it turned out that the Let's Go Road had bypassed the hamlet where we had been hoping to resupply. However, the two nomads who had hosted us had indicated we would soon reach a *ger* restaurant beside the road, and we were relieved when we finally reached it at lunchtime the next day. The husband and wife who owned the *ger* served us bowls of wonderful hot noodles, while their little boy played on the floor with a few toys. Their business would do well with the new road, and increasing traffic, and their ability to just pack up and move to better locations.

A couple of truck drivers, one chubby, one thin, and both wearing tatty, ex-military clothing, sat at the adjacent table, and I noticed a small handgun on their table. 'Wow, this really is the Wild East,' I marvelled to myself, guessing that the route must be vulnerable to bandits.

Leon, meanwhile, was busy fixing his sunglasses, which had cracked in the cold (we had no more spares). He finally finished, put them on, and asked me what I thought.

'You look like some kind of demented desert pirate,' I laughed, explaining that I could hardly see one of his eyes, there was so much tape wrapped around the frame.

The chubby truck driver with the gun looked over at us and grunted. We jolted to attention. He nodded and passed his own sunglasses to Leon. The driver watched carefully as Leon nervously tried them on, then insisted that he keep them. Leon said an extra-polite thank you.

'Cool,' I thought, 'Leon just got given some sunglasses by a gun-wielding trucker.'

The truck drivers got up and left, but the gun remained on their table. Tentatively I leaned over to examine the deadly weapon.

It felt very light, and I realised it was one of the little boy's plastic toys.

9
Genghis

21 NOVEMBER

The Let's Go Road was still not complete, and it soon petered back into the desert, forcing us to press onwards on a grit track. There were, however, still regular trucks rumbling past throughout the day, carrying manufactured goods up from China, or raw materials the other way. Although we were still in the middle of the Gobi, our route was now, broadly speaking, the highway to Beijing. It was a route that had been in use since ancient times, and through the centuries it had seen the passage of fearless traders, devout pilgrims, promised princesses and ferocious raiders, as well as – of course – Genghis and his armies on their way to unleash hell on the world.

I still found it hard to believe that the stories of Genghis's life and achievements were real; even his childhood was the stuff of Hollywood legend. He had been born with the name Temujin, about 800 years ago on the grassy steppes northeast of Ulaanbaatar. At that time, the Mongol people were a series of scattered, competing nomadic tribes: hardy, wild, often fighting. Temujin's father, an important chief, had died shortly after he was born. His mother was left destitute and had to fend and provide for the family herself.

Temujin and his siblings grew up in a dangerous world – and with no shortage of sibling rivalry. This escalated severely when, at thirteen, Temujin got into an argument with his older half-brother about the rightful ownership of a lark and a minnow they had caught. Later that day, Temujin murdered his brother. Not long after this he was kidnapped and held hostage by a neighbouring tribe.

He managed to escape, hiding in an icy river to avoid recapture, and befriending one of his former captors to help him make it safely home.

As he reached manhood, Temujin took up the leadership of his local tribe and, after two decades of fighting and politicking with other tribes, managed to unite them all behind him. He now took the name Genghis Khan – Ruler of All – and from this new position of authority marshalled the most loyal and well-coordinated force of nomads that the world had ever seen.

And a force they were indeed. For more than a century, they swept south like a perfect storm in their tens of thousands, destroying anyone who stood in their way. Impregnable cities fell, armies ten or twenty times bigger than them were routinely defeated. Under the leadership of Genghis's sons and grandsons, the onslaught spread further and further – from Korea to Indonesia, from Persia to Poland; all collapsed before them.

The Mongol's victims in far-flung lands barely knew who or what had hit them. When Christendom first heard about an army on horseback, smashing the Muslim peoples of the Middle East, they thought it was the legendary Christian King, Prester John, coming to aid them in their dreadful Crusades. But the Mongols then encroached into Europe, and when the Christian knights of Poland and Hungary said their prayers and went out to face the horseback warriors, they fared no better – by day's end their entire force had been destroyed, princes and bishops included.

The Chinese, in contrast, knew their pillaging neighbours well, having endured conflicts with them for thousands of years. They had kept the nomads at bay through a mixture of defence (the Great Wall was built partly for that purpose), bribery, marriage alliances, meddling in tribal politics, and occasionally fielding huge armies. But they never thought that the nomadic raiders would be capable of taking the whole Chinese Empire for themselves. However, under the leadership of Kublai Khan, Genghis's grandson, the unthinkable did happen. The Mongols completed their conquest of China, and founded the imperial Yuan Dynasty, which would rule the Middle Kingdom for almost a hundred years.

And what was it like if the Mongols did come your way? Well, one of the great secrets to their success was the fear that came in their wake.* If you were lucky, they gave your city the option of 'surrender or die'. If you did not surrender, you would be caught in a whirlwind of massacre worse than your most infernal nightmare.

While cycling through Central Asia a few years previously, I had gone past many of the cities, or ex-cities, that the Mongol armies had laid to waste: Termez – after a two-day siege in 1220, everyone in the city was slain; in Merv, 700,000 were executed in a single day. In order to take the seemingly impregnable citadel of Bukhara, Genghis forced captives to march into the moats – the siege moved forwards on top of their mangled bodies. The death toll of the Mongol conquests, including lives lost as a result of subsequent famines and sieges, is thought to be between thirty and sixty million. If this figure is taken in proportion to the global population at the time (less than half a billion), the figure becomes even more staggering, amounting to around 10 per cent of the global population wiped out.†

* Other factors behind the Mongols' success included their skill and speed at firing arrows from the saddle; their strategy of fleeing and counter-attacking when in trouble; and their willingness to learn and recruit from those they conquered all across Eurasia.

† Even the Pax Mongolica (Mongol Peace), which enabled the land routes between Asia and Europe to be travelled in relative safety, had a dark side – for these routes eased the passage of the bubonic plague from Asia to Europe. On the other hand, during this time of marginally easier movement, a family of Venetian merchants was able to travel to China and back, and Marco Polo's subsequent account was the inspiration behind Columbus's discovery of the New World, and a whole new epoch of world history.

10
Total *whiteout*

Distance to home: 2,879 miles

22–23 NOVEMBER

I woke again and again in the night to the noise of my tent walls flapping in a rage. Outside, in the cold darkness, a storm was flinging itself down the valley like one of Genghis's thundering armies from eight centuries previously. As daylight dawned, the tent continued to shake violently; hunched in my sleeping bag, the thought of going out into this madness was not appealing. In the last few days I had been starting to feel increasingly tired from the continual walking and relentless cold. But we were short on food, our thermos flasks had cracked, and all the water in our bottles was totally frozen. We needed to keep moving to stay ahead of the winter that, evidently, was rapidly catching up with us.

'You OK Leon?' I shouted above the din, wondering if he was awake.

'Fine thanks, you?' he shouted back.

'Bit of a wind blowing outside.'

'Yes, I just had a look through my door and it's a total whiteout.'

I followed Leon's lead, and unzipped my tent for a peek. Gone was the sparse, open valley of the previous evening; instead we were enclosed in a prison of screaming whiteness, with a high-speed layer of snow dancing across the scrubby desert floor. The road we had been following yesterday was lost from sight.

Inside our tents, Leon and I stuffed away our things, and then, yelling like madmen, burst out into the storm. Immediately the tents tried to fly away. Leon sprawled himself on top of his, while I threw my rucksack inside mine. I suddenly remembered that we had previously discussed the importance of filming when things were most desperate. I grabbed the camera, ran ten metres into the wind and turned it on.

Leon and I wrestled with our tents as the wind roared past. The coldest I had ever experienced had been −40°C in Siberia and with the wind chill, this was feeling almost as bad.

'How are your hands and feet?' I yelled. Frostbite and hypothermia were a real risk.

'Completely numb,' Leon shouted.

We needed to warm up fast. We dropped the bags, and started to run in wild circles, swinging our arms in windmills, doing kung-fu kicks in the air, and singing, 'I feel good' very loudly. After a few minutes the blood began to return to our digits. We quickly finished packing and followed the compass through the whiteout and back to the truckers' track.

As the morning progressed, even marching at full speed, we still felt cold in the blistering wind. To shield our faces, we put on our black balaclavas. They were the old-school 'terrorist' type, with holes only for the eyes and mouth.

Leon turned to me and asked, 'How do I look?'

I burst out laughing. 'You look like a member of the IRA who has taken a wrong turn and ended up in the Gobi.'

Leon smiled sheepishly, and looked even stranger.

The next few trucks coming down the road slowed to say hello, but when they saw our masked faces, they revved their engines and kept going. We were starting to feel thirsty, so we pulled off our balaclavas for the next truck and waved it down. The trucker first of all kindly offered us a lift, which we turned down. Instead, we asked for some water. He handed us a gloriously lukewarm bottle of water, which we gulped down quickly before it froze. In return we gave him one of our frozen bottles, which he could melt inside the warm cab on the way to the border.

As the whiteout gradually subsided, we realised that it was not actually snowing, but rather the gale was picking up snow from the ground and flinging it horizontally across the land. I had taken first turn with Molly, and when we switched round I jogged ahead to keep the blood pumping to my feet. It had been a crazy start to the day, but I thought we had coped well given the conditions. And I was especially happy that we had managed to capture much of the experience on camera.

The filming had been going reasonably well, and on average we had been shooting about an hour a day. In the cold, this was very time-consuming, and sometimes unpleasant, but it was what we had signed up for. I was gradually getting more relaxed when I presented, and Leon was increasingly nifty with the camera, though since the temperature had dropped into the −20°Cs on day five, he grimaced whenever he got it out.

'It's like holding a large block of ice,' he had said. 'All the plastic and metal are basically conducting the cold straight into my hands. They go completely numb, and it always takes an hour to warm them back up.' Our gloves were doing a good job at keeping our hands warm when we were walking, but they were not designed for holding blocks of ice.

When we reached the border in a few days' time, we would send back to Hong Kong a hard drive of the footage we had shot. The TV network that would broadcast the episodes had, at the last minute, outsourced the management and editing of the show to a small local production company – Tiberius Productions – and it was with them that we would have our main contact. We were looking forward to seeing what they thought of our desert filming.

We had met Tiberius just before we left, and found them to be a young, dynamic team; in our initial meetings, lots of creative ideas buzzed around the room. In addition to helpfully lending us a wireless mic and a second primary camera, they also gave us feedback on a test shoot, and took us shopping for extra gear. At the same time, though, it became evident that, as a production company, their priorities were different from ours. Their mandate was to focus on the technical aspects of the production. For Leon and me, the issue was much more about how we were going to pull off the expedition at all.

Leon and I had concerns about whether Tiberius understood our limitations. They would not be travelling with us, and it might be hard for them to grasp how – with our daily regimen of walking twenty miles a day while carrying all the gear, organising our own food, shelter and logistics, not to mention filming – we would not always be able to shoot the same quality of footage that was achieved on higher-budget expedition TV shows, with their convoys of support vehicles and fixers.

Conversely, Tiberius were unsure about whether we fully appreciated the high levels of filming standards that were required of us. Their main concern was with Leon's youth – it was unusual for someone of his age to end up as primary cameraman for an entire show. His main prior experience had been through his film studies at university, a handful of internships and freelance jobs, and the self-filming of his bike trip the previous year. However, Tiberius knew they had no choice: 'We're not exactly going to find another cameraman who is willing to walk across China,' they had joked.

Because our final two weeks in Hong Kong had been so busy with last-minute preparations, these production vs. expedition tensions were still somewhat unresolved when we departed. We certainly felt daunted by the filming pressure, and Leon's confidence was shaken. But I thought that as long as Leon pointed the camera in the right direction and remembered to take the lens cap off, it would all work out fine.

On our final two days before the border, the land flattened into long rolling hills, and the road widened to over a hundred metres. More and more convoys of trucks swerved past, waving and honking. One truck came over the crest of a hill too fast, and was obviously not expecting us. Out of control under its own momentum it came straight at me, and I had to dash sideways to get out of the way. The truck's roaring wheels missed Molly's rear end by less than a metre, and I realised that if she had been hit I would have had no time to detach myself and would have been dragged under too. My heart was beating in overdrive for the next half hour.

On our last night before the border town, Leon asked for another laxative tablet. I woke from my slumber to hear him making several panicked nocturnal outings. When I remarked on this the next morning, Leon laughed. He said he had just remembered a dream he'd had during the night.

'I was on the run,' he said, 'being chased by a man in a suit with dark glasses – like Mr Smith from *The Matrix*. I managed to hide behind some trees, and as I looked out I saw the agent hunting for me. I saw he had a name badge on, and when I looked more carefully, it said: Mr Lax!'

Leon and I were gradually generating slang for various aspects and procedures in the expedition, and from this point onwards, going for 'number twos' would be referred to as a 'Mr Lax'.

The first sign that we were nearing the border came with a sighting of the trans-Mongolian railway, with its absurdly long trains, clattering romantically past on the plain to the east. It was extraordinary to think these trains came all the way from Moscow. Shortly after this, some tall, rectangular buildings started to rise out of the far horizon. They looked peculiar to our eyes after all the emptiness. With civilisation so near, the exhaustion and hunger in my body suddenly felt more pressing. I was excited about having a hot shower, some vegetables, and a chance to talk to Christine.

Slowly, slowly the buildings drew nearer, and as they were starting to take on a clearer shape, we came to a large pile of stones, littered with bottles of vodka and beer cans and with a stake of wood coming out of it. It was an *oboo* – a sacred high point inspired by Mongolia's ancient shamanistic religions, and a site where people prayed for good luck on their journey through the emptiness. While we were filming, a car pulled up and two men climbed out. They drank a can of beer, walked a lap of the stones, jumped back in and drove off into the desert.

For us, the *oboo* was a marker that we had almost made it through the first stage of our long walk home. Distance-wise, we had only travelled about 5 per cent of the way. But walking across the Outer Mongolian Gobi was certainly not an easy way to start, and we had coped quite well, all things considered. As a team, we had had some arguments, but we had got through them without bitter feelings, and were steadily becoming friends. In terms of physical fitness, our bodies were tired and hungry, but in one piece – a satisfactory result given our state of exhaustion before we had even set off. And it had already been a fine adventure, with a few good challenges to overcome, and some wonderful encounters with the Gobi's hardy, hospitable people. I looked up at the *oboo* again, and said a prayer of thanks to my own God. Then I picked up Molly for the final time and set off towards the skyline of buildings on the ever-nearing horizon.

II
Mos Eisley

Distance to home: 2,830 miles

By the time we reached the outskirts of Zamiin-Uud, the sun was setting. The streets were grimy, and lined with an assortment of small concrete buildings and dirty *gers*, all mixed together. A large chimney spewed fumes into the icy air, and cars screeched and swerved down the narrow road. Welcome back to civilisation.

It took us an hour to reach the centre of the border town, and gradually more people were on the streets, all of them inhabiting very different worlds. A dad wheeled his toddler past in a baby buggy and smiled; two gruff-looking Genghises shuffled across the street, smoking; a teenage girl with lipstick and a smart handbag overtook us while writing a text message. Down in the gutter some little Chihuahua-like mongrels barked – too puny to be guard dogs, and too skinny to be eaten, they were simply left to breed and scavenge.

The town centre itself was bathed in murky light from a selection of half-working streetlamps. 'A wretched hive of scum and villainy if ever I've seen one,' said Leon, quoting Obi-Wan Kenobi's description of the space-port of Mos Eisley.

We hid Molly under a stairwell, checked into a cheap hotel and headed to the best restaurant in town, which as it happened did feel a little bit like the bar where Obi-Wan meets Han Solo, but without the cool band. As we sat down, the strange security and warmth of being inside a real building hit me. For a moment I felt giddy with euphoria, and I looked across to see Leon was grinning too. We ordered a feast of steak, chicken, vegetables and beer.

'Cheers,' I said. 'So far so good.' I took my first sip, and felt my cheeks flush.

'We've earned a couple of days off, that's for sure,' said Leon.

We looked out of the window. It was dark outside, and the iPhone showed that it would be in the low −20°Cs again tonight.

'And it's going to be nice to sleep inside.' Simple comforts had become the greatest of luxuries.

Back at the hotel, I took the much-dreamed-of, and very long hot shower. As I re-emerged from the bathroom, Leon told me he had just taken two phone calls from Christine. She was actually in the UK for work, and had gone there just before Leon and I left Hong Kong. A few minutes later she rang again. I felt emotional to hear her voice. She said that she had been coping OK, but now she was starting to dread the prospect of returning to our empty flat in Hong Kong the following week. I felt guilty, and said that hopefully we would be able to talk more easily in China, with its better mobile-phone coverage. It was also less than a month until we would meet up for Christmas.

In daylight Zamiin-Uud was less ugly, but still not somewhere one would stay longer than needed out of choice. Apart from a couple of small supermarkets, the shops were sparsely stocked, and most shopkeepers seemed a bit grumpy. We decided to save our main shopping for China. But before we crossed the border, we had other things to organise; in particular, we faced two potentially far-reaching decisions.

The first was about Molly. Although she had served us well and it was tempting to keep her for the upcoming Chinese section of desert, in China we wanted the freedom to go off-road. We also did not want to draw too much attention to ourselves from the Chinese authorities. Molly slowed us down, too – at our current rate it would take us three years to get home. Furthermore, there would be more regular settlements in China, so we would not need to carry the same heavy loads of food and water. We therefore decided, with a little sadness, that we should give her away.

The second decision was connected – what gear we could send home. Even without the food and water supplies, we still risked injury or over-exhaustion through carrying too much on our backs.

Anything not completely essential had to go. We therefore wrapped our spare camera, stove, batteries and clothes in a pink Mongolian blanket, and put it in a box. We added to this a hard drive of footage for Tiberius, and posted it all to Hong Kong.

Leon went to an internet café and I went back to the hotel and started work on my weekly newspaper article. I had been commissioned to write for a newspaper in Hong Kong; it was a privilege to have this writing opportunity, and it would help pay the rent while I was away. But my eyes were half shut in front of the laptop as I dug around my memories for some stories, and all I really wanted to do was lie down.

Our last task was to get rid of Molly. We wheeled her down to the train station car park. A young man was sitting in a shiny black SUV with his window rolled down. Western rock music was blasting from the stereo, and a huge pile of Chinese banknotes sat on the dashboard. Every few minutes, someone approached his window for a moment, before walking away again.

'Hello,' he called across to us, 'come and sit in my car – we can talk English and listen to music.'

We left Molly by the front of the car and hopped in. The man's name was Urult; it turned out that, despite appearances, he was not a drug dealer but a money-changer.

'I love Ooosis and Coolplay,' he said, putting on his favourite tunes, and then changing each track after they had only half played. Evidently not many people shared his musical taste around here, and he was glad to have a captive audience. Urult explained that his brother was some kind of big man in the town. 'He's a billionaire,' he said, though we thought he meant millionaire, and that he must be the local mafia boss, thus explaining both why the police overlooked this blatant black-market money-changing, and why there was no risk of robbery. Urult also said he could look after Molly, and that he would give her to the next desert explorer he met passing this way.

We could not have conceived it at this point, but those desert explorers would turn out to be Leon and me, returning to Mongolia three months later under the most unforeseen of circumstances.

Part Two

Into China

不怕慢　就怕站

*One is not so much concerned when he is slow
as when he comes to a halt.*

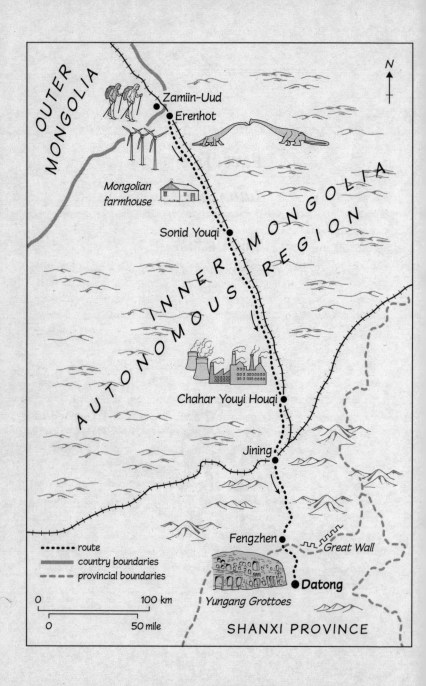

12

Welcome to China

Distance to home: 2,830 miles

27 NOVEMBER

We sat in the jeep and the driver grew in Genghis-like aggression as he slammed the door several times until it stayed shut. Then he jumped in, and we revved out onto the road.

Every expedition needs 'rules', and from the outset our basic rule was that we must walk every metre of the expedition unless officialdom or the police forced us to take a lift. Unfortunately, we had now reached such a moment, because the Mongolian–Chinese border had a strictly enforced 'motorised vehicles only' rule for crossing the two-mile border zone. Hence the jeep.

We drove into no-man's-land and joined a traffic jam of other beaten-up Russian jeeps, each driven by a chain-smoking Genghis. They were all constantly trying to overtake one another, as if they were fairground bumper cars. Our Genghis revved, laughed and lit cigarettes as he tried to barge into a position further up the line, and at one point we felt a scraping sensation along our side. He jumped out to observe that part of his bumper had fallen off, but was unabashed. Climbing back in, he growled something under his breath, leaned forward and revved into the side of the next jeep. Let the joust continue.

Eventually, we made it to the Soviet-era immigration terminal. We were unceremoniously stamped out of Mongolia and, with our adrenaline starting to flow, we entered the next building on which red letters proclaimed:

中国 二连	𐭷𐭷	Erlian* China
(Chinese)	(Mongol Script)	(English)

I held my passport tightly in my hands. I had been to China several times before, on bicycle trips and for work, and I had never had any serious problems with the police or bureaucracy. However, this time I was nervous because we had heard stories about our exact camera model being confiscated at the Chinese border, and if that happened the whole trip would derail. Leon had therefore packed it deep inside his rucksack and we hoped nobody would search us. We also had neither journalist visas nor filming permits, as we had understood that we would almost certainly have been turned down and, in any case, on journalist visas we would be subject to more regular police questioning. Therefore the only viable option was to enter China as tourists. We needed more than the usual one-month tourist visa, so we had paid an expensive visa agent in Hong Kong to fly our passports to Los Angeles and back. The Chinese consulate there was giving out multiple-entry visas, with a three-month stay allowed per entry. This was a lot better than one-month entries, but it still meant that halfway through China, we would have to somehow leave and re-enter the country to renew the visa.

'Good luck,' I said to Leon as we joined the queue.

'You too.' He looked nervous as well.

I reached the front and handed my passport to the officer.

Official (blank face): 'Where are you going?'

Me (broad smile): 'To Hong Kong.'

Official (furrowing his brow): 'You got your visa in Los Angeles?'

Me (smiling even more brightly): 'Yes.'

The official dithered for a moment before looking up and handing me back my passport.

'Welcome to China,' he said, squeezing a brief smile. I nodded back and walked on through into the Middle Kingdom.

---

* Erlian is a shortened Chinese name for the border town. The older Mongolian name is Erenhot, and the two seem to be interchangeable.

13
Dinos

Distance to home: 2,824 miles

27 NOVEMBER

After the Chinese took over the Mongol lands in the seventeenth century, they divided the majority of it into Outer Mongolia and Inner Mongolia for administrative purposes. Erlian, developed only as a tiny desert outpost for the trans-Mongol horse-relay postal system, lay on the border between these two provinces. But as the twentieth century arrived, the two Mongolias – caught like shrimps between the lumbering whales of Russia and China – were to have very different fates. Outer Mongolia achieved independence from China, becoming The People's Republic of Mongolia under Soviet lordship in 1923, and then the fully independent Republic of Mongolia in 1990.

Inner Mongolia, meanwhile, although making some fleeting attempts to unify with independent Outer Mongolia in the 1920s and 1930s, remained part of China throughout the tumult of Chinese Nationalist rule, Japanese invasion and civil war. When the Chinese Communist Party (CCP) won the civil war in 1949, Chairman Mao extended Inner Mongolia's boundaries to encompass much of China's northern frontier, and Erlian became an international border post. By the early 1990s it had grown from a relay station to a small town of 8,000 people, and in 1992, having opened up to international trade, the Han Chinese pioneers poured in. Its population today is pushing towards 100,000.

We were wide-eyed on our short walk into the town centre, gazing up at the ten-storey buildings and glass-fronted shops. The shops sold mobile phones, fast food, sports gear, sunglasses and computers. The streets were clean, cold, and buzzing with traffic. People scampered across the road looking upbeat and talking loudly, and many stared and laughed openly at us. I knew that a fair number of backpackers must pass through here by train, so we were not an entirely exceptional sight. Perhaps we did stick out, though, with our Mongolian fur hats and metal hiking poles.

While the young people were in jeans and branded jackets, the older men mostly sported green People's Liberation Army (PLA) coats, and PLA hats with rabbit-fur earflaps. We eyed the hats with envy – they looked even warmer than our Mongolian hats. Most faces were Han Chinese, but some looked more Mongol, with higher cheekbones and rosier cheeks.

We checked into a cheap hotel, and set out with the shopping list we had compiled in the desert. In search of new thermos flasks, we entered an odds-and-ends store on a side street. A young lady sitting with a baby on her lap was startled by our entry – evidently backpackers did not usually visit odds-and-ends stores. She called out and her husband appeared, and he looked startled too. But after I had said, '*Nihao, women shi yingguoren*' (Hello, we are British people) in my best Mandarin, their expressions softened. Very little English was spoken outside the main cities in China, and on past visits I had relied purely on a magic letter and sign language to communicate. Before this trip, however, I had been learning some Mandarin, and I was delighted that my first tentative efforts were being understood. There was a picture of Chairman Mao on the wall behind the desk, and the shelves were filled with pots, pans, cables, rice cookers, kettles and blankets. No sign of thermos flasks, though. Now came the challenge of explaining what we needed.

Digging deep into my memory banks, I said '*re shui*' (hot water), accompanying this with elaborate mimes of steaming water and some sound effects. The man watched me with devout concentration, and then suddenly smiled. He led me over to a shelf at the back with a line of silver thermoses. We haggled a little, and settled on 100 RMB (£10) each. We bade the shopkeeper and his wife a friendly goodbye and headed back into the street for the next items on our list.

To our delight, after only two hours of lively, jovial miming and haggling with a host of other helpful shopkeepers, we had managed to buy new prepaid SIM cards (for our one iPhone and one basic phone), lightweight blankets (to insulate us from the ground, instead of our cardboard), sunglasses, ice cream, a USB splitter, and PLA sheep's-wool mittens. For boys like us whose key goals when shopping were maximum speed and minimum pain, China was ideal. However, when we returned to the hotel and tried out the thermoses, mine was leaking. I headed back out, on a mission to get a refund from the friendly odds-and-ends store. The shopkeeper was still friendly, but he was not keen to give me a refund. Instead, he boiled a kettle, filled the thermos, gave the lid a very serious tightening and demonstrated to me that in fact it did not leak after all. It has been said before that Chinese shopkeepers are the most determined in the world. I admitted defeat and headed back with the same old thermos.

While Erlian's obvious claim to fame was its status as China's frontier-border town between Inner and Outer Mongolia, it also had another, arguably greater claim, going back to 1922. This was the year that American naturalist Roy Chapman Andrews set off from Peking into the Gobi, with a pistol in his belt and a small convoy of cars and scientists. No one had ever dug for fossils in the Gobi before, and their hope was to find some clues as to the origin of humans in Asia.

They stopped for the night in the tiny Erlian outpost, and a couple of Andrews' teammates went for a walk to do some preliminary digging. Before the sun set, to their astonishment, they stumbled on some fossils lying exposed on the surface of a dried-up salt lake. The fossils were not of early humans, but rather of some far older creatures, including an unknown species of Asian rhino and, most exciting of all, dinosaurs. Electrified by the find, the team crossed into Outer Mongolia and drove deeper into the desert, whereupon the discoveries kept on coming, with more species of dinosaurs, and even the first-ever dinosaur nests – complete with eggs. Although Andrews' fossils were all shipped off to America in the 1920s, thousands of new fossils have since been discovered in the Gobi.

'Wooooooow, look at those!' said Leon, pointing, as we walked into the enormous Erlian Dinosaur Museum Campus. I had recently discovered that Leon was a self-confessed dinosaur-super-nerd, and I had never seen him this excited. The path we were walking down – though Leon was almost skipping – was surrounded by long lines of life-size dinosaur models. The museum was in fact located very close to the site of Andrews' original finds, and we seemed to have the place all to ourselves.

As we entered the first building, robotic dinosaur models in the hallway roared and swayed their heads at us.

'This is so cool,' exclaimed Leon.

I remarked that one of them was sporting some effeminate feathers.

'Oh yes, more and more fossils have been found with feathers,' enthused Leon, 'and some people now believe that many – perhaps most – dinosaurs actually had them. How weird is that!' The feathers further established the link between birds and dinosaurs, which had originally been based on anatomic similarities. In fact, some have argued that we can go beyond saying that birds evolved from dinosaurs to assert that, actually, birds are dinosaurs.

We walked through to the main auditorium, which had a glass floor. Underneath it we could see a dig site packed with dinosaur bones and fossils. It was the same in the second room, though in here we also spotted a hole in the glass. As there was no one else in the building, we took it in turns to kneel down, put our hand through, and for a few magical seconds take hold of a large bone. It felt as if it would have been rather easy to steal, though neither of us wanted to add a dinosaur bone to our already overladen rucksacks.*

---

* In 2012 an American man was arrested for smuggling an impressive Tyrannosaurus skeleton out of Mongolia. It was sold for over US$1 million in an auction. At the time of writing he faces up to seventeen years in prison.

14
Police

Distance to home: 2,824 miles

'Left here . . .'

'Cross the road then right . . .'

This was a momentous day, our first of walking in China, and our first without Molly – I was excited to see how we would fare. Our packs weighed about twenty-five kilograms each, like an overweight check-in bag at the airport. I had tightened my waist-strap to bring 70 per cent of this weight off my back and onto my hips, but I could still feel the pressure bearing down through my whole body. There were still more than 2,800 miles to go.

'Left again . . .'

Leon glanced up and down from the iPhone, and gave directions as we weaved our way through the streets and out of the town. With our Chinese SIM cards we could zoom in on the satellite images from Google Maps, and a little blue dot showed precisely where we were as we walked. As we would not always have 3G reception, for a back-up map we had some pages torn out of a Chinese road atlas. Topographical maps would have been much better, but there were none available for most of China – not a surprise given its paranoid security policies.

In fact, after the Communists took over in 1949, foreigners were almost entirely banned from China until the 1980s. When Colin Thubron visited in 1986, he had marvelled at the unexpected suddenness with which China had opened up – for a well-travelled man such as himself, it was like 'discovering a new room in a house in which you'd lived all your life.' By the 1990s, floods of tourists were coming, and now, in 2011, there were only a handful of rumoured 'closed zones', which were still off-limits to foreign tourists. The trouble with the 'closed zones' was that their locations were also a bit of a secret. Leon and I could only hope that we did not accidentally stray into one.

'Cross this road, and left . . .'

We cleared the final few factories on the outskirts of town.

'OK, it should be straight all the way from here.'

Leon was not exaggerating, for we had arrived on National Highway 208, a smooth, new dual carriageway, blazing south, dead straight ahead of us to an empty horizon, a giant runway into China's heart. We would be more or less following this road until we left the Gobi in about 400 miles. It was already much busier than Outer Mongolia, with a car or truck passing us every few minutes. Half a mile away, running parallel, was the trans-Mongolian railway, and once or twice an hour an implausibly long train clattered past, bearing cargoes of passengers or coal.

Not long after setting out down this road, we found ourselves surrounded by a forest of wind turbines, standing thirty metres high, silhouetted against the big blue sky. The wind was gentle today so only a handful were actually spinning. At the turbines' feet was the familiar sight of life-sized dinosaur models. Tyrannosauruses rex and triceratops, diplodocuses and pterodactyls stood in static poses of fight or flight.

I looked ahead and my smile widened. There before us was a spectacle that we might have expected more in an eccentric corner of the USA than the northern frontier of China. A pair of sauropods (so Leon identified for me) reached their necks across the road and joined lips in a tender kiss. They thus created an archway ten metres high and thirty wide, under which all cars had to drive. Leon set up the tripod and we filmed ourselves walking back into the Gobi, framed by the love birds.

Because of the wind farms and the decent road, at first it had felt as though the desert in China was different to that of Mongolia. But as we went further we saw that we were surrounded by the same barren wasteland of grit, snow and small, defiant shrubs. The Google satellite images, however, showed that we could expect a steadily more developed and populated desert as we moved south. Numerous grey-black stains, like violent bomb sites, marked the presence of open-cast mines for which Inner Mongolia was becoming famous. And every twenty or thirty miles we could see clusters of buildings and settlements, the first of which we hoped to reach by sunset. Although we were slowly getting used to the cold temperatures, it would be good to find a place to stay if we could, especially tonight, as the temperature was forecast to reach −24°C. At the same time, I was in two minds about staying inside because I felt nervous about what the Chinese police might make of us. We were surely both conspicuous and suspicious with our rucksacks, cameras and our insistence on travelling by foot. I couldn't wait to see China properly, but my mind kept replaying worst-case scenarios of arrest, camera confiscation and deportation.

'What would you rather see,' I said, 'a dinosaur or an alien?'

'A dinosaur,' said Leon, without hesitating.

I said that although the combination of Leon's enthusiasm, and the chance to pick up an actual dinosaur bone were making me consider becoming a dinosaur nerd myself, on balance, I would still rather see an alien.

'Really?' said Leon, amazed. But then he wavered and started to ponder whether he might prefer to see an alien too, after all. He was deeply torn and we debated the matter for a while, eventually concluding that whichever we saw, the important thing was that we remembered to capture it on camera.

The sun was about to set, and we were distracted from our conversations by a settlement coming into view on the left-hand side of the road. However, as we got nearer, we saw not village houses, but a complex of faceless grey buildings surrounded by a tall grey wall, flying a large red Chinese flag.

'Uh-oh, are those military barracks?' said Leon.

We stopped. It would not be a good idea to try and sleep in a military village if we wanted to avoid attention from the authorities. We looked over to the right and saw something we had not noticed until now. The whole landscape was fenced off, and behind the fence there was a series of red 'keep out' signs. Behind the signs the desert was strewn with old tanks and large targets.

'I think that's a firing range,' I said.

We looked at each other. The sky was starting to darken, and a heavy, hushed cold was falling. I puffed out some misty breaths, while Leon scanned the iPhone. 'The airport is only four miles away,' he said. 'We could try and sleep there.'

Though it would not be ideal sleeping in an airport this near to a barracks, the wind was starting to numb our faces and the prospect of an airport floor seemed far preferable to camping. We set off at a brisk pace and, an hour later, turned up a side road and saw the small, modern terminal building shining like a little celestial inn out of the darkness. We walked past a couple of taxis and stepped into the light and warmth. Inside, it was sparklingly clean, and a handful of people sat waiting for the next flight.

We perched down next to them and wondered what we should do. It seemed suddenly obvious that such a tiny airport as this would be unlikely to stay open overnight. Two airport policemen started to approach, and my heartbeat quickened. It felt as if the whole terminal was watching us.

'*Women yao kan nimen de hujiao?*' they said in Mandarin, with straight faces.

'Err,' my vocabulary abandoned me and I sat grinning inanely at them. It was one thing shopping for thermoses in Mandarin, another to understand what a policeman was saying to me while I took refuge in a minor airport.

'*Women yao kan nimen de hujiao?*' they repeated.

'Ah!' I said, catching the key word, and translating for Leon, 'they want to see our passports.'

We handed them over. The policemen looked at them for a minute then, to our relief, gave them back. I explained that we were looking for a place to sleep, and they said something else I did not understand. A moment later, they walked away. Unsure what was going on, Leon and I went and sat in a little snack bar in the corner of the airport. It did not sell any cooked food, so for 4 RMB (40 pence) each, we bought some instant noodles which came in cardboard bowls, and a processed sausage (1 RMB, 10 pence). The noodles came with sachets of spices that could be added for flavour and, as we prepared to eat, I noticed Leon pouring all of the powder into his bowl.

'Are you sure you want to do that? That stuff is pretty spicy,' I said.

'Yes, real men eat all the hot powder,' Leon replied, stirring it in with his disposable chopsticks and smiling. I smiled back.

As we ate, we agreed that the Chinese processed sausage was a welcome upgrade from the tins of Mongolian dog food, though Leon's initially rapid pace of slurping noodles quickly slowed as the spice took effect. Mid-mouthful we looked up and saw the policemen heading towards us once more, this time accompanied by an older man wearing a police chief's cap.

'*Hujiao*,' (passports) they said in unison as they reached the table.

We produced them again and I glanced across at Leon. He was looking very solemn – the combined effect of the spices and the police. The chief said, 'The airport will be shutting soon, you cannot sleep here. But Erlian is only fifteen miles away, and there are plenty of hotels there. You can catch a taxi outside.'

We let out a small sigh and thanked the officers. Having filled our thermoses from a hot water machine, we stepped back into the cold. The sudden move from the pleasant terminal to the bitter cold outside felt like a slap in the face, but I was relieved that the police had not interrogated us further. They stood at the window, watching us go; I was not sure if they noticed that we ignored the taxis and simply walked back into the night. Perhaps they were just glad that we were off their turf and not their problem any more.

We spotted a little row of trees on the verge beside the firing range, so we scurried through them and put up our tents. It was illegal for foreigners to camp in China, but I was simply following my usual motto for camping in strange places – as long as nobody saw us and nobody expected us to be there, we would probably be fine.

But that night was our coldest night so far, and in the middle of the night I woke up almost shivering. I started to put on more clothes until in the end I was wearing almost everything I had: on my feet, two pairs of socks; on my legs, two pairs of tights, hiking trousers, and Gore-Tex trousers; on my torso, three thermal vests, a fleece, a windproof jacket and a puffa jacket; on my hands, thin gloves and wool mittens; on my neck, a buff and a scarf; on my head, a balaclava, a woolly hat, a Mongolian fur hat, and my spare boxer shorts. If the army had caught us that night they might have been somewhat surprised by the appearance of the British spy.

We were awoken by a couple of loud cannon booms, followed by some hearty male singing. It was the barracks up the road reporting for action. We packed up quickly and headed back onto the road before anyone saw us.

We marched hard and fast all day, until an hour before dark the next village came into sight. We hoped there would be some kind of basic hostel; spotting an old shepherd leading his flock through the desert, we scrambled across to intercept him.

'Excuse me,' I said, in Mandarin, 'we are British people, we are looking for a hotel.' •

The shepherd stopped walking, looked at us for a moment, and then pointed a weather-beaten hand into the sky above the group of clay brick houses. It was hard to interpret exactly where he was pointing, but we said thank you and headed in that direction.

The village seemed deserted until we came to a little wooden shop. I walked in and three men stopped their conversation in mid-sentence and looked at me. I saw that the shelves were stacked with instant noodles, processed sausages, sweets and soft drinks. There were eggs and vegetables on the wooden counter and I was pleased that we were in the land of vegetables again.

'Excuse me, we are British people, we are looking for a hotel.'

One man led me outside and pointed his hand vaguely into the air, in a similar fashion to the shepherd. 'Chinese pointing', as Leon and I would come to call it, was usually like this – skywards and vague. As we set off again, the man called after us and acted out a climbing motion that was even more cryptic than the pointing.

We pressed on past more empty houses, and a chained-up dog barked at us. Two middle-aged ladies appeared and 'Chinese-pointed' for us to keep going, while again performing a mysterious climbing motion. We reached the railway line, clambered across it, and straddled a fence. 'Aha, the climbing,' we noted.

Another man led us to the next cluster of buildings and into a warm room full of tables, where a middle-aged lady said yes, this was the hotel (though it was evidently a pretty basic one). We beamed as we shed our packs and sat down. The lady brought us some snacks, and Leon laid his camera on the table while we waited to be shown to our room. The lady disappeared into the kitchen, and a moment later some dark shapes appeared at the window and half a dozen smartly dressed police officers walked in.

I groaned and realised Leon's camera was still on the table.

We stood and greeted them with a smile, though they remained straight-faced. They were mostly in their twenties.

'Passports please,' one of them said in Chinese.

We handed them over, yet again. While one officer copied our details onto a form, another stood by the table looking at the camera. This was what I had been worried about. Leon casually picked it up and played him some footage from the current memory card. Fortunately, this just showed us walking down the road, rather than the previous one that showed us camping beside the firing range.

After a short while the policemen started to relax and we joked with them about how beautiful and yet how cold China was, miming the freezing temperatures and the vast desert. One of the policemen challenged his colleague to pick up Leon's rucksack. The man took hold of the bag, but on his first attempt could not get it off the ground. This made Leon and I feel slightly less wimpish about our sore backs. In a second attempt, he squatted down underneath it and staggered to his feet. We all applauded and it was good to see some smiling. With our information copied down, the policemen handed back our passports, wished us luck and left.

We had been in China for less than sixty hours, and we had

already had two run-ins with the police. But we had survived the encounters unscathed and they had not seemed to care about the camera. Nonetheless, I hoped that we would not have to deal with the police every night on our long walk home.

15
Inner Mongolians

Distance to home: 2,789 miles

30 NOVEMBER

The next day we pressed on down the smooth asphalt. For hours the landscape of snowy, undulating plains hardly changed, though from time to time we saw more wind farms and farmhouses in the distance. Conspicuously, we did not see a single *ger*, although Inner Mongolia, too was historically a land of pastoral nomads. Such a way of life had continued even after the arrival of Chinese rule here four centuries ago, notwithstanding the slow tide of Han migrants who had begun to settle in certain parts of the region. It was only more recently, under Chinese Communism, that most Mongolians had been forced to end their itinerant ways. As Leon and I walked into the late afternoon, we wondered if the lonely brick houses dotting the horizon every five miles were inhabited by former nomads. Just before dark, with the temperature plummeting again, we spotted one a mile off the road, and decided to see if we could stay there for the evening.

We walked towards it across the dust; nearing it we saw a large, unchained dog pacing beside the porch and starting to bark. Leon zoomed in with the camera and we could see its breath forming mist in the air. The house was made from brick and concrete, with a glass-screened porch and corrugated-iron roof. A single red motorbike was parked outside, indicating someone was home. We shouted hello a few times. A teenage boy appeared, waved the dog quiet and walked over. He had a scruffy bowl haircut, thick black hair, and was clearly ethnically Mongolian rather than Han Chinese. He smiled, said hello in Mandarin, and led us past the dog and into the house.

We found ourselves in a dimly lit room, with a lone motorbike poster hanging on the bare walls. A bald man with rosy cheeks, presumably the boy's father, sat on a sofa watching television. He looked up, said a quiet hello, said something in Mongolian to the boy, and indicated that we should sit on the other sofa. We smiled and nodded and attempted to make conversation in Mandarin, our only medium of conversation. We tried to address both the man and the boy, but the man only glanced up from the TV occasionally and said very little. Leon and I took it in turns to do our usual party trick of explaining and acting out the walk and the cold. The man laughed a little, then turned back to the TV. It was screening some sort of Chinese obstacle-course game show.

The man muttered something to the boy in Mongol, who explained to us in Mandarin that he needed to go out to do something, though I did not understand what. A moment later we heard him roaring away on his motorbike. Leon and I looked at each other, wondering what we should do. Were we welcome here? It felt quite awkward. Maybe the boy had gone to get the police, like last night? I was really not in the mood to deal with the police again. Perhaps we should just cut our losses and set up camp? But it was unbelievably cold out there, and beautifully warm in here. The man continued to watch TV. It had been hard work trying to hold a conversation with him – perhaps he was shy, or perhaps he didn't want us here? Or maybe he just did not speak good Mandarin – though this seemed unlikely, because the Mongolian language had been banned for much of the Communist era. He must know some Mandarin.*

We did not know what to do and, paralysed by the warmth, we ended up sitting and waiting. Half an hour later we heard the motorbike returning, and the boy walked back in, smiling. Instead of the police, he had brought a hunk of meat, and he now stoked

---

* There was no point in us showing him the Mongolian magic letter because, while the people of Outer Mongolia read and write in a modernised Cyrillic version of Mongolian, the Mongolians of Inner Mongolia still read and write using the traditional Uighur script of Genghis's time.

up the stove and started to cook. I went outside to relieve myself. The cold was brutal, and the sun was setting almost purple on the empty horizon. I saw that the sheep pen, empty when we arrived, was now full of sheep and goats. The boy had been out shepherding in their flock, and getting some dinner.

Back inside, the boy was happily cooking away, and the man now smiled and said to Leon and I that we would be welcome to eat with them and spend the night. We expressed our immense gratitude, and a few minutes later, the boy was serving us with a tasty mutton soup and doughy buns to dip in it. I attempted a bit more conversation but, even with the boy, I was not able to get very far. We all smiled at each other, made appreciative noises about the food, and continued to watch TV.

I mused about the lives of our kind hosts. Where was the woman of the house?, I wondered. Before living in this little farmhouse, had they lived in a *ger* and owned cows, horses and camels, as well as sheep and goats? And what did they think of their Chinese rulers? The man would have been a child during the 1960s and the Cultural Revolution – Mao's megalomaniac attempt to reassert his power and bring the country under more central control. It had been the outer provinces of Tibet, Xinjiang and Inner Mongolia that had suffered the most. In Inner Mongolia, the focus of the terror was a campaign to root out an imagined Mongolian independence movement. Even official estimates admit to tens of thousands of ethnic Mongolians being killed, and hundreds of thousands imprisoned, maimed or injured.* Culture also suffered, with Buddhist monasteries destroyed, and both the Mongolian language and pictures of Genghis Khan being banned. No one who lived through the Cultural Revolution

---

* Dr Kerry Brown, an expert on the Cultural Revolution in Inner Mongolia, quotes reports of 'people being branded with hot irons, having their tongues and eyes ripped out, and being burnt alive'. The extent of the terror was such that 'a visiting soldier describes how, when he drove in an army jeep into one of the villages surrounding the provincial capital, Hohhot, people literally fled for their lives, believing him to be the latest in a constant stream of "clean up" patrols coming to get more victims'.

was unaffected, and in the end even Mao admitted there had been 'excesses'.

Since the 1970s, although such terrors had mercifully ended, a more deliberate policy of Han Chinese immigration into Inner Mongolia had swung into progress. By the 1980s, the Han Chinese were arriving in their hundreds of thousands, and the Mongolian people – who a century ago had been in a majority – were now outnumbered by more than four to one.* At the same time, the government was starting to promote the expansion of industrial zones and the exploitation of rich natural resources. In recent years, Inner Mongolia had become the fastest-growing economy in the whole of China.

Things had also improved somewhat for the ethnic Mongolians, as their culture had now become accepted, at least within officially sanctioned boundaries. The ban on their language had been reversed, to the point that it had become mandatory on all road signs – we had observed the indecipherable scrawls all down the highway. Genghis Khan, too, was no longer blacklisted. His picture was not only permitted, but statues of him had been built in many of the region's town squares. In an implausible volte-face, the Chinese government proclaimed that Genghis was actually a Chinese hero, not a Mongol one. After all, had his grandson, Kublai Khan, not been the founder of a Chinese dynasty? So of course he was Chinese.

However, despite the economic boom and renewed cultural affirmation, Chinese rule was still not a terribly positive thing for the Inner Mongolians. Many had been forced to settle down and cease their nomadic ways for good; most of the new wealth had gone to the Han, and the farming, industrial and mining developments were inflicting severe damage on the ecosystem.

I looked across the room at our host. His hospitality felt even more precious as I pondered what terrors he might have seen or experienced. Even though he must surely have reason to be distrustful

---

* The redrawing of the boundaries of Inner Mongolia also contributed to the proportionate rise in Han Chinese population.

of strangers, he had generously opened his home and shared a meal with us.

It was time for bed and, to top off their kindness, the boy showed us through a doorway and pointed to a bed on a platform that filled the width of the room. It was a *kang* – a special, centuries-old type of bed in northern China. Pipes, connected to the stove, run along beneath it, and so the bed is kept warm. This *kang* had a thin mattress on it, and all four of us climbed onboard and fell asleep side by side.

16
Dr Leon

Distance to home: 2,768 miles

1–3 DECEMBER

We are walking onwards down the highway, day after day, from dawn until dusk, as fast as we can. The landscape around us shifts slowly from one empty panorama to another. Although we are moving south at twenty to twenty-five miles a day, the progress is almost indiscernible on our map of China, and we are clearly not outrunning the winter. It is December now, the night-time temperature is in the low −20°Cs, and it is unlikely that it will get much warmer until February.

But we are falling into a good routine and, whether we sleep inside, or camp, we dutifully rise with the sun and stagger back onto the road. We groan when we heave on our heavy packs, and we gasp with shock when we step into the cold for the first time each morning. But once we are moving, the crisp desert landscape, full of silence and majesty, makes us want to sing.

Time passes slowly, as we stride forwards, one step at a time. For the first few hours we usually walk and talk side by side. By the afternoon, we drift apart, lost in our own thoughts. Leon is proving to be slightly faster than me, both at packing up and at walking, but we always stay within a few hundred metres of each other because we need to work together on the filming. We now store the camera in a pouch on the back of his rucksack, while the tripod is strapped to the side of mine. When we need to film, we do not have to drop our packs, but simply help each other pull the camera and tripod out. We are ready to start recording in a matter of seconds.

We need to capture a wide variety of footage. Most of the time

I am the subject while Leon shoots, but sometimes we switch roles. We take many different types of shot, including scenic shots, interview shots, B-roll (shots of little details that bring a scene to life), buddy scenes and video diaries. I have also strapped our small GoPro sports camera to my chest. With the push of a single button I can turn this on to record exactly what I see in front of me. All being well, the huge mass of footage we take will eventually be edited down by Tiberius into a four-part series when we get back to Hong Kong, but that seems impossibly far away now.

While we are shooting, Leon also directs. Sometimes he makes me walk back and forth in front of the camera several times. Occasionally, his instructions are unclear, or I misunderstand. I walk too far or not far enough. We have to repeat the whole thing, both of us getting annoyed in the process.

But apart from getting in a mood with each other once or twice a week, we are mostly getting on well. We are both movie fanatics, and as we walk we often natter about our favourite and least favourite movies, scenes and stars, sometimes even straying into such highbrow topics as the relative merits of Orlando Bloom and Jason Statham. We agree that Orlando, in his role as an elf, has mastered the art of the 'middle-distance stare'. Meanwhile Jason (or Jase as we call him), England's skinhead tough guy in Hollywood, has three critical expressions underpinning his success: angry look, confused look and ready-for-action look.

Leon uses these insights as a basis for his own directing.

'Give us an Orlando,' he commands, as he films me standing at the roadside. I immediately raise my eyes to the horizon, with a slightly smug expression on my face, imagining Orcs.

'Give us a Jase,' says Leon, as he takes a shot from the front.

'Which one?'

'Ready-for-action.'

I strike a grimace, expectant of combat and head-butts.

Another part of our daily routine is stopping every one or two hours for a break. Both of our new Chinese thermos flasks are already leaking, so our tepid bowls of instant noodles supplemented with processed sausage are not as appetising as they could be. When we run out of hot water completely, we move onto stuffing copious amounts of cheap biscuits and peanuts into our mouths. Leon's appetite for peanuts, in particular, seems inexhaustible. Our breaks are also a chance to do our stretches, which we had been taught by our sports physiotherapists back home as the best way to prevent injury. My physio in Hong Kong has given me a little spiked rubber ball with which I am supposed to pummel my muscles. It is agony to use, and I call it my torture ball.

But though our bodies are doing fine overall, the aches and pains are gradually increasing. One day I start complaining about a mildly sore shoulder, and suddenly Leon pipes up and says it is just a tensed muscle, and that I should take some Ibuprofen and give it a self-massage with the torture ball.

'You sound like a radio agony aunt-stroke-doctor,' I say, heeding his advice, and rubbing my shoulder.

'Indeed, I am,' says Leon. 'Actually, you can call me Dr Leon.'

Over the coming months, Dr Leon will end up making many diagnoses of injury and prescriptions for treatment. His usual advice consists of confidently stating that the problem will probably just get better on its own, and it is best not to worry about it. On this point, I accuse Dr Leon of being no mere optimist, but rather a hopeavist, as in: 'I have no real basis for saying things will work out OK, but I certainly hope they will.'

17
Tones

Distance to home: 2,736 miles

3–4 DECEMBER

Mandarin is not an easy language for English speakers. Firstly, it has no linguistic connection to European languages, meaning words need to be memorised from scratch. Secondly, it does not use an alphabet, but thousands of different characters.* Thirdly, it is a tonal language, with four tones. You thus have to learn not only how to pronounce a word, but also to say it in the right tone. For example, *ma* ('first' high-pitched tone) means mother; *ma* ('third' down and then up tone) means horse. 'I love my *ma*' (first tone) or 'I love my *ma*' (third tone) would mean quite different things: depending on whether you are trying to express affection for your mother, or for your horse.

But I did not want to let any of this put me off, and my motto was 'to learn by making mistakes', meaning that I would speak as much as possible, and not worry about embarrassing myself. I had started teaching myself Mandarin only five months previously, though since we arrived in China I had also been listening to an hour or two of ChinesePod lessons on my iPod each day. Leon was also learning, but he had spent less time studying, and it was usually me who took on the 'communicator' role while he filmed.

So far, the Chinese seemed very forgiving and willing to repeat things, though they did gravitate towards using the same method as English people do abroad – assuming that by shouting the same thing louder and louder we would be more likely to understand.

* There is a system for reading and writing using a Roman alphabet – Pinyin – though this has limitations.

They were also happy to listen attentively to my attempts to speak, and to creatively interpret my eccentric sign language and noises when my vocabulary failed me.

My food vocab was particularly weak; in restaurants I would often be ushered through to the kitchen and shown a plethora of rice, meat and vegetables and I would have to point out what I wanted, with lots of '*hen hao, hen hao*' (very good, very good) encouragements when they suggested throwing them all in a wok and frying them up.

And it was not only us who were initiating conversations – the Chinese were usually very inquisitive about what we were up to, and were nearly always asking us the same questions:

Where are you from?

What are you doing?

Where have you come from?

Where are you going?

Are you married?

Do you speak Mandarin?

Do you have children?

What is your job?

How is China?

Which is better – China or England (or America)?

Why don't you cycle?

Why don't you catch the bus?

In his book about walking through China in the late 1990s, Canadian travel writer Bill Purves described a near identical list of questions. He referred to his rote answers, which he reeled off multiple times a day, as 'reciting his catechism'. Leon and I were getting used to reciting our own catechisms.

As well as my own self-study, Christine, who was fluent in Mandarin, had also helped me to practise before I left. However, this was sometimes frustrating for her because my pronunciation was terrible and I tended to get grumpy when she did not help me in the ways I wanted.

'Pass me the milk please,' Christine would ask over breakfast, in English.

'How do you say "milk" in Mandarin?' I'd ask.

'*Niu nai.*'

'How do you say "pass me"?'

'*Gei wo.*'

'How do you say "milk" again, I've forgotten?'

'*Niu nai.*'

'And "pass me" again?'

'Honey, just pass me the milk!'

During our second week in Inner Mongolia, Christine had arrived back in Hong Kong from England. She told me of the feeling of desolation that had hit her as she dragged her luggage up the stairs and through the door, and saw the empty flat before her. It then truly dawned that I would not be back for many months.

But at least it was now much easier for us to speak on the phone: we were in the same time zone, and the mobile phone signal in much of China, even the desert, was mostly good. Sometimes the conversations we had were comforting and encouraging, but sometimes they just reminded us how far apart we were, and for how long. Christine also gave me some help with my Mandarin on the phone or if I met someone while on the phone with her, she would listen in and correct me afterwards.

It was not unusual for cars that overtook us to stop and reverse back to take a better look, and perhaps ask some questions. One day, a man stopped beside us, and started to reel off questions to which we replied with our increasingly polished catechism.

In answer to the question 'What are you doing?', we replied by saying:

'*Women zuo qu Datong.*' 'We are walking to Datong', using the Mandarin word '*zuo*', which we thought meant 'walk'.

The man looked confused, but beckoned us to his car, offering us a lift at least some of the way.

'*Bu yong le, women zuo qu Datong.*' 'No thank you, we're walking to Datong,' we said.

He persisted a few more times, but after a while gave up on the two mad foreigners and drove off with a honk.

Christine overheard me on the phone and burst out laughing. She pointed out that the way I was saying 'walk' – using '*zuo*' instead of '*zou*' – actually meant 'sit down'. So Leon and I had in fact been saying, 'We are sitting down to Datong.' To avoid confusion, Christine said we should try the words '*bu xing*' for walking instead.

But even after this correction, there were more confused responses. And the next time Christine overheard, she laughed again and said we were now using the wrong tones, thus it sounded like 'not able to'.

So when someone asked, 'What are you doing?', Leon and I were pointing our poles southwards and replying: 'We are not able to go to Datong!'

Travelling on our own two feet, although a hard, slow mode of transport, was certainly helping us to experience out-in-the-sticks parts of China where few other foreigners would find reason to visit. And, more often than not, even in these remote places, we were still able to stay inside and avoid the cold. About once a week, we passed through a proper town in which there would be little hotels called *binguans* – guest places. *Binguans* cost about 100 RMB (£10) per night, and had clean rooms and hot showers. We tried to treat ourselves to a night in one on our days off.

But there were also more local guesthouses called *ludians*: 'road shops'. In villages and smaller towns, they were they only option. They cost half or a quarter of the price of a *binguan*, and they were the usual accommodation of choice for truckers, poor migrants – and us. *Ludian* accommodation was often just the spare rooms behind a restaurant, and typically contained a couple of beds (with a pile of blankets on each), an old TV and, if we were lucky, a coal stove.* Officially, most *ludians* were not registered to accept foreign guests, but we were rarely turned away – perhaps because most settlements we passed through were never (or seldom) visited by foreigners, so nobody knew the rules.

But in all settlements, it went without saying that Leon and I were an unusual sight, our foreign strangeness exacerbated by our

---

* In summer, in the south of China, there was a fan instead of a stove.

huge packs, strange walking poles and increasingly dishevelled beards. We were stared at by virtually everyone we passed: street-sweepers, shopkeepers, shoppers, motorcyclists, children and mothers. On one occasion a young man walking beside us was staring so hard that he walked straight into a lamppost. However, we knew that in Chinese culture staring was not rude, and while being strange-looking might have provoked suspicion in the West, here in backwater China, it often aroused generosity.*

On our first weekly day off in Inner Mongolia, in the old Qing Dynasty fortress town of Sonid Youqi, we went to an internet café. The young manager asked us for our passports – everyone who used an internet café in China was supposed to give their Chinese ID or passport number. When we explained we'd left our passports in the hotel, he pulled open a drawer of spare ID cards, and happily logged us on under someone else's name. After we finished and came up to pay, he said, 'It's free, my treat.'

That night in a restaurant, we chatted to a neighbouring table of Chinese men while we waited for our bowls of dumplings. When we came to leave and tried to pay, the owner told us that there was no bill, the men had paid for us.

But it was not always quite that pleasant. One night, staying in a truck-stop town, we entered a rough-and-tumble trucker restaurant for dinner. We then managed to forget the oldest motto in the traveller's book: ask the price of food before ordering. The lady presented us with some tasty skewers of meat, and it was only after we had finished eating that she hit us with the bill – about five times what we normally paid for dinner. We started to haggle, completely unsure if she had given us the most expensive item on the menu, or if she had raised the price just for us, or both. All the truckers sitting at

---

* I had found on previous expeditions that I was normally treated well across the world, despite my often bizarre, nomadic appearance. On my three-year bicycle ride, having ridden through twenty countries in Asia, it was only in Western Europe, on my home straight, that I was sometimes denied drinking water from petrol stations and cafés for no apparent reason beyond my grubby clothes.

other tables turned to watch the argument, and we sensed an ominous mood building. But a few minutes later, the price was slightly lowered, we paid up, and with everyone having saved face, the room was full of smiles once again.

18
Baijiu

Distance to home: 2,704 miles

In our second week in China, we were starting to share the tarmac road with an increasing volume of traffic. We tucked ourselves against the verge as new cars, old cars, mopeds, tractors and trucks whizzed past. Although the driving in China was, by Western standards, fairly mad, it seemed that the Chinese drove as if they expected obstacles to appear in front of them suddenly – whether it be a donkey, a bicycle laden with large metal pipes, or a couple of foreign hikers with clinking poles. But one day we saw a dead cow lying by the roadside. Its legs stuck out with rigor mortis, and blood was frozen around the corners of its mouth. It was a stark reminder that our gravest danger on the expedition was not cold, police or robbers, but careless drivers.

Leon, who continued to take the lead with navigation, started to scan the iPhone satellite maps for possible alternative routes. One morning he led us off the main road and down a snowy path towards the railway track.

'There should be a kind of jeep track running alongside it,' he said.

He was right, and although our progress was slower on the snowy, dusty surface, there was no traffic, and we enjoyed watching the long trains rattling past us once or twice an hour. We also saw a couple of rail workers walking along the tracks themselves, one of them holding an enormous pair of pliers. The more we watched them, the more we started to think this actually looked like a good idea. The train lines passed through all the little snowy hills in cuttings, and thus it would be a much smoother route. So after we had overtaken the two rail workers, we clambered up the bank, and started marching along the tracks too. The spacing of the wooden sleepers made for an awkward stride, but overall our speed increased. After half an hour, we heard a burst of rhythmic chugging and shrill tooting – a train. Leon wanted to catch its approach on camera. We stayed nervously on the track until the iron rooster appeared from round the corner, and with a good ten seconds to spare we jumped off the track and out of the way as it rushed furiously past.

As night fell, we reached a cluster of small grey buildings beside the track. They looked like some kind of signal control complex. Having knocked on the door and received no answer, we found the door was unlocked and nudged inside. A bare corridor led us to another open door, and peering through, we saw two uniformed men – one lying asleep on a sofa, and the other staring at a wall of ancient computer screens. At first he did not notice us standing at the door.

'*Nihao, women shi yingguoren!*' (Hello, we are British people!) I said.

The man at the computer screens looked up and gasped with an open mouth. The other man woke up and let out a small shout. To calm them down we launched straight into our catechism before they had even asked any questions. We were walking (or not able to go) to Datong; we liked China; it was very beautiful, but very cold outside.

'So you work with trains?' I finished with a question.

The two men had started to recover from their shock, and they said that yes, they did. They gradually warmed to asking us more questions, and the man who had been asleep became increasingly animated. He was about fifty, with a skinhead, a chubby face, and an infectious laugh that made his lungs rasp and body shake.

Mr Cheerful, as we would call him, led us through to an office, where another man sat beside a wooden desk. A little dog leapt to its feet and ran up to us. Mr Cheerful explained what we were doing, and after they had conferred for a moment, the man at the desk, the boss, generously said we would be welcome to join them for dinner and stay the night.

We sat down in the kitchen as Mr Cheerful and a middle-aged lady started to cook. The air filled with hunger-inducing smells, and soon the table was strewn with plates of fried eggs, vegetables, noodles, rice, shrimps, and a bottle of vegetable oil. But when Mr Cheerful poured us each a glass of something from the bottle, we saw it was not vegetable oil.

'*Baijiu*,' said Mr Cheerful with a loud chuckle.

Baijiu literally means 'white alcohol', and is the drink of choice in much of China. It is usually made from sorghum or glutinous rice, very cheap, and needless to say, at 40–60 per cent alcohol level, incredibly strong. We sat around the table, the boss joined us, and the *baijiu* started to flow. Mr Cheerful's enthusiasm seemed to sum up the exuberance of the Chinese people in general. He was loud, fun and tolerant of our bad Chinese, though it was hard to follow exactly what he was saying. As the Chinese expert of the expedition I tried to translate for Leon. It was only when I subsequently watched the footage that I realised how often I had misunderstood.

'Sorry there is too much salt in the dishes,' said Mr Cheerful.

'He's asking if you want some eggs,' I said to Leon.

'*Ganbei*,' said Mr Cheerful, meaning cheers, or more literally, 'dry cup'. In other words, drink up and let's have another. But I was already on my second glass, and beginning to feel light-headed, and so I took only a sip.

Mr Cheerful broke into another drawn-out spasm of laughter, wheezing and shaking his head. He grabbed my little finger and exclaimed to us all how ladylike the British man was. I did not understand, smiled cheerfully back, and said '*xie xie*' (thank you). Next, he picked up a piece of vegetable and daintily held it up to me. I opened my mouth and he popped it in – like a mother bird feeding her chicks, or perhaps two besotted lovers. We all laughed. Before the night was over we had managed to establish that Mr Cheerful's job was to switch the lines, and organise the signals for the trains. He said there were few incidents, but that five or six horses and cows were hit by the trains each year, which always caused a mess. He lived in the city of Jining, about a week's walk away for us. When he knocked off work, he simply hitched a ride home on a passing train.

'After thirty years of hard work, I am very tired,' he said, shaking his head, and laughing sadly to himself. He was a small exhausted cog in the giant machine that kept China running smoothly.

Gradually the desert plains turned into desert hills, and signs of a more ambitious economy started to emerge. Every twenty miles we passed a petrol station. A mess of craters and bulldozers – open-cast mines – were scattered sporadically across the hillsides. Columns of electricity pylons marched across the land like tripods from *The War of the Worlds*. Factories jumbled with pipes and chimneys started to dot the valleys. One morning, we saw a big white bank of clouds rolling towards us, and rounded the corner to see that they were not clouds at all, but a colossal splurge of white fumes rising from a factory. A passer-by told us it was a French fries factory, and we noticed a pile of steaming potatoes, half a mile long, lying inside the fence. Another day we spotted some cranes putting up a new building, and a few minutes later we came to a large poster advertising what was happening: a vast new industrial zone, complete with power stations, factories and wide roads. The development was being constructed entirely from scratch, right here in the middle of nowhere.

There was also a more unlikely intrusion on the land. We had grown used to seeing only an occasional tree, making a lone, heroic stand against the Gobi. But now we also increasingly saw trees planted in ordered lines beside the road and on the hillsides. This was the beginning of the so-called 'Green Wall of China', a government attempt to thwart the advance of the Gobi. The desert was estimated to be taking over Chinese grassland at a rate of 2,000 square miles per year, and the Gobi dust storms that afflicted Beijing had also been occurring more frequently. The government believed that the problem could be curbed by a mass tree-planting campaign, though environmentalists said that the non-native species used sometimes did more harm than good as they damaged the fragile soil and ecosystem.

But whatever its flaws or merits, for us the Green Wall marked the beginning of the end of the Gobi.

19
Rivalry

Distance to home: 2,639 miles

9–10 DECEMBER

At the end of our second week in China, we reached the town of Chahar Youyi Houqi. Menacing-looking factories lined the roadside, and we coughed in the cold polluted air as we stomped past them. Several miles of grey backstreets eventually led us to a vibrant town centre full of shops and banks, though even the hardy locals looked cold, walking fast with hands in their pockets and collars turned up high around their necks. We checked into a hotel and, after our showers, noticed large amounts of dead, frost-nipped skin peeling off our fingers. Just before we reached the town, we had celebrated our passing of the 350-mile mark of the trip, which meant we were officially over 10 per cent of the way home.

The following morning, lying in a warm bed with a day off ahead of me, I woke up early, feeling strangely claustrophobic. The reason, I realised, was that Leon was lying in a bed just two metres away. I was suddenly feeling fed up with being stuck in his company for almost twenty-four hours a day. He was still asleep, so I packed the laptop and headed out in search of a café.

The streets were sleepy, and all I could find was a little noodle restaurant. Dozens of eyes looked up at me as I walked in, and I noticed a poster of Genghis Khan on the wall. I ignored the staring, ordered a bowl of noodles and opened my diary.

'I've been getting stressed with Leon, and I suspect he with me,' I began writing.

In most senses, Leon and I had been getting on well. Many of the long hours on the road were spent in fun conversations. We debated whatever random thoughts and ideas popped into our heads, from every conceivable angle; whether it was what items of our gear we should post home, new filming ideas, or the merits and demerits of environmentalism. But irritations were continuing to mount. Sometimes they were about very specific things – such as disagreements about how to film something, or the increasingly obvious issue that Leon was a faster walker than me. But sometimes it was more a general vexation, arising out of the fact that we just spent too much time together.

The previous day a new form of annoyance had arisen. About once a week we would take a short video on our iPhone to be posted on our expedition website. On this occasion, when we recorded the message, standing side by side on an empty train line, Leon had ended the recording by making a joke about how slow I was. This was a touchy subject, and after we had finished I stomped off in a bad mood.

As I had pressed ahead, I was deluged with negativity about Leon. My thoughts spiralled out of control, and suddenly I was seeing him not as an expedition partner, but a rival. All my time pitching the TV series and appearing on camera had been making me incredibly vain, with the result that I cared a lot about how I came across on screen. And now as I saw Leon pushing himself into the limelight, I felt very jealous. Hadn't I recruited him as merely the cameraman? And yet here he was morphing himself into a co-star. On one level, I knew I was being ridiculous, pathetic and egocentric, but the thoughts were there and I couldn't shake them off.

Such a competitive and negative mindset was classic expedition stuff, and Leon and I had in fact come to label the floods of bitter thinking against each other as 'head games'.* My head game after this little iPhone video incident seemed particularly bad. I was very angry with him. It was only when Leon caught up half an hour later, and took the initiative to talk it through, that we resolved the bad feelings. He apologised for the joke and I apologised for taking

---

* A Google search reveals that sometimes 'head games' is used to refer to people giving one another confusing signals and manipulating each other's emotions in a dating relationship. That is not the sense in which Leon and I were using it!

offence. But although the rivalry head games had been stemmed yesterday, this morning they were back again.

After I had been sitting in the restaurant for a few minutes, a man came and sat down opposite me, jolting me with his knees. He proceeded to stare at me and my diary writing, before slurping his noodles and carrying on an extra-loud conversation with his friend on the other side of the room. 'I'm not in the mood for this,' I muttered, standing and walking towards the door. I glanced up at the Genghis picture. 'And why would people want a picture of a mass-murderer on their wall?'

Back on the street, I went in search of an internet café, intending to take my mind off things by reading emails. As I walked, I realised the other reason I was feeling strange and fed up was because I would be turning thirty-five the next day. I had noticed a few grey hairs in my beard that morning, and all of a sudden felt like a grumpy old man. Wasn't I too old for this adventuring stuff? Shouldn't I just grow up and get a proper job? At twenty-five, Leon was younger, stronger and quicker. An irrational sense of envy started to rise up within me.

The internet at the first café was not working. The second initially refused to let me use a computer because I did not have a Chinese ID card. They were not even friendly about it. Perhaps my bad mood was making everyone around me less friendly. I argued for a while, and was finally given a computer. Not long after, I received a text message from Leon asking where I was and saying he needed to use the laptop. With a darkening mood, I returned to the hotel and gave it to him. I spent the rest of the day in the internet café writing my weekly newspaper article which, given my state of mind, took far longer than it should have.

That evening, back at the hotel, Leon looked tired, but not as bad as me. I felt emotionally, mentally and physically exhausted – worse than if I had not had a day off at all. Because it was my birthday the next day, and we had, in any case, been moving at a good pace through China, I proposed a second day off. Leon agreed.

But the next day, my birthday, I woke up wanting to burst into tears. What was wrong with me? Was the steady, relentless exhaustion of the road getting to me already? I tried to ignore the inner turmoil, but Leon sensed I was feeling unhappy and so took me out for a birthday chicken burger brunch in a little KFC knock-off. Seeing I needed space, after the brunch he left and I sat drinking coffee and reading *There Are Other Rivers*, a book by my old adventuring friend, Al. Like me, Al was an amateur-professional adventurer, and a bit of a tortured soul. In fact, his book was all about why going on exhausting, painful adventures was actually a good thing to do with one's life. We had often debated this, and once, when he had felt like giving up in the middle of a trip, I had told him that the alternative was to work in an office all day – surely pain, fear, hunger, danger, cold and potential financial ruin were better than that? Al and I had been through many adventures together. Sometimes we had got in pretty bad moods with each other and there had been plenty of head games. Yet in the long run, our friendship had become a very solid one. I wondered if the same thing might eventually happen with Leon.

Christine called to wish me a happy birthday, and we talked and prayed about the situation for a while. She helped me see things in perspective, and cheered me on – my number one fan, as always. I realised I needed to see things from Leon's point of view, and there was nothing wrong with him trying to make the most of the trip. Leon had made his own sacrifices in order to come – borrowing money, turning down other jobs and leaving his girlfriend Clare for six months. And in fact I was very impressed at how maturely he handled my little tantrums and was often the first to initiate an apology. Of course, he often got grumpy too, but that was par for the course on expeditions. Really, I should be grateful that he was such a decent and generous person. He could easily have turned out to be a complete nightmare.

That night, I felt a lot better. I explained to Leon that I had been feeling pretty downhearted and, to cheer me up, and because it was my birthday, he gave me a double swig of whisky. Psychologically it had been a hard, dark and deeply testing forty-eight hours, but somehow I had come out the other side. It was frightening how easy it was to get into a negative tailspin of thoughts – the internal trials were sometimes even harder than the external ones. And, unbeknown to us, an even greater challenge was about to come along.

20

My right foot

Distance to home: 2,639 miles

'So how did you meet Clare?' I asked. We were walking out of Chahar Youyi Houqi, where I had had my birthday, on a quiet, snowy, tree-lined track next to the railway.

'At university. We started going out about a year later, and we've been together for three years – though I was away cycling for a year and a half of that, and now I am away another six months.' Leon looked a bit sad.

'Well you can blame this trip on me,' I said.

'That's a good idea.'

We discussed the long-suffering patience of our girls for a while then, just before noon, we stumbled into our first agricultural village. Pigs lay lazily beside haystacks, birds fluttered in the trees, and men piled up wood – all this against a backdrop of frozen, ploughed fields. Signs of the end of the Gobi were coming thick and fast.

On the other side of the village, we clambered down into a dried-up riverbed, and back onto the main road. When we stopped for lunch a few minutes later, I noticed a slight discomfort in my right foot. It did not feel serious, but Dr Leon nonetheless prescribed some extra stretching and some Ibuprofen. I dutifully did as I was told. Our aim was to try and stretch at least twice a day, but in the last few days we had become lazy. Somehow I felt that, having done 10 per cent of the expedition, the risk of injury was smaller.

As the afternoon progressed, the foot pain grew steadily worse; at nightfall we reached a trucker town and checked into a *ludian*. I inspected my foot. It did not look swollen, but it felt very tender.

'Take two more Ibuprofen,' instructed Dr Leon. 'Hopefully it will be better in the morning.'

But to my horror, when I climbed out of bed the next morning, I found that I could not put any weight on it. We decided we had no choice but to continue: a truckers' junction was no place to take an injury day. I leaned hard on my poles and planted my foot on its side as I hobbled back into the world. We passed more and more villages and cultivated fields and, by late afternoon, the desert had virtually disappeared. As the sunset turned the sky purple, we crested a hill and saw our first city of the expedition, Jining, sprawling out before us. The skyline was filled with buildings, street lights and cranes, and a giant chimney towered over everything, like one of Blake's dark satanic mills. I suddenly imagined myself as an eye-witness of the industrial revolution in England two hundred years ago. But this was China and the industrial revolution was still in its prime, and it was happening on a much vaster scale.

A few hours later, sitting in a *binguan* room, I took my boots off and poked my foot. It had deteriorated significantly during the day. Dr Leon furrowed his brow, and said that the next day we should take our first injury day off, after which we both hoped it would be better.

But the next morning, it felt even worse. I had to use the support of the banister to get down the stairs, before limping along the street in search of an internet café. I sat down at a computer and fired off an email to Al, asking if he had any ideas about what it might be. That afternoon I got a reply:

'Your foot injury sounds alarmingly similar to how mine felt when I first broke my metatarsal.'

A broken metatarsal? I had never even heard of a metatarsal before, but after some Googling I discovered that it was the bone behind the toe bone – exactly where my foot was hurting. It was also the bone that David Beckham had broken shortly before the 2004 World Cup, to the distress of all England. His had been broken from a hard impact, but my pain had just begun gradually when I had been walking through the stream-bed two days earlier. I also read that a metatarsal can sometimes break as a stress fracture in response to too much walking.

'Historically, a metatarsal stress fracture has been called a march fracture because it was seen in soldiers who were marching for long periods of time,' said one authoritative-looking website.

The web pages explained that it usually took at least three months' rest to recover. In a panic, I emailed my podiatrist in Hong Kong, who replied recommending an X-ray. I sank into another deeply despondent mood. A serious injury was always at the top of my list of fears about what might undo the expedition, and suddenly it looked as if I might have one. We were barely 10 per cent of the way home; there was no way I could take three months off; and restarting the expedition was not an option.

Back at the hotel, Dr Leon was unfazed.

'Always avoid Googling symptoms,' he reprimanded, 'it is bound to make you think something is terribly wrong.'

But Dr Leon did agree to an X-ray, and thus another day off, and for the first time he also prescribed a 'things are getting bad' double swig of whisky before bed.

In the hospital reception area, people scurried in all directions, shouting, pushing and queuing up at a dozen different counters, each of which had an incomprehensible set of Chinese characters above them. Leon and I walked into the crowd.

'What do you think?' I said.

'No idea.' Even Dr Leon was at a loss.

A Chinese man walked up to us.

'Hello, can I help you?' he said in perfect English.

The man's name was Hugo. He was in his forties, smart and well spoken – it turned out he taught English at the local teacher training college. We explained our problem and he kindly showed us to the correct counter, spoke to the receptionist, and told us to pay 20 RMB (£2) for an appointment slip.

'Follow me,' Hugo said, and led us up some stairs. Along the way, we were spotted by the hospital's head of security, who joined us as a second escort.

A white corridor led us to a room full of people, and the head of security bustled us to the front where an elderly doctor in a white coat sat talking to a patient. The doctor looked up, a little surprised.

Ignoring the fact that there were at least twenty other people in the queue, the head of security told me to sit, and I removed my boot and sock, while Hugo translated. The doctor nodded, and started to press my toes in various places until I yelped. There were murmurings in the room as other patients came up with their own diagnoses for the strange foreigner. Dr Leon looked rather sheepish, and hid behind his camera.

The doctor told me to go for an X-ray, and the head of security led us through the maze to another room, where I lay under an X-ray machine, while Leon and the others joined the technician behind a screen of glass. I noticed the technician was happily puffing away, despite the no-smoking signs.

We returned to the doctor, who squinted at the X-rays against the light.

'I cannot see any broken bones,' he said. 'Your foot is strained because you have been walking too much. You need to rest for at least ten days, and it should get better.'

I felt elated that there was no broken bone, though the doctor's advice to take ten days off was going to be hard to follow. We were only a week's walk from Datong, and our Christmas break. Christine had already bought tickets to come to see me. We decided that we had to keep going, and would just have to be extra careful with my foot, and hopefully it would recover during the holiday. I emailed Al explaining the good news, but just before bed I got his reply:

'Good news on the foot. But be careful: when I first got the pain I was X-rayed and they said nothing was wrong.'

Al went on to explain that his broken metatarsal had started in exactly the same way as mine, with a gradual pain, and no indication on the X-rays. After resting it for two months, his foot had apparently recovered, so he ran the Marathon de Sables in North Africa. However, in the middle of the race, he felt a sudden crack in the same spot. After he had limped to the finish and flown home, this time the X-ray showed a fracture in the exact same place.

'I suspect what happened is that originally it was a stress fracture which more or less healed, but then I did a sudden clean break on it in the marathon,' he concluded.

Leon and I could not stop walking on the basis of Al's email, but my worries were back, and that night I did not sleep well.

21

Breaching the Wall

Distance to home: 2,549 miles

18 DECEMBER

'*Qing wen. Chang Cheng zai nar?*' (Excuse me, which way is the Long Wall?) I said.

The young man with a round face and brown jacket looked confused for a moment, and then said, 'Beijing.'

I thanked him and kept going. It was dawn in the town of Fengjie, and the sun was tearing through a polluted mist and turning the air golden. We had spent the previous two days walking here from Jining. With the help of some strong anti-inflammatory pills from our first-aid kit, and some careful limping, my foot had felt stable, though still painful. But today we had a mission to invigorate us: to breach the world's longest and most famous barricade, the Great Wall of China, or as it is called in China, the Chang Cheng, or Long Wall. Our map showed it lay just a few miles south of the town, precisely on the border between Inner Mongolia and our next province, Shanxi.*

The man I had asked was referring to the most famous segment of the Wall, but that was 300 miles to our east, a little north of Beijing. The Great Wall over there was fully bricked, and had been touched up for the millions of tourists who visited it each year. Out here, in the sticks, I knew it would be less impressive, but I had at least expected people to know it was on the outskirts of their own town.

---

* Technically, Inner Mongolia is an 'autonomous region', not a province, though in most senses this is just doublespeak for province, as there is no real autonomy.

We kept walking and met an old man with a toothy smile and a black cap.

'Chang Cheng?' I asked.

He looked confused. I repeated my question several times, varying my tones a bit, but his look of miscomprehension widened. I knew that in Chinese road atlases, the universal symbol for the Wall was ⊓⊔⊓⊔⊓⊔ so I pulled out a pen, and quickly drew the symbol on my hand.*

'Chang Cheng, Chang Cheng?' I said, showing it to him.

The old man's face lit with recognition.

'Ah, ChurChur.' He said, in his thick local accent, delighted to understand me. But although he now knew what we meant, he pointed in the opposite direction to where I thought it was. We smiled enthusiastically at each other for a moment, and then Leon and I soldiered onwards on our quest.

Since local people apparently did not know it was only a couple of miles away, I started to wonder if the Wall would be visible at ground level at all. On Google Maps, even when we zoomed in, it was not distinguishable as a Wall, but looked like a dusty road. This confirmed what I had already heard – the notion that you can see the Great Wall from space is a myth.† And this is not the only Great Wall myth. Another common, but false belief – this one started by a member of Britain's first diplomatic mission to China – is that the Wall is one continuous stone wall, spanning the whole of China. In reality, however, there is a network of Walls, built and rebuilt by various Chinese dynasties through the centuries. It was the Ming Dynasty, in the fifteenth and sixteenth centuries, who had built the most impressive and famous Wall, which included the stone

---

* I first came across this in Peter Hessler's modern classic about China, *Country Driving*, and we had also noticed it in our own torn-out atlas pages.

† As well as the evidence of many astronauts denying they could see the Wall from space, an article in the *Journal of Optometry* states that seeing the Great Wall from the moon would be the equivalent of being able to see a 2-cm cable from a thousand kilometres away.

sections near Beijing. However, much of their Wall, like the older Walls, was made from earth, not stone, and it was an earthen section of the Ming Wall that we were hoping to find.

A car slammed on its brakes beside us, apparently not concerned about blocking a busy lane of traffic. A smart man in his twenties jumped out and asked in English, 'Can I help you?'

We told him of our quest, and he pointed enthusiastically, encouraging us to keep going in the direction we thought we should be going. This was good news, and as we continued there was gradually more agreement: a couple of men bashing a metal pole nodded their heads and yelled that we were going the right way; a gathering of tough, gruff labourers puffed their cigarettes and in unison confirmed that we should carry on; another car stopped beside us and agreed. We were homing in. A sooty road led us out of town to a towering power station, where a group of taxi drivers at the gate looked at us expectantly.

'Chang Cheng?' we asked.

'Go straight and then turn left then turn right,' they said.

Around the corner, a gathering of cheerful street-sweepers, but still no Wall.

'It's just up there,' they said.

The area ahead of us broadened into a coal-processing zone, the breadth of several football pitches. The land was spread with wooden huts, piles of coal, bulldozers, and sooty-faced labourers – both male and female.

All of a sudden, Leon shouted: 'There it is!'

Through the haze, behind all the coal, stood the Wall. It was an earthen bank, covered partly in grass, three to four metres high, and cutting across the landscape at right angles. A hole had been cut through it for the road.

We scrambled up and let out a little cheer for reaching this monumental landmark.

Underfoot, the Wall was made of brown earth, and it ran away from us in both directions, rolling onwards forever through the flat landscape until it disappeared into a haze of hills. As well as tying east to west, it also split north from south. To the north, where we had just come from, there was a montage of power stations, electricity pylons and dirty black coal fields – it reminded me of the industrial wasteland outside Isengard in *The Lord of the Rings*. To the south, there was a spread of ploughed fields that spilled away into a blue skyline and blur of brown mountains. From our vantage point, with the south looking so tranquil and settled, and the north so grim and industrial, the old Chinese stereotype that north of the Wall was the land of the (non-Han) barbarians and south the land of the enlightened (Han), seemed very plausible. And now it was south of the Wall, and into China's historic heartland, that we had to venture.

22

The idea of China

Distance to home: 2,548 miles

18 DECEMBER

I still found it hard to grasp the idea of China, and in my formal
education I had been taught only a few random factoids about the
place: it had a Great Wall, it had pandas, it had lots of people, it
had a one-child policy. But now, in my own ponderous and amateur
way, I was trying to grasp more of what this 'China' really was.

I looked over my shoulder as the Wall receded into the haze
behind us.

'So do you think that thing worked in keeping out the Mongol
raiders?' I said, limping on the side of my foot.

'I suppose it would be quite hard to get a horse over it,' Leon said.

'But once you're through, you're through, like Hitler and the
Maginot Line in France.'

Leon nodded.

The truth was, although historical records showed the Wall had
sometimes stopped raiders from breaking in, the 'single line of
defence' vulnerability was a severe one.* As masters of tactics, the
Chinese were usually aware that the huge resources required to
build, maintain and man the Wall was not a cost-efficient way to
defend the Empire, and for much of Chinese history, therefore, Wall
building was shunned.†

---

* This was well proved in 1644, when a force of Manchurian tribesmen
were let through the Shanhai Gate on the northeast edge of the Empire.
Once through, they swept down to Beijing and set up their own dynasty,
the Qing, which lasted for more than two and a half centuries.
† Sun Tzu's fifth-century BC classic, *The Art of War*, does not talk about

But besides defence, the Wall played other useful roles. It was a giant artery along which troops and supplies could travel the breadth of the Empire. More importantly, it was a boundary marker that made visible the lines of the frontier, and laid claim to all the land that lay within it.

This was particularly symbolic in the reign of the first Emperor, Qin, who in 221 BC had conquered his rivals to create a united Chinese Empire for the first time. He had then joined and bolstered a network of existing Walls into a reasonably continuous rampart running along his northern frontier, thus defining where his Empire lay, what was the Qin's, what was China.*

Long before Emperor Qin marked out his kingdom geographically with the Wall, the foundations of Chinese civilisation had already begun to emerge.

These ideas had started in a much smaller territory in the lower reaches of the Yellow River, which even by 1000 BC knew itself by the title of Zhongguo, meaning 'Middle Kingdom'. The sense of being the centre of all civilisation was an important first foundation for China.

Another foundation of China's identity and future was the notion that a dynasty would rule by divine authority. This was known as the 'Mandate of Heaven'. When an old dynasty collapsed or was taken over, the new dynasty seizing power would be seen to have received the mandate to rule instead. Therefore changes in the ruling dynasties were possible without disturbing the foundations of the Empire. Four thousand years of Chinese history would recognise eleven major dynasties that governed by the 'Mandate of Heaven'.

---

building expensive walls, but rather about being adroit at the politics of keeping your enemies fighting each other. If possible, it was better to pay them off or make them dependent on you for trade rather than fight them head on.

* This Wall was located about a hundred miles north of the Ming Wall and, according to a historical map, we should have crossed it about a week previously. We did not, however, manage to spot it. It has apparently mostly crumbled into the dust.

The teachings of Master Kong – Confucius – made for a third, more ethical, building block of Chinese culture. From the fifth century BC, Confucianism emphasised the need for all members of society to know and accept their place: children must show respect to parents, and subjects to rulers, who in turn had to govern well. The ritual of paying due respect to one's dead ancestors was also vital.

Thus, with these (and other) conceptual foundations already in place, Emperor Qin had politically united the Chinese landmass and built the first Wall to help define the extent of the Empire.* He further deepened the sense of unity by building roads, and standardising writing, legal codes, and weights and measures. The Emperor and his state thus became the ultimate patriarch, holding the whole place together with an extraordinary bureaucracy. Emperor Qin's dynasty in fact lasted only a few decades, but the Han dynasty that followed solidified the foundations, and thus the idea of China – Zhongguo – was destined to endure.

In comparison with Europe, China has enjoyed enduring unification. In the third to fifth centuries AD, both the Roman and the Chinese Empires were going through a period of disintegration. While Rome failed to recover and Europe would never again be lastingly reunited, China was reunified under the rule of a new dynasty. By the seventh century, when Europe entered its so-called Dark Ages, the Chinese Empire was entering a golden age of art and literature. And in the centuries that followed, surrounded as it was by mountains, oceans and deserts, China remained self-sufficient and self-contained. It thus continued to see itself as the Middle Kingdom, the centre of the world and the heart of civilisation.

China's sense of superiority in the world was well founded. For seventeen of the last twenty centuries, China has had a bigger economy than Europe, and in many other ways it also often far surpassed the West – from poetry to philosophy, from science to government. The Chinese invented gunpowder, the printing press,

---

* Though Qin had actually rejected Confucianism himself, it would resurface in a major way soon after his death.

the rudder, the magnetic compass and paper money. By the 1100s, China was producing a quantity of iron that Europe would not attain until six hundred years later.

The system of imperial dynasties lasted until 1912; even to this day, China still calls itself Zhongguo. Many Chinese continue to revere the core teachings of Confucius, and the first, mythical emperors from five thousand years ago are still commemorated as the founders of the nation.

I talked to Christine about this. She was Hong Kong Chinese and definitely knew more about Chinese history than I had learned back home, but she was still amazed to grasp anew that 'we are the only ones who have survived as a civilisation.' For me, an Englishman, I found the best way I could appreciate the idea of China, and its stupendous age, cultural wealth and longevity, was to imagine a Europe in which everyone was still celebrating the achievements of Romulus, founder of Rome, still using surnames from the time of the Roman Republic, and still reading and writing in Latin.* And yet, in a sense, that was what China was like.

South of the Wall, the air temperature was still in the bitter mid −20°Cs, but my foot, although painful, was still stable enough to walk, no doubt helped by my continued consumption of strong anti-inflammatories. The physical landscape, though, was beginning to change. The scrubby agricultural fields petered out and gradually we found ourselves amid an ocean of hills. These hills were not

---

* The spoken version of the Chinese language did change, and there were, in any case, many different dialects spoken across the Empire. But the characters used for the writing remained fundamentally the same – another vital foundation (perhaps the most important one of all), which helped maintain the continuity of the Chinese civilisation and the unity of the Empire. Even today, there are still 292 dialects in China, and it is only in modern times that Mandarin has become more universally spoken. Sometimes, as Leon and I attempted to chat to local people in our poor Mandarin, but failed to understand them, they would try writing Chinese characters, assuming that even if we did not speak their language, we would at least be able to read it, which unfortunately we could not.

made from the Gobi earth, but rather loess. Loess is a soft, pale-brown soil, formed from the finest dust of the Gobi, which over millions of years had blown off and been deposited all over northern China. The resulting hills had been weathered into smooth shapes, but were also regularly lacerated by gullies and canyons. The Wall also acted as a rough environmental marker, dividing the extreme dryness of the Gobi, and the moderate dryness of northern China. And so this new landscape of arid, loess hills would be our home for the next two months.

That evening we reached the town of Xinrong, and over dinner Leon spoke on the phone to Clare. She was teaching in a secondary school near London, and was looking forward to the long Christmas holidays, but it was obvious that Leon felt sad that they would not be able to spend them together.

'So what are you going to do on our days off in Datong?' I asked him after he had got off the phone.

'Oh, I'll watch some Jason Statham movies, and eat lots of peanuts,' he said.

'Sounds fun.'

At this point, Christine rang, and we chatted for a while. I could not believe that I was going to see her in just three days' time. Leon might have overheard Christine and me talking about mince pies, by which I suppose he must have assumed Christine was bringing the good old traditional English Christmas treat with her.

But he was wrong, because 'mince pie' was actually the codename for the plan that Christine and I had been hatching: to fly Clare out to meet him for Christmas too.

23
Grottoes

Distance to home: 2,528 miles

19–20 DECEMBER

The next day we set off feeling exhilarated, because in the afternoon we would be reaching our first tourist destination in China – the ancient Buddhist caves of Yungang, sometimes known as the Yungang Grottoes. The grottoes were not quite in the same league as the Forbidden City or the Terracotta Warriors, but they were a UNESCO World Heritage Site, and featured in the guidebooks. Seeing tourist sites was not a core aim of the expedition, but when they fell on our route, we were glad to visit them. We wondered if we could still blend in as respectable tourists after being wild men of the desert for the previous few weeks. We decided to be on our best behaviour.

In mid-afternoon our iPhone map led us to the northern gate of the large, walled tourist park in which the grottoes were located. However, a pair of hulking wooden doors barred the entrance, and there was no one in the ticket booth. We spotted a side exit with a guard, but when we asked him where we could buy a ticket, he shook his head and pointed over the large hill behind the park. This was not mere skyward Chinese pointing; he was indicating that the main entrance to the complex was on the opposite side of the hill. It could take us two hours to walk over it, by which time it would be dark and the park would be shut.

We stood outside the closed gates and considered our options. A marshy, semi-frozen river ran beneath the park walls and we noticed a small path leading down to it and weaving its way through the swampy land. After a short debate, we concluded, in true hopeavist fashion, that the path must continue all the way to the main entrance.

We scrambled down the bank. The guard gave us a disapproving look and shouted something, but we were already on our way through the frozen mud and reeds and did not look back.

We had only been going a couple of minutes when we reached a channel of running water, one metre wide, with more solid ground on the other side. Leon was behind me. I paused for a moment, before, feeling confident that I could jump over without getting wet, planting my poles on the other side, and pushing off hard with my left foot.

In midair, I realised my mistake, and a second later I screamed as I landed with my full weight on my injured right foot.

'Aaagh, stupid, stupid idiot,' I shouted.

Dr Leon landed behind me, and looked concerned. I muttered something about needing to keep moving, and hobbled onwards. I had felt the injury was getting steadily better, but the impact had felt terrible – as if I had done some real damage. But nothing would be gained by stopping in the middle of the swamp. So I kept going, again limping on the side of my foot to prevent any more damage.

We snaked our way downstream, until we were on the left bank of the river, beneath the walls of the grotto complex, which rose vertically four metres above us. We could see the road bridge to the main entrance half a mile away, but with me limping in the swampy terrain, it would take us another hour to get there. At that moment, to our surprise, we came upon a homemade wooden ladder leaning against the wall.

Leon and I looked at each other and raised our eyebrows, and then I started carefully climbing the ladder using my uninjured foot, while Leon filmed. I felt suddenly very nervous, as if I was back at school and sneaking into some out-of-bounds area. I reached the top of the ladder and looked in. The top of the wall was level with the grounds of the park, and beyond an area of woodland I could see a couple of Chinese tourists walking around. But there were no guards in sight, so I slung my rucksack inside and rolled in myself. I squatted on the ground. A moment later Leon rolled in beside me.

'Shall we go?' whispered Leon.

'OK,' I said, adrenaline pumping.

We stood up and, looking as nonchalant as possible, Leon strolled and I limped through the trees. We followed signs towards the caves and engaged in a loud, airy conversation about how happy we were to be visiting the Yungang Grottoes. We were failing rather badly in our attempt to be conventional tourists for an afternoon, but at least we were in.

Round a corner, we found ourselves standing before a long, pale thirty-metre-high sandstone cliff face. Its surface was pockmarked with ancient eroded patterns and dozens of large caves. The cave entrances were at ground level, with additional openings set in the rock face above them. A few Chinese tourists strolled around taking photos with their mobile phones, and a uniformed guard stood expressionless in a corner.

We walked into our first cave, and immediately saw an enormous fifteen-metre-tall Buddha growing out of the rock. He sat in the lotus position and his broad, muscular chest was thrust out. One hand was raised, palm out, while the other rested calmly on his knee. His Gandharan face* was set in a ghost of a smile, beguiled and beguiling, and his eyes gazed dead ahead in a perfect Orlando. The cave walls were painted in blue and green patterns, and interspersed with worn sandstone and dozens of smaller Buddha statues.

The Yungang Grottoes are in fact home to over 51,000 Buddha statues, most of them having been carved out in the fifth and sixth centuries AD.† The message of Buddha is thought to have arrived in China several hundred years before this. It came primarily with traders from Central Asia, who crossed the western deserts on the fabled Silk Roads. At first the Buddha was looked upon as little more than a new foreign deity in the pantheon of native Daoist gods, but gradually, as scholar-monks progressed with the difficult task of translating Buddhist texts, the religion took root. By the end of the first millennium, there were thousands of monasteries

---

* The Gandhara style is a fusion of Persian, Indian and Greek influences, examples of which are still strewn across Central Asia.
† The earliest evidence for Buddhism in China comes from a mention of 'the gentle sacrifices to Buddha' in an official history written in 65 AD.

and pagodas dotting the countryside and filling the cities. And a significant proportion of the population – of high and low class – had become Buddhists. The flourishing of Buddhism in China is a case in point that, especially in the first millennium AD, China was not nearly as closed to foreign ideas as is sometimes supposed.*

Leon and I continued on through the next caves, and saw dozens more statues, but still only a fraction of the thousands that had been built. It was amazing to imagine the countless monks at work, chiselling and painting amid the rock faces, 1,500 years ago. All the other tourists around us were Chinese, and as far as we could tell, none was Buddhist. Most seemed intent on taking photos, despite the signs saying 'no photography'; although occasionally a guard told everyone to stop, as soon as he turned, the snapping resumed. Some were also keen to take photos of us, and we made friends with a group of students who gathered round with victory signs and happy smiles.

It was starting to get dark, and the guards ushered us back towards the main entrance. We walked and chatted with the students, feeling nervous that somebody at the gate might notice we had not come in that way. But as we walked past, the guards did not give us a second glance.

The next day, I hobbled into Datong alongside Leon. It was another important landmark, though my own elation was tempered by worries about whether my foot would recover in the coming week off, especially because of the previous day's swamp-jumping. We passed through grids of bland apartment blocks and shopfronts before reaching the hotel. As we went through the revolving doors, I saw Christine had already arrived. She was sitting in the lobby,

---

* The perception that China was consistently closed and xenophobic was based largely on the experience of the Jesuits who arrived in China in the 1600s, a time when China was indeed very closed. But in the broader run of history, China was actually sometimes a very open Empire – as the flourishing of the foreign religion of Buddhism in the fourth–seventh centuries AD demonstrates.

facing away from us. I could hardly believe she was really there. She turned and smiled at me.

'Hi Robbie,' she said, giving me a hug, but then immediately starting to wince.

'I'm sorry, I haven't had a shower for days.' I said.

She held her nose. 'That's OK, I brought some clean clothes for you.'

Leon was standing looking like a gooseberry. Christine said hello, and produced several large packs of chocolate for me, and two boxes of cereal for Leon.

'I brought something else for you too, Leon,' she said.

'What?'

At that moment, Clare appeared and said, 'Hello there.'

Leon nearly dropped his camera. His face changed from exhausted to shocked and then into a beaming, incredulous smile. 'Clare!' he said, 'what are you doing here?'

'I thought you might want to have some company for Christmas,' she said, giving him a big hug.

Leon's grin broadened further as Clare pulled out a bottle of whisky.

'Chocolate, cereal, whisky, and a beautiful wife, what more can a man want?' I said.

'Why does the wife come last?' said Christine, smiling.

And so 'Operation Mince Pie' had succeeded, and we had completed the second leg of the expedition. It had been a tough walk to get this far, but whatever our ailments and woes, we were 15 per cent of the way home, and now we had a week off with our girls.

Part Three

Towards the Yellow River

不到黄河不死心

One will not give up until the Yellow River is reached.

祸不单行

Disasters never come alone.

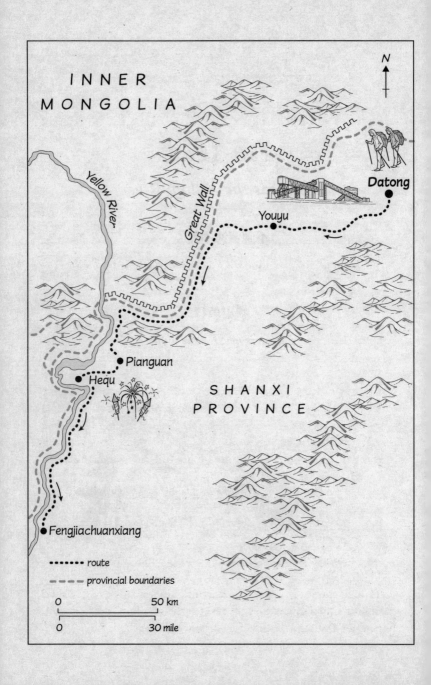

24
Christmas and Christine

Distance to home: 2,503 miles

21 DECEMBER–3 JANUARY

My week off with Christine was glorious. Instead of rising early to walk into a frozen Chinese dawn, I slept at least ten hours a night in our warm, comfortable bed. Twice a day, I took long hot showers, and every morning for breakfast I stuffed myself with handfuls of chocolates. Christine and I spent much of our time lounging around watching DVDs in the refuge of our room, often only venturing outside to have lunch and dinner at a local restaurant.

But readjusting to being back together was not without difficulty. Without a female civilising influence, and under the harsh conditions of the road, Leon and I had been slipping into brutish habits. We blew our noses on the backs of our gloves; we burped and farted constantly; we unpacked our bags by emptying them on the floor. Christine found all this somewhat bewildering to deal with. One day, at the end of lunch in a restaurant, I wiped my mouth with a serviette and threw it on the floor. Though this is the normal custom in much of China, I looked up to see her startled face, and had to apologise quickly.

As well as seeing our degeneration into wild men, Christine was also catching a glimpse of what we had been going through.

'It's a bit cold,' I said, as we stepped out into a –20°C afternoon without really noticing it.

'My toes are going numb,' she said. 'I can't believe you guys actually camp out in this.'

Though ethnically Chinese, Christine had previously only visited Mainland China's more famous cities such as Beijing and Shanghai. Backwater Datong was therefore a new experience for her.

'Why does everyone keep staring at us?' she asked. Mixed couples were unusual around here, but I had forgotten that being stared at was not normal.

Christine and I also spent time talking about how she had coped with being alone in Hong Kong. She had been keeping very busy with running the Viva office. We hoped we might raise £80,000 for the charity from the expedition, so she was building a following through social media. She had also helped us with much of our expedition research and admin. But, despite being busy, coping with an empty home was far from easy, and the months apart still stretched ahead of us.

In fact, the expedition had been growing in length since the moment I started planning it. When I had first come up with the idea and looked at a map, I had thought it would take about four months. By the time we set off, because of the route we were taking, I already knew it would be nearer five. And now, because we were moving more slowly than I had hoped, and I had the injured foot on top of this, I thought it would probably take us a total of six and half months. Leon and I had realised that the earliest we could realistically be home was late May. I explained this to Christine, and she accepted it with resilient resignation. I felt bad, and I was now committed to not letting this new deadline slip.

After six short but wonderful days, it was time for the girls to leave. With heavy hearts, we caught a taxi back to the airport. Christine was taking home our remaining stove, a hard drive's worth of footage and some excess clothing to help reduce the weight we carried. In return she had brought us shockproof thermoses, new blank hard drives, high-quality roll mats and, for me, a new pair of walking boots as my first pair had worn out. Leon hugged Clare goodbye, and I hugged Christine goodbye, and as they disappeared I gave Christine a final smile and wave. And then she was gone, and I felt desolate.

Leon and I could not dwell on missing our other halves because, unfortunately, during the holiday, my foot had got worse, not better. I thought it must be because the muscles had stiffened up. We would therefore need to stay in Datong for longer, and hope it started to improve. We sat in a cheap restaurant and brainstormed our options.

'I think it will take at least two weeks for the foot to fully recover,' I said, 'but if we wait that long there is no way we'll finish by late May.' Leon had made a similar promise to Clare about finishing in this timeframe.

Leon thought for a minute, and said, 'How about we give it another five days, and hopefully then, even if it is not fully recovered, you will at least be able to walk again. And we will still have just about enough time to finish by the deadline.'

'It will probably start deteriorating once we set off,' I said, 'but I guess we've got no choice.'

We decided to set ourselves a short-term goal of walking to the Yellow River, about 150 miles away, after which we would reassess. If at that point the foot was still causing significant delays, we would switch to a contingency plan: 'Plan B'.

Plan B would involve buying a couple of old bicycles and riding them for a few weeks to allow my foot to get better (I assumed I would still be able to cycle). This would at least allow us to keep going, but it would undermine the purity of the trip. Unfortunately, it seemed like our only real option.

On Christmas Day, the previous week, Christine and I had gone to a local church in the city centre. It was the size of a small cathedral, and was packed with thousands of people. We had arrived in the middle of the Christmas service, which seemed to involve various members of the congregation taking to the stage to perform a hymn or dance. Everyone else chatted and cheered appreciatively. We were warmly welcomed, though we declined the invitation to give a performance ourselves.

With Christine gone, I limped back to the church on my own. It was empty, apart from a caretaker. I sat in an empty aisle and, as I have done many times before in far-flung churches across the world, leant my head against the back of the pew in front and closed my eyes.

The stresses and worries about what now awaited us flashed through my mind. I felt powerless that there was literally nothing I could do to fix my foot. We had a Plan B, yes, but I was not happy about the compromise. Using bicycles would feel like a face-saving failure. On the other hand, it was a good thing that this expedition was proving so hard that we might fail. What kind of adventure would it be if there was no chance of failure?

I prayed and wrestled through these emotions and thoughts for a while, and tried to lay down my burdens. When I left the church, I did not feel any happier, but I did feel more resolved to accept the problems. We had not failed yet. The foot was not going to be the last of our problems, and the important thing was to keep going even when things went wrong. I liked Bunyan's old story, *The Pilgrim's Progress*, about the pilgrim who sets out on his journey, but then messes up and falls down. He gets back up and keeps going. Not long after, things go wrong again, but once more he gets back up and keeps going. Onwards he goes, falling and rising time after time, and slowly getting closer to his destination. Eventually the pilgrim makes it.

Leon and I had also tried to catch up on admin on our extra days off. Since we had started, we had not had much contact with our production company, Tiberius. The day before we left Datong, I sent them a long email giving an update. Overall, I felt we had done a good job of filming so far, especially given the cold and exhausting conditions. The hard drive we had sent from the border had been delayed, though. This meant the first they would see of our footage would be when Christine gave them the back-up hard drives that week. I was confident they would be impressed with the filming we had done: our stunning desert panoramas, our raging snowstorms and our silly adventures. I looked forward to hearing their feedback.

25
Coal country

Distance to home: 2,503 miles

3–4 JANUARY

We set off on 3 January, with Leon marching ahead and me limping behind. The frozen air and our heavy packs were a shock after eleven days of lying around inside. I had taken more of the strong anti-inflammatories, but still my foot felt delicate. Our road followed the Shili River out of town, the same route we had come in, and the dry valley walls on both sides climbed up to barren ridge lines. But the ridge was also dotted with occasional brown beacon towers, which had once relayed messages to and from the Great Wall, a hundred miles away. Although we had already crossed the Wall as we entered Shanxi Province, in fact it looped round to the south and the west, and we hoped to intercept it again in a few days' time. Now, however, we would actually walk along it, cross-country, all the way to the Yellow River.

But there was other ground to cover first. Just after lunch, we found ourselves entering a broader section of the valley, which in fact showcased one of the things that Shanxi was famous for: coal. The valley floor brimmed with activity. Small, privately owned mines clustered along the roadside, with rusty machinery churning coal out of the ground and dumping it in piles. Dwarfing these were the much bigger, government-owned mining complexes. They were the size of towns, and packed with homogeneous, rectangular accommodation blocks and administration buildings. Towering above all this were chimneys spewing grey smoke, and huge blue and white refining cylinders.

Coal was the essential ingredient in China's industrial revolution. In 2009, China had become the number one energy consumer in the world,* and two thirds of this energy came from coal. To keep up with demand, the nation's coal production increased three-fold between 2000 and 2010, and continued to grow at 10 per cent a year, with an average of two new coal power stations opening every week. Although Inner Mongolia had recently taken pole position as the province producing most tonnes, Shanxi was the traditional coal heartland, and its output was still vast – and growing. As we walked, we sometimes caught sight of the railway that ran down the valley. A coal train rumbled past every ten minutes, pulling 200 carriages. The road was full of coal trucks, interspersed with buses transporting miners, and shiny, chauffeur-driven Audis transporting the mine bosses. They all roared past, honking their horns, and we kept ourselves tucked against the verge.

We camped behind some trees, and the next day continued through more of the same landscape. But that night, instead of camping, we decided to try our luck with staying in one of the coal-mine complexes. We walked through the entrance, and immediately found that up close, the complex town was not as dreary as we had imagined. The streets were brightly lit, clean, and lined with manicured trees and hedges; red Chinese lanterns hung from the lampposts in preparation for Chinese New Year in a few weeks' time; a broad public square was dominated by a five-metre-wide TV screen showing the news. The buildings, which included shops and restaurants, were freshly painted in a colourful mixture of oranges and greens, and many of them sported the green and white logo of the 'Datong Coal Mine Group'.

Small groups of off-duty miners wandered the pavements. Their faces were a little glazed and, unusually, they did not stare at us. We asked a couple of them about a hotel, and were eventually pointed towards a building. We walked through the main entrance and into a corridor, unsure of which door to knock on. A young man appeared on the stairwell.

'Can I help you?' he said in English, with a smile.

We explained our situation, and the man, whose name was Duan,

* Though it still has a far lower per capita consumption than North America and Europe.

led us through some rooms and into another block. He chatted to a caretaker lady, and we were shown to a bare but beautifully warm dormitory with four beds. We dropped our packs with relief and gratitude, and Duan said he would come back later with some friends – we could all go for dinner.

'All four of us are engineering graduates,' said Duan, as we sat down at a round table in what seemed to be the smartest restaurant in town. He had brought three friends with him, and they were all in their early twenties, wore leather jackets and spoke good English. They were happy to be able to practise their conversation skills, and Leon and I were glad that we would not be limited by our Mandarin for a change.

'We are in the technology department,' said one of the friends. 'We only go down in the mine about once a week and most of our work is to do with maintenance and machinery design. This is a very modern mine; the miners here do not use picks and shovels.'

We had caught a glimpse of this as we passed through a control room on our way to the accommodation blocks. There was a wall of TV screens showing CCTV footage of the various mine operations: conveyor belts, miners loading them and buggies driving around, all far beneath the ground.

As the food arrived, Duan and his friends told us that this mine was 300 metres deep, and produced an astonishing 20,000 tonnes of coal a day. There were many such mines in this valley.

'The coal that comes to the surface is loaded automatically onto the trains,' they explained. 'They carry it to the port of Qinhuangdao on the coast, where it is shipped to wherever it is needed.'*

---

* Until recently, one of the major problems of China's coal was its location, buried here in the arid hills of Central China. Martin Jacques, author of *When China Rules the World*, claims that a major reason that England had an industrial revolution in the 1800s, and China did not, was not because of any cultural or intellectual superiority in the West, but rather because England had much more accessible coal. Shanxi's coal was, after all, over a thousand miles from the nascent industries that were developing on the Yangtze River at the time.

I mentioned that Western media often ran stories about horrific accidents in Chinese coal mines.

'The government mines like this one are safe,' said Duan, piling a piece of chicken onto my plate. 'Most of the accidents happen in the smaller, unregistered mines.' He explained that although being a miner in this mine was tough, with fourteen-hour shifts followed by two days off, it was a decent regular wage. As far as we could tell from how well things were organised above ground, this mine did seem well run and modern – though it was hard to believe there were no accidents at all. I had spotted a shop selling life insurance at the complex entrance.

'What about non-government mines?' I asked.

'They are very dangerous, especially the illegal ones,' said Duan.

He clearly did not want to elaborate further, but I had been reading that there were still tens of thousands of illegal mines in China, despite government clampdowns. Since the reform period started three decades ago, at least 170,000 miners had died in coal-mining accidents. According to official statistics, in 2012 – the year I was walking through China – more than three miners were killed, on average, each day. But miners in these dangerous, illegal mines had little choice, because their meagre wages were still more than they could earn as farmers. The mine owners, cast as villains by the state media, reportedly lived the high life, with expensive sports cars and multiple Beijing apartments.

When Duan's friend asked about coal mining in England, I said that most of the British coal mines had been closed by Margaret Thatcher in the 1980s, resulting in furious marches and protests.

'That could never happen here,' said Duan, shaking his head, 'there are too many workers. One hundred thousand work in the mines of this valley, and with their families there are three hundred thousand people. No, they could not shut the mines here.'*

---

* The other important issue raised by Chinese coal is the damage that it is causing to the environment. In many Chinese cities, the air is unsafe to breathe for much of the year. In terms of global impact, China's increasing coal consumption is effectively wiping out the benefits of the Kyoto Treaty.

It had been a good evening and, as we walked back to our warm beds, our stomachs full of meat, fish and beer, we felt content: we were back on the road; my foot, although sore, had survived two full walking days. I was looking forward to getting into the routine again.

We got back to our room and checked the iPhone for emails. Something had come in from Tiberius, our first email from them since we had sent back the footage.

It turned out there was a major problem.

26
The fiasco

Distance to home: 2,463 miles

5–7 JANUARY

> Subject: Emergency!!
> Hi Rob and Leon,
> We've been going through all the footage from Cards 1–22, and there
> is a very serious problem . . .
> Most of the exterior shots, 90 per cent, are out of focus.
> Please find out what is wrong a.s.a.p.!
> Best wishes
> Kate

'What?' said Leon, sitting up in his bed, as I read him the email
from the iPhone.

We pulled out the laptop in a panic and plugged in the back-up
hard drive of Gobi footage. For the first minute we could not spot
anything wrong, but as we scrutinised the small screen more closely,
to our horror we saw what Tiberius meant. The shots in the bright
sunlight were indeed slightly blurred. Not badly blurred, but bad
enough to make most of it unusable for a high-definition TV show.

Leon had gone pale. 'How can this have happened?' he said. 'The
cameras were mostly on autofocus.'

'I don't know.'

I was in shock too. This was a very serious situation. It meant that
most of the best footage that we had shot with great effort, freezing
hands and back-breaking pain in the beauty of the raw, frozen desert
was probably useless. Our dreams of making an inspiring documentary suddenly seemed dead in the dust, like a pile of camel bones. In

fact this was so serious that it might not be possible to make the show at all. In that case, we would be in such dire financial straits that we would probably have to abandon the trip.

We sat on our beds, looking at the blank walls and feeling numb. 'Well, what shall we do?' I said at last.

Leon looked up and said he didn't know. I thought I could almost see tears in his eyes.

'I think we should go back to Datong,' I said. 'We can get fast internet access and have a proper conversation with Tiberius. Hopefully we can figure out what has gone wrong and how to fix it.'

Leon agreed. We slept after midnight, our minds and emotions in turmoil, and hoping we would wake in the morning to discover that it was just a nightmare.

It was no nightmare. The next morning we squeezed in beside some coal miners, and a bus chugged us back down the valley to Datong. Two days' worth of walking fled past the windows in an hour, and our recently renewed sense that the expedition was getting back on track fled along with it. We checked into a hotel, and Leon shot some test footage outside, changing the settings on the camera for each clip. We uploaded the clips for Tiberius and, a short while later, they phoned us from Hong Kong.

We were nervous as the phone rang, wondering what they would say. To our relief, they did not start reprimanding us, but rather they wanted first and foremost to sort out the problem. It did not take long to establish what had gone wrong.

'The loss of focus is because of something called diffraction blur,' they said. 'You need to set the Iris Limiter, and turn the Auto-ND filter on.'

We knew vaguely the importance of an ND filter (yet it had somehow been turned off, and we had overlooked it) but the Iris Limiter was a new concept to both of us. It was good that the problem was fixed. But the damage was done, and it could not be undone.*

---

* In more technical terms, what happened was this: on a camera, as with the human eye, there is something called an iris, which expands and

We continued the discussion with Tiberius. Like us, of course, they were incredibly disappointed about what had happened. Suddenly their concerns about whether Leon and I were up to filming a whole TV show on our own seemed starkly well founded. 'Hopefully we can save some of the footage, but it's too early to tell how much,' they said, hinting that perhaps the series could still be made. 'You should just keep going for now, and we will send you more detailed feedback in a few days' time. You will also need to send footage back to us much more often, and we will need to have more regular phone conversations.' Leon and I would now need to do exactly as they told us. This was fair enough, but we felt daunted about coping with more pressure from them, on top of the foot injury, the severe cold, and our huge daily quota of miles to walk.

We stayed in the hotel that night, planning to catch a bus back to the coal mine the next day and keep walking. But the next morning I was awoken by the sound of my phone ringing very early, before my alarm went off. It was my father, in London. He had some sad news about my grandmother, he said. I knew what that meant. My grandmother, his mother, had died the previous day, peacefully, at her home. She was 106 years old.

After I hung up, I went into the bathroom and looked in the mirror, taking a few deep breaths, tears welling in my eyes. I had last seen her about a year previously. I remembered her stories of growing up in another world, and things long past, such as the day she came home to find out World War I had broken out. I recalled, with a smile, how, at the age of a hundred, she had read *War and*

---

contracts to control how much light comes into the lens. However, if the camera iris contracts too much, the light coming in will be diffracted, so that even if the camera is on auto-focus, the footage will be out of focus ('diffraction blur'). This is a law of science. To prevent the problem it is important to limit how small the iris can become using the Iris Limiter function. A second setting to prevent the problem is called the ND (Neutral Density) filter, which filters the light to stop the iris from contracting too much. Technically speaking, in our case, we had therefore been undone by the double mistake of the Iris Limiter having not been set, and the Auto-ND Filter having been turned off.

Peace. 'I'd been meaning to read it for ages, so thought I should get on with it,' she had said, before explaining that she had preferred the peace bits to the war bits. She had been a dear grandmother to all her fifteen grandchildren. We had been fortunate to have her around so long, and we would miss her greatly.

I went back into the bedroom and told Leon. He was very understanding, and asked if I was going to fly back for the funeral. As much as I wanted to be with my family, I knew I couldn't.

We caught a bus back to the coal mine and restarted our walk west. We were into new territory once more. Leon and I walked separately, with him walking faster and up ahead. I felt detached from the landscape, and simply ignored the coal trucks that gave us friendly honks as they roared past. My mind plodded from one downcast thought to the next. Most of all, I grieved for my grandmother and missed my family in England. But on top of this, my mind kept flooding with questions about how I was going to walk the next few hundred, let alone few thousand miles on my painful foot. I also lamented all the wasted effort we had put into the filming, and dreaded the implications for the show.

I wondered whether it had been a mistake to get involved with TV in the first place. In a sense, I had always felt a little ashamed for wanting to make a second show. It was so narcissistic and self-absorbed. On the expedition, it meant that sometimes I was thinking more about filming an experience than experiencing it. But the TV deal had helped fund the trip and also would help my freelance work, and thus justified me leaving wife and home for a big chunk of time. In other words, it was the price of being a 'professional' adventurer; though, right now, I felt neither professional nor adventurous. I just felt like a bit of an idiot carrying a very heavy rucksack down a very cold and very polluted coal valley.

If I felt bad, Leon was feeling worse. For him, this trip had been his chance to 'make his break' as an adventure cameraman. But now he had filmed the most scenically spectacular part of it largely out of focus. It would have been funny, if it had not been so serious. 'I'd offer to resign if it would help,' he had said to me on the bus ride to Datong. I was impressed by his willingness to take responsibility without making excuses, but quickly said no. He had been working in almost absurdly difficult conditions: filming his first full TV show with a camera he had never used before; sleeping in an icy tent with torn cardboard for a bed; walking over ten hours a day in blisteringly cold temperatures with a 25-kg rucksack; eating dog food or processed sausage, washed down with a laxative pill when nature required it; and putting up with grumpy old me for his companion. And for all this, although most of his costs were covered, he was taking joint liability for debts we incurred and was not getting paid a penny.

Despite these difficult conditions, Leon had not shirked from his technical responsibilities. He stayed up late watching through much of the footage when he backed it up, and was so conscientious that he spent hours polishing the lens to clean off specks of dust. However, it was part of his job description to monitor that the footage was being recorded at the required standards, and somehow he had not spotted the focus problem. On the other hand, neither had I when I had watched it with him, and so I knew the same thing would have happened to me. This was not the equivalent to leaving the lens cap on, by any measure, but it was something we definitely should have noticed. So how on earth had it happened?

There seemed to be a number of factors. Firstly, we had acquired the cameras very late, and in the rush before we left they had somehow been set up wrongly and we had not had time for sufficient test shoots; secondly, as we were usually using the autofocus, the last thing we were expecting was a focus problem (it was a meta-phorical blind spot); and finally, our laptop screen was small and we had been watching the footage on a freeware programme (which jolted the images) and so it had been hard to notice the blur.

This made good sense of what had happened. But at the same time, the more I ruminated, the more some dangerous thinking started to grow in my mind. Leon was the cameraman. Despite the mitigating factors, and although he had owned up to his mistake, offered to resign, and shown great remorse, he had still potentially jeopardised the whole expedition. My mind began to turn with resentful thoughts about Leon's ceaseless hopeavism and eagerness

My first day
in the Gobi

Leon and Molly

e Gobi

Stretching before bed

The desert monastery of
Khamariin Khiid

Welcomed into a *ger*

Childhood
in the dese

The best way to warm up in a Gobi blizzard – dancing

Sauropods, Leon, me

The biggest danger is the traffic

Leon's hands are losing skin

A shortcut ⟨along⟩
the trac⟨ks⟩

Mr Cheerful and friends

Leon self-filmin⟨g⟩

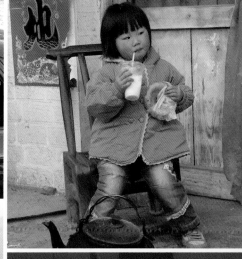

The French fry Factory. We had thought there were clouds in the sky before we saw the factory

The Yungang Grottoes

Leon and Clar
Orlandos a
better than mi
and Christin

A single swig (straight from the bottle)

e Great Wall with Leon climbing into a gully

A *yaodong* village

A warm *yaodong* stable
where we slept

Camping by the frozen Yellow River

Along the scree slope

Chinese New Year's Eve with Gaoyu and his family

to be involved in non-filming aspects of the expedition – if he had concentrated fully on his camera duties, perhaps he would have spotted the problem straight away.

Sensing a gigantic head game in the making, I knew I had to get things back in perspective quickly. Leon had been very unlucky, there was no doubt about that, and the somewhat cavalier attitude that I had brought to the expedition, right from the planning stages onwards, had definitely not helped. On another level, I did not want to become a bitter person, and in the long run, nursing grudges led only to misery. Finally, if I let my head run riot with these poisonous feelings against Leon, it would be more disastrous for the longer-term prospects of the expedition than this focus fiasco in the first place. I had to nip these thoughts in the bud.

When we stopped for our next break, I explained my lurking anger to Leon. I said outright that, even though he had made an unfortunate mistake, it would from now on be water under the bridge, forgiven, and – to the best of my ability – forgotten. Leon was grateful for this, and I could see him steeling himself to increase his efforts. He had fallen down, but he had got back up. We walked onwards together, still determined to make the expedition – and the show – work.

After two days we left the coal valley and entered an open brown plain, flanked by gentle hillocks. Leon suddenly piped up.

'I've just had an idea,' he said. 'You know that when our Chinese visas run out in February, we need to somehow get them renewed.' Our current plan was to leave the country on the cheapest flight possible, spend a night in a foreign airport, and then fly back in again to get another three-month entry stamp. It was a ridiculous plan, but we felt it would work.

'Go on,' I said.

'What if,' Leon said, 'instead of flying to South Korea or wherever is cheapest, we fly back to Mongolia.'

I raised my eyebrows.

'And then we go back to Zamiin-Uud,' he said, growing more animated. 'We retrieve Molly and head back into the desert for a few days and do some filming. That way we can get some non-out-of-focus desert footage that can be slotted into the show.'

'Wouldn't that be duping the viewers?' I said.

'Not really. It's not as if we are filming something we have not already done. And we are still in the middle of the trip. It is just a very expanded version of when I ask you to walk down a street a second time because I wasn't happy with the first take.'

Leon stayed quiet to let me think about it for a minute. It was true. We needed to leave the country anyway. And Leon's crazy plan would make our lives harder, not easier. I did not think it counted as 'cheating'.

'Actually,' I said, letting out a deep breath and shaking my head, 'maybe this could work.'

Leon was delighted. He told me that he had feared the focus fiasco would hang over him for the rest of his life, but now he had a chance to redeem himself. We had already abandoned our Plan A (walking at a reasonable rate), and were waiting to see whether we would proceed with Plan B (buying the bicycles if my foot did not recover). The 'Plan A, B, C' terminology was growing stale, and we needed an altogether grander, more militaristic title for Leon's idea. We decided to call it our 'Code Z'.

27
The cave village

Distance to home: 2,423 miles

8–10 JANUARY

The plains led us to the town of Youyu, where we took two more days off. My foot had started to deteriorate again, and we also felt emotionally washed out by the stress of the week. We were now slipping so far behind schedule that we could hardly bear to think about it. And despite the Code Z idea, Leon was still feeling depressed about the focus fiasco. On our second day off, I went shopping and bought a huge lightweight blanket. I paid a tailor's shop to cut it in half and sew up the edges. Returning to the hotel, I gave half to Leon. This cheered us up because we were still getting very cold when we camped, and the extra layer would make things more comfortable. The night before we left, Leon spoke to his mum on the phone. She reminded him not to forget what a privilege it was to be walking across China, and that many people dream of doing things like that and never get the chance. She had a point, and it was something we needed to hear.

The next morning, our rucksacks loaded with four days' supply of noodles and processed sausages, we were ready to make a fresh start of things. We set out westwards, following a flat road lined with willow trees and stubbly yellow fields. There was almost no traffic, and according to our map the road only led to a few villages – but beyond them, in the hills, also ran the Great Wall. At lunchtime, with more and more ridges rising from the horizon, we arrived at a village enclosed in a ten-metre-high earthen wall. The narrow streets were a jumble of run-down houses, and we wandered through until we found a small restaurant where we ate a plate of egg fried rice each. While we sat eating, I realised that even though the day's first anti-inflammatory pills had worn off, I hardly felt pain in my foot. That morning, before we set off, I had dug out my ankle support, and tried wearing it in reverse, so that it was covering my foot instead of my ankle. The improvisation seemed to be working.

Through the afternoon, a land of pale brown hillocks gradually replaced the fields, and we spotted more and more beacon towers on the hilltops. As the sun went down, we crossed a frozen stream, found a beautiful patch of grass, and pitched our tents. Strangely, neither of us felt hungry. We went and sat beside the stream as a slow moon rose. Leon dug out the hip flask and, beacon towers aside, we could have been in Scotland.

I told Leon I was feeling much more optimistic about my foot.

'A single swig to celebrate being able to walk again,' said Dr Leon. Dr Leon not only used his whisky as a cure, but also as an incentive for patients to get well quickly.

'Cheers Dr Leon,' I said.

In the middle of the night I was awoken by a gurgling in my stomach. Something was not right. I lay still for a moment, hoping it was not what I feared, but seconds later I was unzipping the tent, throwing on my boots and running into the cold bushes to relieve myself. I had not taken any Mr Lax pills for weeks. This had to be something we had eaten or drunk. In the course of the night, I made three more rapid exits. In between my outings, I was slightly consoled when I heard Leon swearing and fumbling with his own tent zip and running into the bushes as well. Whatever it was, we had both got it.

The next morning, we got up feeling weak, queasy and in no mood for breakfast.

'I think it was the egg fried rice in the walled village,' I said, digging out our first-aid kit yet again. We took a Ciprofloxacin antibiotic pill each – or anti-Mr-Lax, as we called it. This would stop us needing to run into the bushes all day, and hopefully kill the stomach bug, but it would still take a while for our appetites to return.

The previous day's road now became a dirt track and led us beside a frozen stream and into a maze of green-brown canyons.

Since the end of the Gobi we had had 3G reception almost constantly, and had been growing reliant on our iPhone's ability to pinpoint our location on Google Maps. However, our increasing remoteness and the high canyon walls were cutting off our reception, and by the afternoon we did not know where we were. Although we had still barely eaten, and were running out of water, we had no choice but to keep going. We spotted a partially melted section of a stream, and I edged out onto the ice to fill our bottles, adding iodine to kill any germs. I was shivering by the time I put on my gloves, and felt unsteady as I hauled the rucksack onto my back.

We were relieved when we eventually arrived at a hillside village, but it did not consist of normal village houses. Rather, everyone lived in caves. We had heard about these villages of cave houses, or *yaodongs*. They had been popular in this part of China for centuries, and there were said to still be 30 million people living in them.* We walked up the dusty street. Each of the little dwellings was fronted with bricks, windows and semi-circular entrances, and their grass-covered roofs merged into the hillside. Most of them also had a walled courtyard out front, but as far as we could see, the place was deserted. We needed to eat something soon and so started calling out 'hello' through the gates in the hope that someone might be able to give us hot water for our instant noodles. At first only the dogs noticed us. Eventually an old man appeared, and walked slowly towards us. He frowned as he tried to understand what we were saying. Another old man appeared, and joined his friend.

I dropped my rucksack, pulled out a thermos and asked if they had some hot water. The men hesitated and talked to each other. They spoke in a local dialect, not Mandarin. I saw a little girl staring at us from around a corner, but when I smiled at her, she and her blue-ribboned pigtails quickly fled. However, within a few minutes, she was back, along with a crowd of a dozen people – the whole village had turned out to see us.

We explained we were walking to the Wall, and there was general

---

* Even China's new President, Xin Jinping, spent several years living in one in the 1960s.

agreement and some unusually specific Chinese pointing that we were heading the right way. I held out the thermoses again, and an old man pointed at the half-empty plastic bottles in the back of my rucksack. 'Your bottles are frozen,' he said in a thick accent. A child giggled. A lady stepped forwards, took the two thermoses and walked into a *yaodong*.

The crowd stared and discussed our rucksacks. Almost everyone was either elderly or very young. Most of the young adults, it seemed, had left the village to work in the towns and cities. The lady came back with our thermoses. We thanked her and then, feeling cold from standing around, and with my appetite starting to pick up, I asked if there happened to be a restaurant.

'No, there's not,' several people said, and then, after more discussion, and to our immense gratitude, an old man and his middle-aged son said we could come back to their house to eat. We followed them into a courtyard containing a noisy pig, an old tractor and a satellite dish resembling a giant wok.* Entering the *yaodong*, we passed through a hallway piled up with boxes and crates, and turned left into the main room. Three metres wide and six deep, the walls were lined with smoke-stained plaster. On one of the four walls there was a window. Half of the space was taken up by a *kang*, and the other half was dominated by a simple wood stove, a cheap DVD player and a large, square TV. The room seemed to function as kitchen, living room, dining room and bedroom combined.

The men told us to make ourselves comfortable, and as I sat down on the *kang* I felt relief sweep through my body. I was even more exhausted than I realised. The son started to stoke the stove and fan it with a hand-powered air pump, and the room quickly warmed. He used a huge cleaver to chop up pieces of pork and threw them plus some potatoes and generous amounts of salt into a deliciously sizzling wok. Then he set to work with flour, a rolling pin and some scissors to make noodles. The old man meanwhile put on a DVD, which showcased a middle-aged couple wearing

---

* The Chinese word used for satellite dishes is in fact the same word as used for wok.

gigantic 1980s sunglasses and garish grins, waving flags and singing a cheery tune. We leaned back on the beds, rosy cheeked and near delirious at the respite from the cold and the thought of hot food on the way.

When the old man said that we would be welcome to stay the night, our powers of resistance were at their weakest. It was only mid-afternoon, and stopping early would put us still further behind schedule, but we reasoned that we needed a good night's sleep to recover from the stomach bug. We asked how much it would cost, and the man said it was free. We thought we could leave him with a parting gift, and gratefully accepted. A few minutes later we were served a fine meal of deep-fried noodles, potatoes and pork.

Over the course of the rest of the evening, more and more villagers trooped in to take a look at us. All of them smoked, so combined with the belching stove, the room became thick with fumes. Again and again we were asked the usual questions, and our answers were repeated and discussed around the room. Wanting to change the subject, I pulled out a photo of Christine and me on our wedding day, which I carried in my wallet. I sometimes looked at it when I was missing her. It was passed around to various exclamations of 'very pretty'. Everyone seemed pleased that I was married to a Chinese girl.

Someone asked if we had any foreign currency. Leon had told me that on previous travels he had sometimes shown foreign currency to people he met when he ran out of things to talk about. I thought it sounded an amusingly high-risk strategy for losing banknotes, but I dug out a Hong Kong twenty-dollar bill, while Leon pulled out a US ten-dollar bill and a Mongolian one hundred-tugrik note. The notes were passed around with more murmurs of interest and conversation. The old man who owned the cave seemed especially interested in the US ten-dollar note. This was worth more than the price of a night in a *binguan* with hot showers, so we were not keen to give it to him, though I did say he could keep the Hong Kong note. The man thanked us, but kept holding onto the US dollars until, with a firm smile, we asked for it back. It was time for bed, and the old man and his son rolled out their blankets on the *kang*.

Leon and I produced our sleeping bags, and all four of us lay down to sleep.

The next morning we put on our packs, said our thank yous and stepped out of the door. As we were about to leave the courtyard, the old man came out and asked to see the ten-dollar bill again. We handed it to him. He smiled, and then, without handing it back, walked back into his house. Leon and I looked at each other and shrugged. He had taken good care of us and certainly earned it. I felt slightly ashamed that I had not let him just keep it the night before.

Leon and I soldiered out into the morning and set our sights on finding that Wall. Brown hills, brown beacon towers, brown ridges. Everything around us was brown, apart from the blue sky above and a frozen stream beside our path. Around the next hill another *yaodong* village came into view, and a man hacking ice out of the stream pointed us up a steep track. We walked up it and when we reached the top we stopped. There, once again before us, running brazenly through the empty hills, was the Great Wall.

28

The Wall, our guide

Distance to home: 2,410 miles

11–15 JANUARY

A line of imperial earth, three metres high and a metre wide, runs ahead and behind, up and down, veering and swerving through the contours of this twisted, rolling land. It is a line of defence to keep out the barbarians, a boundary line to mark the frontier between the land of the civilised and the wastelands of the uncouth. It is bold, confident, unfazed, enduring, magical and ancient. It is from another age, another world, from the time of uncrossed oceans and unknown continents, tyrannical emperors and horseback armies.

We walk beside it on goat-herders' paths; when these disappear, we push through brambles, or trudge through forests carpeted with snow. Occasionally we walk along the top of the Wall, our eyes minding each step – it is a three- or four-metre fall from either side. The walking, although hard and slow, also makes us feel liberated and joyful, for we are back in the wild beauty of China, and roaming free amid its ancient loess hills. Our worries about the filming, the foot injury and the Chinese police are falling back into perspective, and though it is still deep in the −20°Cs, we are finally toughening up. And we no longer need fear getting lost – the Wall is our guide.

Like the land, the Wall is made from loess. Every few hundred metres there is an earthen watchtower – a simple, large mound, without an entrance or room inside. Sometimes we can see ten or more such brown towers in either direction, stretching to the furthest ridges. And often there are beacon towers on the hills behind, and even another wall – a second line of defence or a wall from some other dynasty, we do not know. And made as it is from the earth, the Wall is crumbling from the centuries. When we scramble over it or along it, little pieces crumble into the dust. The hills, meanwhile, are riddled with gullies. Once the Wall would have bridged its way across these, but these sections have long since been washed away. Regularly, we have to scramble down the steep hillsides to the gully floors and launch into a long clamber and crawl back up the other side.

Often, we feel entirely alone, as if we have the Wall to ourselves, but we do encounter the occasional grizzled goat-herder and, once or twice a day, a cave village. The yaodongs are built into the south-facing slopes to get more sun and, because we are approaching from the north, sometimes it is only when we spot a chimney at our feet that we realise we are on someone's roof. But the villagers are always friendly and happy to resupply us with hot water, and are intrigued to see Leon's camera. In one village he flips the screen round and a beautiful old lady stares at it, wondrous at being able to see a digitised image of herself, possibly for the first time.

My diary entries, meanwhile, reflect an increasingly exhausted mind and body:

15 January: Foot feeling stable – foot support really helps.
16 January: Falling further and further behind schedule – what can we do about that? Things are turning into a bit of a blur as we are walking pretty hard, working hard filming. I'm not sure how sustainable this is?

At night, we camp amid the hillocks beneath the wall though, even with our new blankets, it is still too cold to really enjoy our sleep. One evening, at dusk, we come to an abandoned yaodong stable, its floor lined with hay. Even though there is no glass in the window, or door in the doorway, it is still a luxurious few degrees warmer than outside. I fall into a slumber, as happy as a horse in a hay-filled stable in the cold mountains of northern Shanxi.

One dawn, just after we have packed up camp, I climb a watchtower and stand looking along the Wall continuing through the hills. Leon and I are finding even walking beside the Wall hard work, so what *kind of a gargantuan task must it have been to build it? Here, the Wall was built using the tamped earth technique – a wooden casing was constructed, and mixed earth packed inside to leave a solid earthen wall. It was built by corvée labourers; this was a form of taxation imposed on the common people whereby they not only had to pay tax in money and produce, but also by labouring for the state. The work of corvée labourers often included the hard, dangerous tasks of building elephantine public projects, like the Wall.*

I imagine the mass of labourers, their quiet, hunched footsteps and groans as they dig and pack the earth. In winter, the cold would soon be deadly for those without thick clothing, good food and good shelter. In summer, forced to work in the heat all day, with insufficient water, it would have been no less dangerous.

An official history from the first century BC *claims that a million people perished building the Wall for Emperor Qin. It is also said that the bodies of dead labourers were sometimes not given proper burials, but just incorporated into the rampart itself, which has resulted in the Wall sometimes being described as the world's longest cemetery. One day, some village children tell us a story about a girl called Meng Jiang Nu.*

Meng Jiang Nu married the man she loved. However, no sooner had they married then he was taken away for corvée duty, building the Wall. Meng Jiang Nu was distraught, and went to look for him. But when she reached the section of the Wall where he was working, she was told he had already died. And so she wept and wept, and her tears were so many that they swept away a section of Wall.*

I now look up from the Wall to the hills, and suddenly I am imagining myself, not as a corvée labourer, but as a conscript soldier, sent to guard the frontier, keeping watch from this very tower, on some frozen dawn 600 years ago, underfed and cold. As I scan the

---

* We later discovered that this was a famous Chinese legend, and that there were many different versions of it, some of which included the peculiar detail that Meng Jiang Nu was hatched from a melon. Although it was impossible to establish its origins, it painted a vivid picture of the grief and death toll exacted all those centuries ago.

ridge line, the sound of horses' hooves echoes into my imagination. The raiders are coming. A moment later, a line of horses appears, bearing rugged men, outlandish, dangerous, ready to kill – though it is unusual for them to attack by day. I can almost smell the blood in the air. I freeze in terror. I cannot run; I'll be executed. And besides, behind me are my farmlands and my village. I light the beacon, a signal alerting reinforcements. But they will not get here in time. I will stand and fight, but I will not last long – I am arrow fodder for the Empire.

29

The Mother and the Sorrow

Distance to home: 2,355 miles

16–18 JANUARY

To speed ourselves up on our Wall walking stretch, we sometimes hiked along tracks in the valleys, the watchtowers marching along the ridge above us. As we walked, we also now got sporadic reception on our phone, so we spoke further with Tiberius. It turned out that enough footage could be saved to hopefully still make the show viable. We shared the Code Z idea with them, and they enthusiastically agreed to it. They said it would be a good way to fill in a few gaps, especially for the more epic desert panoramas. In addition, they sent us a feedback email explaining that we needed to use the tripod more to get steadier shots, and the radio mic more to get better sound. It had been hard, and sometimes unrealistic to do these things in the harsh weather, and we felt demoralised that their feedback focused on the things we needed to improve, rather than praising anything we had got right. But at the same time, although we had been working very hard, perhaps we could work harder still. At the end of the day it was not Tiberius's job to show us sympathy but to make sure we shot the necessary quality of footage. And so that was what we were going to have to do.

After five days, a twisting road led us away from the Wall, and we began to descend into a deep canyon. As we wound down through pine forests on endless switchbacks, we could see a steep cliff face on the other side, several miles away. After an hour, we still could not see the bottom. We spotted a beacon tower, and clambered up to it for a better view. And from here, finally, we caught sight of our next major landmark: the Yellow River, the Huang He.

The river's tumultuous flow was imprisoned by the cliffs, scree slopes and crags and, at the point where we sighted it, it was also unnaturally split in half by a giant dam. Upstream of the dam, the river was fifty metres higher, and its surface was frozen. Downstream, the water – a murky brown-green colour, not yellow – gushed out of the dam's base, liquid again. It swirled rapidly under a bridge and down to a bend two miles away, where it froze over once more.

The Yellow River has always been a central character in the history of China. It was sometimes referred to as 'the Mother River', which was appropriate, for the heart of Chinese civilisation had grown up in its fertile valleys downstream. But it was also known as 'China's Sorrow' on account of its frequent, terrible floods – over one and half thousand of them since China was unified two millennia ago.

Both the floods, and the river's famous yellow-brown colour, are caused by the heavy load of silt that the water picks up on its path through the loess plateau. The river carries over thirty times more sediment per cubic metre than the Nile. In the final 500 miles to the sea, as it decelerates amid the flat plains, much of the river's load is deposited on the riverbed. This causes the riverbed to rise continually and so, down through the ages, the only way to stop the river flooding had been to build huge dykes to contain it. But as the riverbed continued to rise, the river channel itself now flowed many metres above the surrounding countryside – with nothing but the dykes to hold it in. In a flood, or if the dykes burst, the river would gush out across the plains, sometimes rampaging around in different directions for years before finding a new channel in which to make a home for a while.

These floods not only killed millions through drowning, famines and epidemics, but also severely destabilised the whole Empire. The mythical Emperor Yu of the third millennium BC was the first emperor to attempt to control the river, and was attributed as saying, 'When the Yellow River is at peace, China is at peace.' This is linked to the widespread belief in China that natural disasters – whether they be earthquakes, famines, or floods – were omens from heaven indicating disfavour with the ruling dynasty, and that soon a new dynasty would be given the 'Mandate of Heaven' instead. There was actually a very literal link between such calamities and the implosion of the Empire, because huge numbers of displaced people often led to mass rebellions. Yellow River flooding had in fact been a contributing factor to the outbreak of the Boxer Rebellion at the end of the nineteenth century – often noted as a key event leading to the downfall of the Qing Dynasty, the last dynasty, in 1912.* And yet even after the death of the dynastic Empire, the Mother River, the Sorrow of China, kept on flowing.

* Sometimes, rulers tried to use the Yellow River as a weapon, deliberately bursting its banks to wipe out or block an advancing enemy. But the river was a Pandora's box; once unleashed, its power could not be tamed or controlled. In such an attempt by a Ming Dynasty governor in the seventeenth century, he had ended up accidentally flooding his own city, with three quarters of the population dying as a result. In 1938, Chiang Kai Shek had tried such a tactic against the Japanese, but while up to a million civilians died in the ensuing floods, there was little benefit to the war effort.

30

Hemmed in

Distance to home: 2,295 miles

We clambered down towards the river and, on the way, caught a much better view of the dam. It was an impressive sight, with its smooth wall of concrete, and series of James Bond-like control buildings and watchtowers. This was one of dozens of dams on the river. Although they had virtually put an end to the river's terrible floods, they are frequently prone to silting up, making their hydro-electric power redundant. As we continued downwards, a shopkeeper in a solitary petrol station told us there was a path beside the river that would lead us downstream.

At the bottom of the canyon, we saw that the river was flowing fast: aggressive and silent, like a fiercely disciplined army marching off for a surprise assault. It seethed with ice shards, and shelves of ice jutted several metres out from the banks on each side. In the earlier stages of planning the expedition, we had considered carrying small inflatable kayaks with us to paddle down the Yellow River. We had abandoned the idea when delays meant that we would not reach it until winter, which turned out to be the right decision. Paddling in these conditions would have been suicidal. We saw the track mentioned by the shopkeeper and, as we started walking, we found ourselves sandwiched between the silent, icy river on our right, and towering cliffs on our left. The opposite bank was also cliff-faced. All being well, we would cross over to it in two weeks' time, 300 miles downstream.

After two miles, we reached a bend where the river surface was completely frozen again, and the indignant water swirled under-neath. We continued walking, hopeful that this track, although not on our map, would continue all the way to where the asphalt road met the river again, ten miles further on. It would be a good shortcut compared to the truckers' road that ran through the mountains. However, as the end of the day drew near, the track petered out into a small field. Beyond it, there was no path. It would be too dangerous to walk along the frozen river surface itself – we could see water splurging up through numerous cracks in the ice beside the bank. The only way forward would be to pick our way along a crumbly scree slope between the cliffs and the river. It looked dangerous. While I was hopeful that we could make it, Leon, in a rare display of non-hopeavism, was not sure. Perhaps all the problems with the camera had shaken his confidence.

I found the thought of walking all the way back and round, and up to the top of the canyon to join a smelly truckers' road, very unappealing. I therefore tried to persuade Leon for a few minutes, while he umm-ed and err-ed. We did not reach a conclusion, but it was getting dark anyway.

'Let's camp here and decide in the morning,' we agreed.

By morning, Leon was also keen to try the scree slope, and we began to pick our way along it. It was slow work. The ground was crumbly and, ten metres below, the frozen river chewed at the bank. The cliffs shot vertically above us for almost a hundred metres, and we were constantly alert to the sound of falling stones. I felt jittery but alive.

Stepping carefully from stone to stone, trying to stick to the more solid-looking sections, we gradually made progress forwards and upwards, until we reached the base of the cliffs, where the ground was more solid. My optimism was increasing that we could get all the way to the road, but by this point Leon was unconvinced again and kept looking further ahead. Several miles away, we could just see the river turned right and, from where we were, it looked as if the cliffs dropped straight into the water.

Suddenly Leon said, 'The Wall!'

My eyes followed where he was pointing, and saw a crumbling brown watchtower, standing on the edge of a low cliff just ahead of us. We scrambled up to it. A small section of wall ran along the ledge – not a part of the Great Wall, just a part of the river defences. But our hopes that we might be able to follow this little wall were quickly dashed, as the small cliff turned out only to be a ridge of land, sticking out into icy water. It was not long before we had to climb down into a gully and back up another ridge, and then back down yet another gully, all the time paralleling the river. We kept moving, but the further we went, the harder it became. It was now twenty-four hours since we had seen any humans. If we were to twist an ankle, it would be very difficult to get rescued. We were also starting to run out of water, and our progress was so slow it looked unlikely that we would reach the proper road before sundown.

Leon stopped walking and frowned at me.

'I think we should follow this ridge back into the hills,' he said. 'There is no way we can make it along the next seven miles of river like this.'

'I think we'll find a way through,' I said. 'I can't believe people would not have made little paths along here.' I strained my head to try and see round the next bend.

Leon pointed. 'Look up there, it's all just cliffs.'

We each contended our point of view for a few minutes, but I stood my ground and this time Leon gave in. We had now survived two major tests as a team – my foot, and the focus fiasco – and as a more robust friendship developed, we were handling disagreements more easily.

However, as we tried to descend into the next gully, we came to a much steeper slope, and I had to admit that the way forward was blocked. Three of the oldest rules in the book for hikers are: make sure you know where you are going; make sure someone else knows where you are going; don't underestimate how quickly a seemingly safe situation can turn precarious. We had managed to break all three, but we were too far along to contemplate going back now.

'Sorry,' I said, 'we'll have to try your route.'

We started climbing Leon's ridge instead, but this too led to more cliffs. We returned to the previous gully, and started clambering up the dried-out stream-bed. We had no idea if this would lead anywhere either, and the sky had now turned a menacing grey. It looked as if it might snow – a whiteout was the last thing we needed.

For an hour we scrambled over the stream-bed's smashed boulders, and eventually we found a small sheep path zigzagging up a slope. We climbed up and along, and into the mountains, and impressively, in the midst of all this, Leon still regularly stopped to set up the tripod and do some careful filming, sometimes even on the edge of narrow cliff ledges. He also insisted that I clip on the radio whenever I spoke to the camera. He was pushing our standards up.

Eventually, exhausted, we reached the summit. Far below, we could still see the frozen Yellow River, but as we looked around us, we were relieved to see a couple of scrubby terraced fields and, beyond them, a cave village. A cheerful, wrinkled farming couple met us outside their *yaodong* – the first humans we had seen in almost thirty-six hours. We were very happy to see them. They filled our thermoses while talking continuously, though their thick accents – combined with the fact that they were both chewing something and speaking simultaneously – meant we could hardly understand a word. Still talking, they led us down a path, and to our surprise we came to a brand new asphalt road. It carved across the mountain, connecting their tiny village to the outside world. Three hours later, in darkness, we arrived back on the truckers' road, thirty miles further back than we had hoped. There was a little *ludian* on the junction, and we checked in, glad to have made it back to safety.

31
Ice wine

Distance to home: 2,300 miles

Overnight, the grey clouds dumped a heavy snowfall, and the next morning the world had turned white. It was good that we were not still stuck on the Yellow River scree slopes. We spent the first three hours of the day skidding and stomping down a long hill to the town of Pianguan. It was now only two days until Chinese New Year, and the markets were buzzing with fireworks stalls, fresh poultry being sold, and live fish getting clobbered bloodily around the head. Our aborted shortcut along the river had effectively cost us another whole day. We were so tired we felt we still needed our weekly day off, though we were so badly behind schedule we could not really afford it. We sat in our hotel room assessing our progress and options. My foot was still painful and continued to slow me down because I could not push with it; I had noticed my right calf muscle had shrunk considerably. But with the help of the foot support, it was stable, and even slowly improving. The trouble was, if we were going to make our deadline of reaching Hong Kong by the end of May, we now had no choice but to start upping our distances by five to eight miles a day – an increase of about 25 per cent. And this was not just a short-term measure: we would need to keep this up all the way to Hong Kong. We reconsidered the idea of riding bicycles to make up time and let the foot recover. But it felt like a cop-out. I told Leon that I was determined to at least attempt to tackle the extra mileage on foot.

'Are you sure?' he said.

'Yes. If the foot completely starts falling apart, or I can't make the distances, we can always switch to bicycles. But that has to be a last resort.'

The next morning we set off into a frozen dawn, and the air was thick with smog. Smoke plumed from the chimney of every house and, even this early, fireworks zipped across the sky and popped. Some 1.4 billion people were waking up in anticipation of Chinese New Year's Eve. Chinese New Year is dated according to the lunar calendar and always falls between late January and late February. It is a tradition that goes back thousands of years, and in Mainland China the celebrations last for fifteen days. The most important event is New Year's Eve – the equivalent to Christmas Day – and this is an occasion when family members try their hardest to get back home to be together for the traditional evening meal. This results in the world's largest annual migration. Hundreds of millions of Chinese are on the move, and between them make over three billion trips by road, rail, ship and plane.

Over the past week, we had noticed the roads were getting steadily busier, and today was the final push. We reached a clifftop road above the Yellow River, and tucked tightly into the verge as cars and buses drove past even faster and more recklessly than normal. They were apparently paying no attention to the 'Danger Yellow River' signs – it was a fifty-metre drop off the cliff's edge. Halfway through the afternoon, with Leon somewhere ahead of me, I stopped to do some stretching. When I turned back to the road, I saw a huge cloud of dust swirling into the air 100 metres ahead of me. As I drew closer I saw several cars had stopped, and a small crowd was peering over the cliff edge. Leon was among them in his orange jacket, with the camera out. I caught up and looked down to see a car wedged in a gully ten metres below. It was facing uphill, with a smashed in bonnet. To my relief I could see the car was empty.

'What happened?' I asked Leon.

'I'd just stopped at that building to fill up my thermos, and we heard a screech outside. We came out and saw this.'

I followed Leon into the clifftop building, and saw the three survivors: two men and a seven-year-old boy. They looked shaken, and had dust all over their faces and clothes. But they were uninjured and smiling. Smiling was the expression of choice in China when someone is embarrassed or nervous, though I suppose in this case they were also genuinely happy to have just narrowly avoided an icy grave in the Yellow River.

As darkness fell, the sky above us boomed with a continuous series of fireworks; it felt as though we were entering a war zone. We reached the outskirts of Hequ, the riverside city where we would be spending our own New Year's Eve. At ground level, the street was lined with red lanterns hanging outside each house, and on each porch sat a one-metre-high pile of burning coal and a little mound of oranges.

'The fireworks are to scare away a mythical beast called a *nian*,' said Leon, who had been doing some reading on Chinese New Year. 'And the oranges are a food offering for him.'

'What happens if you don't leave the oranges?' I asked.

'The *nian* will kidnap and eat your household's youngest child.'

Through the windows, we could see families getting ready for their celebratory meals. The atmosphere around us was magical. But at the same time, after almost thirty miles, this had been our longest day yet. My feet were bruised, and I felt sorry for myself that we had to spend Chinese New Year tramping the cold, dark pavements, while the rest of China celebrated with their families. Apart from us, the decorations, and the occasional pair of young boys sneaking outside to let off a chain of firecrackers, the street was totally empty. I missed Christine.

Two miles before we reached the town centre, a black SUV drew up beside us. A man yelled out of his window in Chinese. 'What are you doing?'

We recited our catechism.

'Jump in,' he said pointing to his back seats, 'come back to my house for dinner.'

'No thanks, we're walking.'

'Oh come on, come to dinner.'

Leon and I looked at each other. Leon said, 'We could just mark our spot, and start walking from here in the morning.'

And with that our decision was made. We threw our packs in the boot, and jumped in. We had no idea what the night might hold. The man, whose name was Li, shouted into his mobile phone as we drove, explaining something along the lines of, 'You're not going to believe who I've picked up for dinner – these two bearded foreigners. They've walked here from Mongolia. Lay two extra places!'

The car pulled up in a dimly lit street, and we followed Li through a courtyard and into a simple-looking house. The first room was a small kitchen, where an old lady and two middle-aged women were busy rolling dumplings, while an old TV played loud Chinese opera. We were ushered into another room, with a round table in the middle. The walls were decorated with red patterns – the colour for good luck and prosperity. Two men and a boy walked in. The oldest man was the father of the house – another Mr Li, and the brother of the Mr Li who had picked us up. The younger man and the boy were his two sons.

'Please, let me take your coats,' said the older boy. His name was Gaoyu, and he was a twenty-year-old university student, home for the holidays. I pulled off my two coats, two hats and a scarf. Gaoyu took each item and hung them up and I dreaded to think of the smell that I might be emitting now that my protective layers were gone. At Chinese New Year, it is an age-old tradition to wear new clothes, and have a haircut, but Leon and I had turned up with bedraggled clothing, scraggly hair and bushy beards. The Li family was far too polite to show they noticed.

'I am sorry my English is not good, I have never spoken to a foreigner before,' said Gaoyu. We assured him his was the best English we had encountered for weeks. As we sat chatting we discovered Gaoyu was studying economics, was a serious Liverpool FC fan, and also played football himself. His father, who spoke no English, owned several steel mines.

Just before it was time to eat, the three men all gathered at a family shrine at the back of the room. A line of miniature 'lucky gods' sat in a row, and at the front there was an urn of ashes. The men lit a joss stick, and placed some food before the shrine – the ancient rite of venerating their ancestors.

Delicious aromas billowed into the room as the food started to arrive: fried sliced potatoes, braised bean sprouts, fried bean curd, steamed Chinese fungus and vegetables, steamed fish head, steamed fish body, fried and steamed chicken and several large bowls of dumplings. The dishes completely covered the round table in the middle of the room. I looked at Leon, and could tell that we were both thinking the same thought: tonight's dinner was going to be a lot better than the usual processed sausages.

We all took our seats at the table, and Gaoyu's father stood up and shook our hands. 'As representatives of the Chinese people, we welcome you,' he said with a huge smile.

A bottle was produced.

'Ah, *baijiu*,' said Leon and I.

'No,' said Gaoyu, showing us the label and smiling proudly, 'this is Canadian Ice Wine.' Western luxury imports were becoming all the rage.

A glass of wine was poured for everyone, including Gaoyu's little brother, and then we all took a sip and the feast began. In Chinese culture, rather than each person having a large plate of food each, everyone instead just plucks individual pieces of food from the large dishes in the middle. Chopsticks are ideal for this, as are the harmonious round tables. We ate away, gorging ourselves on the meats and vegetables. Everyone smiled at each other and looked content between mouthfuls. We found that we did not have to pluck items from the middle ourselves, because as soon as we ate something, Gaoyu placed another dainty morsel into our bowls. When I first started dating Christine, I had learnt that serving your guests – as Gaoyu was doing – was excellent manners.

Suddenly, Leon yelped.

'Ah, sorry, you must be careful because some of the dumplings have coins inside them,' said Gaoyu gently. He smiled and added, 'You are very lucky, because this means you will become rich this year.'

Leon choked a little, before producing a coin from his mouth and waving it around triumphantly. We all cheered.

'I wonder if you will get one, Rob?' said Gaoyu, waving his chopsticks at the bowl of dumplings.

I felt a little jealous, but a few minutes later, I too bit down on a hard coin in my dumpling and produced it for all to see. But soon after, Leon got another one. The evening ended with a score of 2:1 to Leon; though I was happy for him, the reality was that neither of us expected to get very rich this year.

After supper, as Gaoyu's little brother set off firecrackers in the yard, Leon and I realised we had no idea where we were going to sleep. But then Gaoyu and his father insisted on driving us to the local hotel. We arrived at a smart building and followed them through some automatic doors into a glitzy lobby. It looked way beyond our normal budget, but to top off their amazing hospitality for the night, Gaoyu's father insisted on paying for a room for us.

After our hot showers, we collapsed. It had been a long day, but China had again treated us well, and the New Year had got off to a good start.

Part Four

Into Ancient Heartlands

————

车到山前必有路

When we get to the mountain, there'll be a way through.

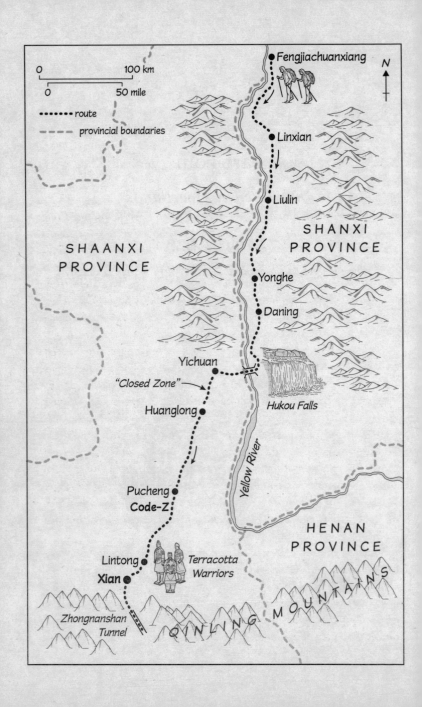

32
Big Nose

Distance to home: 2,200 miles

It is a week after Chinese New Year, and we have maintained our speed, rising each day at dawn, packing fast, walking fast, often into the frozen night. We are still in Shanxi Province, east of the Yellow River. But we have left the riverside for a while in order to follow a network of roads that runs southwards through the valleys that parallel it. Walking on these roads is not always as peaceful as when we guessed our way down shepherds' tracks by the Wall, or followed the looping Yellow River bends, but it is certainly more direct.

Sometimes our route takes us along winding ridges, surrounded by cascades of steep, brown earth that falls away into deep canyons on one side, and rises above into crumbling hillocks on the other.

Much of the soft land has been cut into terraces for growing corn, though as the winter drags on, they are carpeted only with rows of dead yellow stubs and leaves. There are still occasional beacon towers on the ridge lines, but fewer and fewer as we move beyond frontier territory and deeper into the core of China. More common are the electricity pylons running from ridge to ridge, connected by high voltage cable. The farming villages are a mix of cave, brick and concrete dwellings. Old and new China are colliding before our eyes.

We have also re-entered coal country, and the wild, tainted beauty of the more remote ridges alternates with huge mining developments. However, rather than running along a valley like they did near Datong, the mines here are up among the hills themselves. We often see giant conveyor belts pouring inexhaustible rivers of coal onto thirty-metre high piles.

We also occasionally glimpse less official mines. One night, walking up a mountain road with our head torches on, we pass some makeshift mines dug into roadside cliffs. The roofs are held up by homemade wooden staves. Two-man teams are still working away in them, digging out seams of coal. They stared at us as we walked past in the dark, as if we were ghosts. It looks like miserable, dangerous work. But they will get better pay for this than for farm work, so they probably have little choice.

The whole region, meanwhile, is full of coal trucks. Sometimes when we stride round a corner, we see a battalion of red trucks queuing up outside a large mine to collect their loads. These trucks also fill the valley roads, and the fields beside them are sprinkled with truckers' defecations and toilet paper. Along with pollution and jobs, the coal has brought money to this region, and many of the towns are clearly growing in prosperity. When we arrive in the towns at night we are dazzled by brand-new, neon-emblazoned hotel complexes, rising out of impressive metropolises of sculpted fountains and riverside promenades.

My diary entries continue to reflect our gradual physical deterioration:

29 January: Well yesterday was a serious slog, bashing down a main road – lots of trucks and cars and slushy snow on the shoulder, not much fun . . . Lots of hooting and sudden swerving . . . Blisters starting to develop lots on the end of my toes . . . Our bodies rather beaten . . .

2 February: A slog day – but we moved fast and slept well last night . . .

6 February: Wow, another incredible but exhausting but unpredictable day! Is this trip changing me?

Now we are walking further and for longer each day, with less time off, we notice a difference in how our bodies are coping. In the first two months of the trip, we had walked a maximum of just twenty miles a day, and apart from my right foot and a deepening tiredness, we did not have many physical complaints. But now we have upped our distances to twenty-five or thirty miles a day, our physical ailments are starting to pile up. Leon partially twists an ankle climbing a slope to do some filming; I develop a sore knee; Leon gets a sore back; I start to suffer from bruised feet every night; Leon gets stress-induced toothache so he has to take some Chinese antibiotics. When I pull my socks off in the evenings, I often see ugly white blister bubbles under my skin that I need to pop with my penknife to get the puss out, and douse with iodine to disinfect. But remarkably, however beaten up we feel at the end of a walking day, the next morning, with the help of a reasonable sleep and a few plasters, we are ready to go again.

On the other hand, our descent from civilised human beings into wild men seems intractable. We burp and fart still more. Instead of words, we speak in groans and grumbles and with increasing references to Orlando, Jase and dinosaurs. When we stop for breaks, we sit down in the dirt (though still checking that we are not about to sit on a trucker's toilet) and shovel instant noodles and processed sausages into our mouths like they are fuel. At the same time we look forward to reaching towns that have a restaurant, now a regular occurrence, where for about 10 RMB (£1) we buy bowls of dumplings or fried rice – much better nourishment than instant noodles. Our Mandarin improves slowly, but we still continually confuse shui jiao (second and third tone: dumplings) with shui jiao (fourth and fourth tone: sleep). We get bemused looks when we try to order a bowl of sleep. In fact, we would usually be happy with either – food and rest are our two great concerns.

When I look into a hotel mirror one night, I blink in surprise at the sight of a heavily bearded man looking back at me. His moustache is growing into his mouth and his hair is sticky, unwashed and moulded in strange directions from wearing a woolly hat for too long. His eyes, meanwhile, are crazed with exhaustion. The suggestion of insanity is exacerbated by the layers and layers of clothing, which make him look like the Michelin man.

Amazingly, my right foot is still stable, though in addition to wearing the foot support and taking at least two anti-inflammatories a day, it is essential to regularly and strenuously stretch my muscles.

In particular I find that stretching out my calves helps. So we stretch when we are taking a break in roadside fields, we stretch when we are in village shops buying instant noodles, we stretch when we are in restaurants having lunch. Apart from Clare and two tourists we had spotted in Datong, we have seen no Caucasians since we arrived in China. It is probably rare for local people to encounter foreigners first-hand, let alone foreigners who are constantly stretching. And yet the Chinese people are uninhibited with us. One day, during a stretch break in a warm roadside shop, the shopkeeper comes over and competes with me to touch his toes – and gets a lot closer than I do. Another time, as I lean against a tree, stretching my calves, a labourer approaches and gives my legs a good squeeze. 'Very strong,' he says, before offering me a cigarette.

On a quiet path, a goat-herder catches sight of us, and shakes his head in disbelief. He garbles questions at us in a strong accent that we cannot understand, before suddenly reaching up and grabbing Leon's cold pink nose. 'Da bizi' – Big Nose* – he shouts with a triumphant chuckle, as if pleased to confirm that we are real and not imaginary, and that we do indeed have big noses, just like he has always been told.

One night we hear a man walking towards us, and singing loudly.

'Waaa . . . yeeeee . . . hoooo . . .'

He sounds very drunk and, after he has passed us, he turns and starts walking along behind, still singing at the top of his lungs. As we reach the next town, the singing stops, and the man appears beside us, walking peacefully.

'Where are you going?' he asks. Up close he does not look drunk after all.

We explain, and then compliment him on his singing.

'Ah, singing is how I let off steam after I've had an argument with my wife!' he says. 'Tonight we had a pretty major one.'

But some people are intimidated by us. When we wave at a group of young boys playing on a frozen stream, they scream and run away. One night we stagger into a small dark town, and I approach

---

* A common derogatory slang for Caucasians in recent centuries.

beards

IRA in the desert

rough a tunnel

Insanity sets in

Instant noodles and
processed sausage –
our diet for breakfast,
lunch and dinner

The fifteenth day of
Chinese New Year

The Yellow Riv‹

quick dip in the Yellow River

Onto a motorway

short cut that went well

A short cut that
didn't go so well

A very steep terra[ce]
near the Yangt[ze]

A dip in the Yangtze

A good way to travel

Waking up to frost
on our bivvy bags

A friendly
Chinese policeman

Blisters

Ploughing

Getting hot

Beautiful China

My favourite shop name on the ro

20 RMB note

A quick dip in
the Pearl River,
Guangzhou

Hong Kong harbour, back with Christine at last

Over eighty friends joined us for the final few miles

The finish line

a lady walking past and ask in my best Chinese if there is a ludian nearby. I forget how I look with my beard and pack, with Leon standing beside me, even taller, and smelling worse too. I have barely said hello, when she lets out a shriek and runs headlong to the other side of the road.

And amid our exhaustion, we keep filming, keep trying. Perhaps it is this, on top of everything else, that is making us go a little round the bend. One night, we stumble through a small town dominated by an immense, floodlit coal mine. Its massive structure has conveyor-belt corridors running over the top of the road, and it is surrounded by a high, sinister wall. From within the compound we can hear a hearty, apocalyptic Maoist male choir, belting out over a PA system.

The next morning, as we start walking Leon tells me about a dream he had had.

'We were inside that coal mine from last night, the one with the choir. But actually, we had discovered that it was not a coal mine – it was a storm trooper clone factory. We were running around, trying to find a way out of this maze of corridors, but suddenly I realised that I had forgotten to bring the camera! Can you believe it, this was one of our best adventures yet, and I was not able to film it?'

'That sounds almost as bad a disaster as the focus fiasco,' I say.

33
Chinese Li

Distance to home: 2,110 miles

3 FEBRUARY

Without realising the precise moment it happened, we left the coal region behind us, and found ourselves walking through quiet farming valleys once more. The weather was warming up a little, and the stream beside the road was starting to melt to reveal huge gluts of rubbish caught in the reeds. A few goat-herders and their flocks ambled along the hillsides, and for the first time we saw farmers out on the terraces, piling up dead vegetation from the winter.

That evening, we would reach the town of Yonghe; after a week of walking twelve to fourteen hours a day, we were looking forward to a day off. With only six miles to go, we passed through a village where a troop of teenagers poured onto the road and started taking photos of us with their mobile phones. We found that when a small crowd gathered in China, there was often an exponential effect, as passers-by joined in to see what was happening. While the teenagers snapped away, even cars were reversing back to have a look.

After a few minutes, we broke away from the crowd, walking fast. Our followers had to run to keep up. Most people started to saunter home. But no sooner had we got going again, than a black car stopped beside us.

Three young men jumped out and ran over.

'Let us give you a lift to town,' the driver shouted in friendly, husky Mandarin. He was in his late twenties and had a faint moustache.

'No thanks, we are walking.'

'We are not bad people,' said another of the men, in a high-pitched voice.

'We know, but we are walking.'

We moved off again to prove our point, and the men jumped back in their car. They quickly overtook us, stopped and jumped out again.

'It's not far, come on, let us give you a lift, we'll buy you dinner,' said the husky driver.

'We love guests,' added his high-pitched friend.

I launched into our usual response about having walked here all the way from Mongolia, but the men ignored me, amicably, grabbing our poles and throwing them in their boot. By now the crowd had caught us up.

I began to protest with a smile, but the driver shouted: 'Let's go, let's go, let's go.'

As Leon and I started chuckling, the driver subtly moved behind Leon and suddenly grabbed his rucksack. Because Leon was filming, he had to protect the camera from getting damaged, and the driver managed to slip the straps off Leon's shoulder quite easily. A moment later he was bundling the pack into his car triumphantly, with a satisfied, 'Ha ha!'

Now it was my turn, but I was ready. The driver moved towards me, and we began to hustle and tussle as if we were in a slapstick movie. The crowd grew. The children giggled. An old man puffed on his pipe and watched silently.

'We have walked here all the way from Mongolia,' I said again, 'we can't take a lift.'

'We know, we know,' said the men, 'but time is precious, and we can give you a lift back here later.'

The last thing we wanted to do was come back out here after dinner. We said we would meet them in town when we arrived in a couple of hours.

'Oh come on, it's only a few miles,' said the driver, puffing with exasperation. Leon had meanwhile managed to retrieve the rucksack and poles; when the driver saw this, with another big puff, he finally admitted defeat. He gave us his mobile number and then pointed to himself and said (in English): 'Chinese Li.' Li was the most common name in China, so who knows why he included 'Chinese', but it suited him.

An hour later, we arrived in Yonghe. The map had suggested it would be a similar size to the glitzy coal-money cities, but it was actually much smaller and had just one scruffy shopping street beside a river. We phoned Chinese Li and, a moment later, he skidded up beside us in his car, delighted. We squeezed into the back, along with several of his friends, and soon after arrived at a smart hotel-restaurant.

'We welcome you enthusiastically,' said Chinese Li as we sat down at a round table in a private room at the back of the restaurant, 'and I am going to treat you to dinner.'

After shouting some orders at the waitress, he started to open an ominously large bottle of *baijiu*.

'Just a little cup,' he said as he poured me a huge one. The whole bottle managed to fill only four cups. He opened another bottle.

'We are very hospitable,' he said, grinning and raising his drink. 'Unlike you and the eight foreign powers who invaded China.'* We all clinked glasses, and took a gulp. The sudden drink at the end of a long week made my cheeks flush.

'It's fate that has brought us together,' said Chinese Li, accidentally knocking over his cup. 'Tonight, as well as dinner, I will also treat you to a room at this hotel.' It was fortuitous that he was treating us to both dinner and a hotel room, because Leon and I were almost out of cash. We thanked him, and dishes of food started to arrive. Chinese Li put chunks of bony meat into our bowls. 'Meeeeeeer, meeeeeer,'† he cried out, growing more animated.

'OK, this must be lamb,' we said as we started eating.

We discovered that Chinese Li was a fertiliser salesman and his friend with the high-pitched voice was a goat-herder with five hundred goats. Two women soon arrived, one of whom turned out to be Chinese Li's wife – she was a mobile phone salesperson.

---

* It was only when I later watched the video footage that I realised Chinese Li was referring to the European–Japanese–American coalition's destructive encroachment in China in 1900, in order to put down the Boxer Rebellion.
† Chinese people do not go 'baaaa baaaa' but 'meeeeeer, meeeeeer' in their sheep impressions. Their noise for frogs is 'gwa, gwa' rather than 'ribbit'.

'And her name is horse, neeeaaayyyy!' shouted Chinese Li, pointing to the other woman, 'and she is a policewoman.'

I'd never met a Chinese policewoman called horse before. We all clinked glasses again.

Sitting in the lovely warm room, as I ate more food and took a few more gulps of *baijiu*, I started to feel very tired, and had to work hard to stop myself from falling asleep. But Chinese Li continued to talk away rapidly, and enthusiastically. As we skipped from conversation to conversation, I was only able to pick up bits and pieces of what was being said.

'Did you see Chairman Mao's house?' asked Chinese Li.

'Yes,' we said. We had passed a roadside *yaodong* the previous day with a sign announcing that Mao had lived here during the war against the Japanese.

Suddenly Chinese Li sprang to his feet, saluted into the air and burst into song:

The East is red
The sun is rising
China produces Chairman Mao.

He sat down again. The song 'The East is Red' had virtually been the national anthem during the Cultural Revolution.

'And how is Shanxi Province?' I asked. 'It looks like it is getting very rich.'

'A lot of people here have a lot of money,' said Chinese Li, suddenly looking a bit sad, 'but even more have very little money. And the environment is not good, and the air is not clear.' He had nicely summed up China's most pressing, and potentially destabilising issues – inequality and the environment.

As the evening went on, more and more of Chinese Li's friends arrived, until the room was bursting. I was definitely ready for bed, but just when we thought it was time to call it a night, someone suggested karaoke. It was our first karaoke invitation in China, so we summoned our strength and said yes, we would absolutely love to go to karaoke.

The next morning – perhaps unsurprisingly after my appalling rendition of Michael Jackson's 'Beat It', and a bit too much *baijiu* – I had a sore throat and fluey head. The exhausting week followed by a night out with Chinese Li had hit me hard. While Leon went to get some food and withdraw some money, I sat on my bed writing a newspaper article.

Two hours later, Leon returned, with some bad news. Firstly, although there were various local co-operative banks on the high street, there were no national banks. Therefore, none of the machines accepted our foreign bank cards. We had only 220 RMB (£22) left, and Daning, the next town large enough for a bank, was two days' walk away.

Secondly, it turned out that Chinese Li had not paid for our hotel room after all. We therefore owed the hotel 340 RMB (£34). We had an additional US$35 'emergency money' which, combined with 120 of our RMB covered the hotel, leaving us just 100 RMB (£10). Having spent three quarters of this on dumplings for lunch, and a big supply of instant noodles and processed sausage to get us through the next forty-eight hours to Daning, we were left with just 26 RMB (£2.60) to our name.

34

Down and out on the Huang He

Distance to home: 2,085 miles

I am sitting in a restaurant in the International Finance Centre shopping mall in Hong Kong. A waitress comes over, and I start to order some food from the menu. The burger and chips look good. She takes the order down and starts to walk away. Suddenly I remember. I do not have any money. I panic. What should I do? This is going to be very embarrassing, but I am so hungry.

I woke up, and realised that I was not in Hong Kong. I was in my tent, in the middle of a cornfield, on the side of a Chinese hill. The previous day we had left Yonghe, made good progress through the hills, and camped ten miles short of Daning. My stomach rumbled, and the thought of more instant noodles for breakfast was not appealing.

'Are you awake, Rob?' I heard Leon call from his tent.

As we packed up, we were looking forward to reaching the town, getting some money out, and having a good, greasy restaurant meal.

Christine called a few minutes later to give me an update on the flight bookings for Code Z (our visas were nearing their expiry dates). As we chatted, I joked to her about our financial straits.

'How much have you got left?' she asked.

'Twenty-six kwai,' I said.

'What!'

'Don't worry, we're only three hours' walk from the next town.'

As we marched onwards, Leon remarked that today, the fifteenth day of the lunar New Year, was also the first full moon of the year, and last day of the Chinese New Year celebrations. 'We should look out for some good parties to film,' he said.

We felt our filming had been going well recently, but we were continuing to push ourselves hard. The pressure from Tiberius had not relented, as they regularly sent us instructions on how we needed to improve or upload more footage. This was helpful in many ways, but the one to two hours of daily filming or searching for a hotel with an internet connection made the difference between finishing the day's walk in glorious daylight with time to rejuvenate before bed, and finishing in depressing darkness with barely enough time to eat before collapsing into slumber.

Halfway down the hill, we heard the sound of drums and *suonas*. *Suonas* are Chinese reed instruments, which look like a large oboe but have a squeaking brassy sound. The band was playing traditional yet upbeat music. As we drew nearer, we saw the band members were sitting on the edge of a village, and a group of villagers were marching in a procession around some kind of tented shrine. All the villagers wore white robes, and large white cylinder-shaped hats.

'It looks like a chefs' convention,' said Leon. 'Let's go take a look.'

We wandered over, camera running.

'*Xinnian kwai le!*' (Happy New Year) I exclaimed with a smile to the white gathering, while Leon filmed.

The man at the front of the procession, about my age, looked up at me, confused and unsmiling. That was an unusual response when we said Happy New Year.

I turned to survey the scene in more detail and three facts dawned on me. Firstly, I noticed that the shrine did not have statues in it, but rather a photograph of an old man. Secondly, I recalled that Christine had told me that white was the colour of mourning in China.* And thirdly, I saw that the people looked not only confused, but also rather sad – not how you would expect people to look if they were indeed celebrating the last day of Chinese New Year.

'Leon,' I said, starting to tread backwards and away from the procession, who were now all standing and staring at us, 'I don't think this is a Chinese New Year celebration, I think it's a funeral.'

---

* It is rude to give white flowers to a Chinese person in hospital – it is like saying, 'You're going to die.'

'Ah,' said Leon, lowering his camera. We bowed solemnly and made our way back to the road. I felt bad, and hoped I had not added to the pain they were feeling that day.

We arrived in Daning at 10 a.m., eyes peeled for a cash machine. But as we approached the high street, we saw a huge crowd gathering, and we could hear the whizzing of fireworks and a cacophony of drums and other instruments. Reaching the throng, we looked over everyone's heads to see several lines of colourful floats, musicians and dancers. This was no funeral – it was a bona fide street carnival.

We walked onwards, enjoying the crackling fireworks, cheerful music and vibrant performances. Colourful dragons on sticks swirled past, held aloft by ladies in bright red costumes; a unicyclist pedalled by, juggling batons; forty women in a perfect square beat drums and cymbals as they danced; a big troop of men with *suonas* hooted out lively tunes, trying to keep in time with a group of drummers who bashed out their rhythms faster and faster. One man played two *suonas* at once, and in the middle of the song opened his mouth to reveal a lit cigarette held in his tongue. He pulled the cigarette back inside, tooted his *suona* some more, and then flicked the cigarette out again and took a puff. We all cheered.

Amid all the jovial bangs, dancing and crowds, and while Leon filmed, my stomach was rumbling. I dashed into each bank I saw and tried to withdraw some money. However, as in Yonghe, all of them were rural co-operatives, not international Chinese banks. Every one rejected our cards, so I rejoined the crowd next to Leon. A Chinese girl started speaking to us in English. She was called Faith and was home from university for the New Year holidays.

'The performers are all farmers from the villages,' she shouted above the noise, 'they have been practising for months. Most cities don't have local performances like this any more. You are lucky to be here today.' Faith said she would like to treat us to lunch, and we were immensely grateful as we sat down in the little restaurant. A huge plate of dumplings arrived, and Leon and I had to restrain ourselves from eating too quickly.

After we had thanked Faith profusely, we walked back into the street and discussed our options. From here, we would be rejoining the Yellow River, and the next town, Hukou, was another three days' walk away. Hukou did not look large on the map, but it was the site of a tourist attraction – the famed Hukou Waterfall, the biggest on the Yellow River. Because it was a long way from anywhere else interesting, Hukou was still only a small-to-medium-sized attraction, but we still hoped it would have a cash machine we could use.

On our way out of town we spent our final 26 RMB in a small shop. We bought ten packs of instant noodles and one processed sausage, leaving us with just three *mao*, the equivalent of two English pence. A road beside a small frozen stream led us back towards the Yellow River. As we walked we discussed our latest rookie error – running out of money. We had assumed that all towns of a reasonable size would have national banks but, in hindsight, this was not very clever of us.

As the cold dusk started to settle, the craggy brown cliffs above us glowed orange in the fading sun, and after two hours' night marching, we pitched our tents beside the frozen stream.

The next day, from a high, clifftop road, we caught sight of the Yellow River again. It now appeared a dirty white colour and, from our vantage point, seemed completely frozen. But as we looked harder, we saw that the pale mass was actually seething and flowing. When we reached the bottom of the canyon, we saw there was so much ice in the water that it looked like a torrent of white lava. Some ice slabs were the size of minibuses, and the canyon echoed with deep clunking and cracking sounds as they bashed into each other.

Apart from a very occasional motorbike, there was no traffic on the riverside road, and the canyon's stark beauty was breathtaking. For the next five hours, we also saw no villages, and by the afternoon we were running low on water. Deprived of nutritious food, and now liquid, and exhausted from having walked almost a marathon that day with the insanely heavy pack, my energy levels started to drop. Leon, the young man of the expedition, seemed to be doing better, and urged me to keep the pace up. 'Walking more slowly is not going to solve our problems,' he said. I nodded feebly, put on my iPod, and tried to walk faster.

Two hours before darkness, Leon spotted a *yaodong* village built into the cliffs, just above the road. He now looked as tired as me. I told him to have a rest while I scrambled up the little path with our thermoses and water bottles. Luckily, I also took a walking pole, because as I approached the door of the first house, a dog suddenly appeared, barking viciously. I shouted, waved my pole, and backed away. A boy in his late teens opened the door and I asked for some water.

'We do not have much,' he said, 'I can only fill two bottles.'

He took the thermoses and went inside. As I looked more carefully, I saw that this *yaodong* village looked even poorer than the others we had been to. Many of the houses seemed abandoned and dilapidated. From the boy's response there was clearly no running water, and although we had noticed the occasional, precarious terraced field on the cliffs beside the river, it must have been hard to eke out a living around here. The boy re-emerged and, after I had thanked him, I managed to fill our other two bottles from the next house.

When I got back to the road, Leon was lying on the verge, asleep. I gave him a kick and, after more noodles, we set off again.

On our final break of the day, at sunset, we sat on the empty road in silence, looking at the icy river, and bracing ourselves for a final hour of walking. The last part of a long day was always the hardest.

Leon suddenly perked up: 'I've just remembered something!'

'What?'

'You're not going to believe this, but for our roadside snack today I've got none other than . . . authentic instant cheesecake!'

Leon grinned and pulled the vacuum-wrapped packet out of his rucksack. Back in Mongolia, he had mentioned the legendary cheesecake, which he had been given at the start of his bike ride across America, two years ago. He had kept it as his emergency rations throughout the ride but never needed to eat it. He had also brought it on this trip, and planned to take it on every expedition he went on for the rest of his life – and never eat it. But now, on only his second expedition, its time had come. He poured in some hot water, and we took it in turns to eat from the packet. It consisted of mushy sugar, and was beyond its expiry date, but to us it tasted like a Michelin-starred dessert. We licked our spoons until they were gleaming, and then Leon wistfully stuffed the empty cheesecake packet back in his rucksack.

35

To Hukou Waterfall

Distance to home: 2,060 miles

8 FEBRUARY

The next morning, the road wound upwards again to a clifftop village. The Michelin-starred cheesecake had long since been digested, and we felt weak. The sky was overcast, causing the temperature to drop into the −20°Cs. As we passed through the village, some old men filled our thermoses, and also gave us an unexpected but very welcome gift of a dozen beautiful red apples from a huge crate. We sat on a sofa in the reception of a small rural co-operative bank (which would not accept our bank cards), and ate noodles and apples.

By the afternoon, we were back by the river, approaching the Hukou Waterfall, where we hoped to get out some money. After that, we would cross a bridge onto the other side and bid it goodbye. I realised that we were into our final few hours of walking beside the famous torrent and it was, therefore, also my last chance to fulfil a little dare I had with myself. We took our next break just above a small sandy beach, beside which there was a calm patch of unfrozen water. There were a few pieces of ice floating on it, and it was protected from the main river by some large rocks.

'It's now or never, old boy,' I said to Leon, gulping down some warm water from my thermos. 'This is where you prove if you are a man or a mouse, or in your case, a girl.'

He knew about my dare, and did not look keen, but smiled back. 'It is not I who is the girl.'

Feeling suddenly cold, and nervous, we walked down a little path to the water's edge, and surveyed the ice. Leon set up the camera on the tripod and we stood in front of it.

'Go!' we shouted. We needed this, I thought, as I tore off my clothes and started to shiver. We needed this to inject some life and fun back into our world. I'd discovered before: there is nothing quite like jumping in a river to cheer you up. Furthermore, the sight of Leon and me jumping heroically into the icy water might repair our waning tough-guy status in front of the camera, especially after our recent grumbling, bad singing, blisters, and running out of money and food.

However, as we frantically got undressed, we both started to yelp like schoolgirls. I managed to strip faster than Leon, and shouted at him in a high-pitched voice to hurry up, while I stood looking cold and pathetic and the camera kept on rolling. When Leon was finally ready, together we shrieked and shuffled tentatively into the water. Suddenly Leon cried out, 'Ah, there is ice at the bottom,' and plunged his hands underwater to pull out a large, sharp shard.

'It doesn't matter, let's just do this quickly,' I squeaked. The beach was a gentle incline. I was only knee deep, and my legs were going numb. It was too full of ice to go much deeper. So instead of a swim, I just lay down where I was and submerged my head; as I did this my face hit a semi-floating piece of ice. That was enough of a swim for us and, seconds later, we dashed out of the water and, with lots of whooping and puffing, hurriedly threw our clothes back on.

It was not the finest hour in our quest to be tough guys. However, as we hit the road again, we walked fast, with huge smiles. I had a small cut from the ice on both my nose and my foot, but I felt alive like I hadn't done all week. At that moment, Christine phoned.

'Hi honey, did you manage to get some money out?' she asked.

'Err, not exactly. A nice student bought us lunch yesterday, and today some villagers gave us some apples.'

'Oh. How much money have you got left?'

'Err, three *mao*.'

'Three *mao!*'

'It's OK, honey, we just went for a swim in the river and we feel great now.'

'A swim! I thought it was frozen?'

I explained as best as I could. Perhaps we truly had become wild men, where going for a swim in an icy river was the highlight of our week, walking remote, frozen roads with empty stomachs just another day at the office, and running out of food and money just another humdrum problem to solve.

We were only a few miles from the Hukou Waterfall, but it was already late afternoon. I wondered whether we would hear the waterfall long before we saw it. It looked so breathtaking, glorious and majestic in all the photos I had seen.

'It should be in the next mile,' said Leon, a short while later, looking at the iPhone map.

We walked another mile, it started to get dark, and it looked as if the river beside us was beginning to freeze over. The road led into a car park, and Leon said, 'Right, we should be here.'

We looked around us and saw an entrance booth by the car park gate. We walked onwards, a little more slowly. Through the dimming light, we could see some giant billboard photos of the waterfall. They showed a leviathan of brown water, the lifeblood of China, crashing down into a gorge, before churning and spinning downstream. But we could see nothing on the river except a mass of ice, which seemed to protrude all the way across.

'It must be a bit further,' we mumbled to each other. 'The waterfall can't have frozen over.'

We kept walking, and emerged from the other end of the car park, where Leon abruptly stopped.

'I think we've passed it,' he said, zooming in on the iPhone map.

'What do you mean?'

'I think it was back there, beyond the frozen river. We must have walked straight past without realising.'

This was definitely not the triumphant sighting we had been hoping for. We stood looking back, but it was now almost pitch dark. We could barely even make out the frozen river.

'It's too late tonight anyway,' said Leon. 'Let's stay in the town and come back tomorrow morning.'

We kept walking, and a few minutes later saw the lights of Hukou town emerging through the darkness. There was a bridge across the river, which we would cross the following day, and also a promising-looking main street, full of tacky tourist restaurants and a hotel.

'Why don't you wait there and rest?' I said to Leon, pointing at the hotel. 'I'll go and look for a cash machine.'

Leon pulled out our last two apples, our last two items of food, handed me one, and I set off up the street. I walked past a dozen restaurants, and the people inside, all Chinese, stared at me through the glass, and I stared back at their dishes of meat and vegetables. I found two cash machines, but yet again they belonged to the rural co-operatives, and I walked back to the hotel, dejected.

Leon had just finished his final apple when I broke the news. We were now completely out of food and money. The next town was yet another three-day walk away and, even then, there was no guarantee that it would have a cash machine we could use. On the road we had brainstormed a plan of last resort: find a taxi driver, pay him to drive us to the nearest city (almost 100 miles away), withdraw some money, and drive back here. The time had come to put it into action.

The hotel receptionist called up a cabbie and, a few minutes later, in he walked. He was short, with a cheeky, boyish expression on his face. It did not take him long to figure out that Leon and I had no bargaining power whatsoever. After pretending to haggle with us for a few minutes, he magnanimously agreed to take us to the city of Xiangning and back, for the hefty sum of 450 RMB (£45). This was probably three days' wages for him, and three days' living expenses for us. But it was almost 9 p.m., and we were too tired and hungry to argue. We shook hands to prove that we were all gentlemen, and then we jumped in his car and off we went.

The high street fled past, and we whooshed up into the hills. I slumped into my seat at the front. The cabbie was eager to make sure we were comfortable and turned up the heating.

'Is it too cold?' he asked.

'No, this is fine,' I said, enjoying the hot blast.

'Music?' he asked, to my surprise putting on some acoustic jazz guitar.

'Thank you,' I smiled.

I looked behind me and saw Leon sprawled out across the back seat. 'Well, this is expensive,' I said, 'but I don't think we had any other option. I just hope this guy knows where the cash machine is, or he's not going to get paid, and we're not going to get dinner.'

'He seems pretty confident,' mumbled Leon, with his eyes still closed. 'I actually think he's a bit of a Mr Wolf from *Pulp Fiction*.'

'Yeah, he does seem that way.' I turned to the cabbie and said in English. 'We think you're a bit of a Chinese Mr Wolf, is that right?'

Mr Wolf did not understand, but grinned and put his foot down on the accelerator.

Leon seemed to have fallen asleep. I reclined my seat, pulled my woolly hat over my eyes and let out a contented groan. After months of walking at four miles an hour in the extreme cold, it was wonderful to move at such speed and in such comfort. I felt as though I was travelling first class on British Airways.

After two hours we descended a long hill, and arrived in Xiangning, where Mr Wolf pulled up beside an international Chinese bank. We nervously inserted our first card, and to our relief 3,000 RMB (£300), the maximum limit, churned into our hands. We used our other card to get out 3,000 RMB more – we did not want to make the same mistake again. We cheered and gave Mr Wolf the thumbs-up sign as we got back in the car. He gave us a grin, and roared us round the corner to a Chinese KFC rip-off to celebrate. We bought ourselves two huge portions of fries and four giant chicken burgers. Once we were back in our first-class seats, Mr Wolf flicked his cigarette out of the window, and we disappeared back into the night.

'Next time I do an expedition,' I said to Leon, taking a huge bite from my second burger, 'I want to do it by taxi or, at the very least, hitchhiking.'

'I'll second that,' said Leon with his mouth full, sprawling out further.

Mr Wolf swerved around another corner, and smiled at the pile of banknotes that we had paid him, now laid out on his dashboard.

36
Mr Wolf

Distance to home: 2,029 miles

In the cult movie *Pulp Fiction*, John Travolta and Samuel L. Jackson play two eccentric hit men who, while driving their car down a busy urban street, accidentally shoot their colleague in the head, splattering blood all over the windows. Knowing they are likely to get spotted by the police, they urgently phone up their boss, who tells them to go to a location where they will meet an apparently infamous man called 'Mr Wolf'. Mr Wolf arrives, and quickly reveals himself to be a businessman type, highly decisive and no-nonsense; a man who can keep a calm head when disaster is imminent; a man who gets you out of your predicament, whatever that predicament may be. Within minutes of arriving, he has cleaned the car, disposed of the body and, therefore, in short, fixed the problem.

As we arrived back in Hukou, Mr Wolf told us we could sleep at his friend's house. 'How much does it cost?' we asked, a little wary of how much he had already extracted from us.

'Don't worry, don't worry,' he said, waving his hand, as if to say the least he could do after the cab fare was to find us a free place to sleep. He led us up to a small, freezing box room, full of crates of apples. It was simple, but ideal for us, and we dropped our packs in relief. Mr Wolf then told us, with another grin, that it would cost 50 RMB (£5). This was good value, but we still felt he had outfoxed us. As he left, he said he would take us to see the waterfall the next morning – he knew just who to talk to. We asked how much, and although Mr Wolf responded with another cryptic wave of his hand, we still agreed to his offer: it was hard to say no to Mr Wolf.

*

The next morning, shortly after we woke, Mr Wolf appeared. While we packed, he started grabbing handfuls of apples from the crates and insisting we take them. We were not sure whose room we had just slept in, or whose apples these were, but Mr Wolf was happily in charge.

We screeched back to the riverside car park. Just as we had seen through the dying light of the previous evening, the river seemed entirely frozen, or at least an ice shelf stretched most of the way across it. But we could now also make out that the ice was spread thinly over a layer of rocks. An icy concrete path led through the rocky-icy jumble, presumably to the waterfall. But it looked precarious, and was blocked by a chain.

Mr Wolf shook his head and said, 'You cannot see the waterfall; the river is all frozen, and you're not allowed out along the path.' Suddenly, as if on cue, an old man wandered towards us. He looked like a car park attendant, and seemed to know Mr Wolf. They chatted for a moment, and with a nod and a smile the attendant lifted the chain that blocked our way.

'This man works here,' said Mr Wolf. 'He says we can go out onto the ice and have a look at the waterfall. But we have to be quick and get back before the ticket sellers arrive.'

So, following Mr Wolf, Leon and I walked cautiously out onto the concrete path. It weaved through the frozen build-up until we found ourselves walking on the ice itself. A little further on, we started to hear the sound of thundering water; all of a sudden a chasm opened up before us, and we could see a mass of river rapids swirling into it. Mr Wolf held out his arm.

'Stop here,' he said, and indicated dramatically that we were now standing on a shelf of ice overhanging the waterfall – if we were not careful, the whole thing would collapse into the gorge.

We inched a tiny bit closer and, by standing on tiptoes, could see the top of the waterfall. It was a gap measuring some fifteen metres wide, and through this squeezed millions of gallons of water, and millions of tonnes of yellow earth. It all crashed down and into oblivion. We did some filming and Mr Wolf kept pulling us back.

We concluded that if even Mr Wolf was afraid of the ice shelf collapsing, indeed there must be danger.

After a few minutes, Mr Wolf insisted our time was up. We retreated to the car park and he drove us back to town. As we prepared to say goodbye, he produced a couple of dog-eared entry tickets to the Hukou Waterfall, and announced we must pay him another 300 RMB (£30).

Mr Wolf had got us with the expensive taxi ride last night, and a place to sleep, but now he had overreached himself – the tickets were obviously old, and it was he who had no bargaining power now. We gave him 30 RMB – small change, but still more than the cost of a taxi ride to the waterfall and back. Mr Wolf held out his hand with a forlorn expression. 'Not enough,' he said.

'Sorry, Mr Wolf,' we said, smiling, and pointing out that the tickets were clearly second-hand.

He saw that the game was up but, rather than getting angry, he gave a 'you can't blame a man for trying' shrug. Then he flashed his cheeky smile again and asked if we wanted a lift to Yichuan, the next town on our route.

'No thank you, we're walking,' we explained, shaking his hand goodbye, and we all laughed. That was something I loved about China – even if you had a tussle about money with someone, once the negotiations were over, whatever the outcome, there was usually an attitude of 'no hard feelings'.

We popped into a shop to buy more supplies because it was two days' walk to Yichuan, and as we came out we saw Mr Wolf driving past in his taxi.

'Are you sure you don't want a lift?' he yelled, without stopping the car.

'No thanks Mr Wolf!' we shouted back. He gave us a toot, flipped a U-turn in front of an oncoming coal truck and revved merrily away. We would not see him again. Good luck, drive carefully, Mr Wolf.

As we crossed the bridge we took a final look at the Yellow River. It seethed underneath us in a cauldron of rapids and ice, and disappeared out of sight around the bend. It would now run down, down, down to the ancient floodplains, and ultimately out into the Yellow Sea a thousand miles away to the east. But we needed to keep going west. On the other side of the bridge, as another mass of loess cliffs rose before us, we took our first steps into our third Chinese province – Shaanxi. It was a confusingly similar name to the previous province of Shanxi, and we wondered if we would be able to pronounce it correctly.

37
Foreigners not allowed

Distance to home: 2,024 miles

Two hours after we left the Yellow River and climbed back into the loess hills, we reached a fork: to the left, a minor lane wound down into a gorge; straight on was a motorway. The motorway had a sign banning tractors, mopeds, animals, cyclists and pedestrians. A police car was parked beside the slip road, and three policemen watched us approach.

'Well, both roads lead to where we want to go,' said Leon, scanning the iPhone, 'but I'm not sure those officers would appreciate it if we took the motorway.'

We gave the policemen a friendly wave and forked left onto the smaller road. It descended steeply, while above us the motorway bridged the gully on giant concrete stilts. As we rounded the corner, we saw that as the motorway reached a mountain, it simply tunnelled straight through it.

'The motorway must be half the distance, and it doesn't have any climbs or descents,' said Leon as we puffed back out of the gorge. A truck roared past, and we leant against the barrier to get out of its way.

'And it's definitely more dangerous down here,' I said. 'There's probably a hard shoulder up there.'

The smooth motorway continued to taunt us, and we started debating whether we should try sneaking onto it for a while. We had had a few more police encounters recently − usually when a patrol car stopped to see who we were. All they did was look at our passports and let us go. Feeling hopeavistic, therefore, we convinced ourselves that if the police caught us on a 'Pedestrians not allowed' road, the worst they would do was tell us off and make us go back on the small road. And besides, it would be a fun and adventurous alternative to the country lanes for a while.

With our minds made up, we scanned the broken slopes until we spotted a sheep track that led us up to the edge of the motorway. A few minutes later we were strolling onto the beautiful smooth tarmac. It rolled ahead of us, across chasms, and through mountains, without turning, twisting or deviating, like an ideal Roman road. Immediately, our pace increased to our maximum speed of four miles per hour. As hoped, we also had a wide hard shoulder, and this turned into a slither of pavement when we reached the tunnels. The tunnels were up to half a mile long, and they bore us effortlessly through the mountains that blocked our path. There was also little traffic – probably because the toll fees were hefty. Most local traffic would prefer the free but slow road below. As we passed over a bridge we saw the little road twisting along beside the stream, and we were elated to be making double the progress we normally would in this terrain.

We had been going less than half an hour, when a police car appeared.

'Just keep walking,' I whispered at Leon. There was nowhere to hide.

We watched the highway patrol car out of the corners of our eyes. It was new and polished, and two young policemen stared at us through the windscreen, mystified. But although they slowed slightly, a moment later they accelerated away.

We relaxed again. 'I guess if they pretend they haven't seen us, we're not their problem,' said Leon.

Two days of smooth motorway cruising later, we needed to turn south. Our next landmark was the ancient capital of Xian, about 200 miles to the southwest. We climbed off the motorway embankment and continued along a smaller road, which led down a narrow valley. Fertile fields lined the roadside, and the valley slopes were filled with dense pine forests. The air was fresh and fragrant and the daytime temperature had warmed to only a few degrees below zero. Just as we were beginning to enjoy striding through this new environment, a car pulled up and a man wearing glasses leaned his head out of the window and spoke to us in English. He nodded down the road and said, 'Foreigners are not allowed on this road, or in the town at the end of this valley.'

'What do you mean?'

'Foreigners are not allowed,' he repeated. 'The police will catch you, and turn you back or arrest you.'

We tried to press him further, but he did not want to go into details and, after advising us again to go around the valley, he drove off.

Leon and I looked at each other. What did he mean?

'It's at least an extra two or three days if we go around it,' said Leon, looking at the iPhone. 'I don't think we've got any choice. I think we probably just have to go for it, and hope we don't get into trouble.'

'Or at least too much trouble,' I said. We shrugged and started to walk again.

I held my poles more tightly in my hands, and found myself scanning the tree line. Leon pointed out some red signs planted in the fields. We could not read them, but they had a distinct 'keep out' feel. Could this be one of those small, scattered localities of China that was still a 'closed zone'? From what we had read about 'closed zones', they existed because of a military, possibly nuclear, presence. After being a bit cavalier about our recent police encounters, I was suddenly nervous. If we got caught, would they be more likely to take issue with the cameras? I tried to push images of imprisonment or deportation out of my mind, and we decided to keep the main camera out of sight, and film only with the GoPro strapped to my chest.

The town at the end of the valley, Huanglong, was still twenty miles away, so that night we would have to camp. As it got dark we approached a village, which we hoped to slip through unnoticed before pitching our tents somewhere on the other side. To be more discreet, we turned off our head torches and started to carry instead of clink our poles. A lady walked out of a shack in her yard and entered her house. We thought that she had not seen us, but then a light shone against the trees beside me – she had seen us, and had come back out with a torch.

'Just keep walking,' we muttered to each other, and a moment later we were safely back in the gloom, and invisible. Fear now tainted our world.

'That lady's shack looked like a Vietnamese torture cell,' joked Leon in a whisper.

A few minutes later we heard some loud bangs coming from the village.

'Those sound more like gunshots than fireworks,' I said.

A mile beyond the village, we pitched our tents quietly in the corner of a cornfield.

After an uneasy night's sleep we were back on the road at dawn. Although the valley looked less menacing in daylight, we still walked hard and fast. At 8 a.m. we dared to stop at a little cluster of bungalows to fill our thermoses. Some wrinkled, toothy farmers grinned and gave us hot water and sweet-bean-filled buns. Thankfully they did not look as if they were going to perform a citizen's arrest on us.

Later, some dreamy snow started to fall, and by mid-afternoon, everything had turned white. We began to think we might make it to the town, after which we would just need to sneak through its outskirts and out the other side. When we had just eight miles to go, Leon was walking a hundred metres ahead of me, and the snow had almost ceased. But suddenly a police car was driving towards us, its lights flashing. It stopped beside Leon and two policemen climbed out. They handed something to him. Adrenaline started to thump through me. Leon was speaking to them, though I was still far out of earshot. He appeared to be pointing up and down the road, and telling our usual joke about walking through beautiful but cold China. However, as far as I could tell, the police were not amused. A second police car arrived, and another policeman climbed out.

I drew nearer, and they all stopped talking and turned to watch me arrive.

'Hello,' I said. No one replied and a policeman handed me a piece of paper. I looked at Leon, who looked very sombre and raised his eyebrows at me.

The paper had some big official-looking stamps on it and, printed in English, was the following:

Foreigner, you have broken the law. You are trespassing in a region of the People's Republic of China where foreigners are not permitted. You must make yourself completely obedient to whatever the police officers command of you.

My breathing became shallow. This was a potentially grave situation. Were we being arrested? Were they going to search our bags?

'Get in the car,' one of the policemen said, opening the door.

The car did a U-turn and headed towards the town – in the same direction we had been walking. It was warm inside, and I felt a strange mixture of comfort and jitters. Although the police had only spoken to us in Chinese so far, I thought they might know some English. Both Leon and I spoke a little Spanish and French, so we switched to a sort of English-Spanish-French hybrid to make sure the police would not understand.

'*Que pasa tu penses?*' (What's going on?) Leon said.

'Don't ask me,' I said, 'let's just *jugar* the *estupido* foreigner card.' (Let's just play the dumb foreigner card.)

A few minutes later we entered the town. It looked completely normal – no big missile bases to be seen, just the usual bustle of people, and shops selling clothes and televisions and fish. At the police station we were led into the office of the most senior policeman. He told us to sit on the small hard sofa, and again questioned us about what we were doing.

'We are walking through China – what a beautiful country it is!' we said several more times. One of the other policemen came in and asked for our passports and walked out with them. A part of me was still dreading that they would search our bags and take issue with the camera, but gradually, as we continued making small talk, the policemen softened. Another policeman brought in cups of tea. Everyone suddenly seemed a bit awkward.

A few minutes later a lady in her twenties came in to join the tea party. 'I am the daughter of a policeman,' she said in excellent English. 'I work as an airline hostess for Qatar Airways.' She talked with the boss for a few minutes, before turning to us and apologising that we had been arrested but, unfortunately, foreigners were not allowed in this area. We apologised in return and said we hadn't realised, which was reasonably true since we had not known how credible that one random man had been.

'There were no signposts saying it was a restricted area,' we said.

'No, there are no signs,' everyone agreed.

'We were not to know.'

'No, you were not to know.'

'Maybe you could put up some signs for the next foreigners?'

Everyone smiled politely.

The conversation continued with more questions, more explanations, more friendly apologies from both sides. Increasingly, they were happy to hear about our walk, and pleased that we were walking through huge, beautiful China, and meeting lots and lots of friendly people. The mood softened, and some smiles cracked at last, even on the chief's face.

After an hour, they told us we could soon leave, but because the closed zone continued on the other side of the town, they would give us a lift through it.

The police car drove us on through the town and dropped us in the mountains on the other side of the closed zone. As we said goodbye, the policemen took it in turns to take cheery photographs with their arms around our shoulders.

38
Spring

Distance to home: 1,894 miles

13 FEBRUARY

I felt relieved that we had made it through the closed zone without serious trouble, though it was a shame that we had been forced to 'cheat' a little by taking a ride in a police car for twenty miles. However, it certainly counted as 'legitimate cheating' because we had no choice. We wondered whether there would be any more closed zones on our route and hoped that by doing more research we could avoid them.

The road led us down onto a hazy plain – the first large area of flat land since the Gobi, and the start of a new landscape. The next day, we passed through a deep canyon. As we walked downwards, the temperature rose above zero for the first time on the trip. The river at the bottom ran smoothly, without a hint of ice, and it was getting so warm that I even removed my gloves. We stopped for some noodles and I was astonished to see a fly buzzing around my feet: our first insect of the expedition. In the afternoon we met some villagers sweeping up dross and burning it in little bonfires beside the road. All these signs led to only one conclusion: we were on the cusp of spring.

A lot had happened in the last seven days. We had seen the magnificent fifteenth day Chinese New Year celebrations in Daning, swum in the icy Yellow River, run out of money, walked down a mountain-piercing motorway, and even been arrested for walking through a closed zone. Throughout all this, our tiredness had been steadily deepening. Life felt out of control in many ways but, by pressing forwards, we were doing OK. And if the weather was going to warm up – well, surely things were going to get easier.

But we could not start to enjoy the temperate climes quite yet, for the time had come to put into action the plan – conceived in desperation – to return to the wintry wastelands of Mongolia.

39
Code Z

Distance to home: 1,819 miles

14–22 FEBRUARY

One could be forgiven for romanticising the lifestyle of an adventurer, if one's views were based solely upon TV documentaries and glossy travel books. The reality is somewhat different. Much of an expedition is full of monotony – slogging through day after day of hard, painful footsteps; endless identical conversations with strangers; growing bored of one's own company. While there are plenty of magnificent moments of extreme beauty, hospitality, adrenaline and hilarity, there are also long hours when nothing much happens at all. And when something does happen, it is often in the form of an obstacle to be bypassed, or a problem to be solved. On previous expeditions, I had to do a number of slightly ludicrous things to overcome such obstacles and problems, ranging from sneaking through military checkpoints at 3 a.m. in Tibet, to balancing a bicycle on a canoe to cross unbridged rivers in Papua New Guinea. These were all part of the adventure, and a healthy sense of the absurd was one of the most important traits necessary to prevent everything becoming too stressful.

Throw into the mix the challenge of making a TV show, however, and the challenges take on a whole new dimension.

Our 'Code Z' had two key goals. Firstly, to leave China and re-enter it, thus renewing our visa for another three months (which we needed to do at this point anyway). Secondly, to shoot, in focus, two days' worth of footage of ourselves walking around the Mongolian desert with Molly.

Implementing this plan was far from simple. We would have to fly to Beijing, successfully apply for a new Mongolian visa, fly to Erlian and cross the border back into Mongolia, retrieve Molly and head back into the desert for filming and finally cross back into China again and fly back to the place where we had stopped walking. The whole operation would take nine days – days we could ill afford – and would use up almost our entire contingency budget of £1,000. But we felt it was worth it, because it was the one way we could fix the grievous focus fiasco. At the same time, it was quite a risky plan, and there were a number of things that could go wrong: missing flights (we had four to catch within eight days), not getting the visas, trouble crossing borders, and failing to find Molly.

Our first flight was from Xian airport, and as the airport was not on our route, we planned to get as close as possible to it, mark our spot, and catch a taxi. The flight was on 16 February. However, as if to illustrate the unexpected problems that can arise, on 13 February, when we were nicely on track, Christine double-checked with the Mongolian Embassy and found out they were about to shut for Mongolian New Year. This would prevent us from getting our Mongolian visas in Beijing. We scrambled for a new plan – rebooking the flights for the following day, 14 February. We marched quickly to our next city, Pucheng, and jumped in a taxi. A few hours later we were in the air.

'The captain has switched off the seat belt sign, please enjoy your flight. Our arrival time in Beijing will be 12.05 a.m.'

I looked across at Leon who was already dozing in the seat next to me. Outside the world was black. But I knew well what was down below – the loess mountains of Shanxi. It had taken us almost two blister-filled months to walk through them. Memories of walking along the Wall, getting lost by the Yellow River, and trudging through coal valleys flooded through my head. And yet the flight to Beijing (which was over 200 miles beyond Datong) would take barely ninety minutes.

We had two days in Beijing, and were kindly hosted by Christine's old friend Enoch and her fiancé Tim. We set out early the next morning to hand in our passports at the Mongolian Embassy. This done, we wandered the streets of the capital in an elated daze. After the *yaodong* villages and remote frozen valleys, Beijing felt like a different country. Everything was bigger and greater – wider roads, more traffic, grander buildings. The grey blanket of hazy pollution was thicker. There seemed to be a Starbucks on every other street corner. It was also a welcome novelty that people no longer stared at us, for there were plenty of other Caucasians around – business people and travellers, old and young. In the evening, we went to a party with Enoch and Tim, where everyone was looking chic in the latest fashion, and Leon and I, wearing our matching 'his and hers' sponsored puffa jackets, felt slightly out of place.

We successfully picked up our Mongolian visas, and boarded a plane back to Erlian, the border town on the Chinese side. As we landed I stroked my face with my hands, and was surprised by its smoothness. In Beijing, I had shaved off my beard, because for the reshoot to work it was essential that I resembled as much as possible how I had looked when we started the walk. Leon, meanwhile, was not keen to shave. We agreed that if he appeared on camera at all, he would have to wear his balaclava – the mysterious man with no face. But the most crucial thing for continuity was that we found Molly, and to find Molly we would have to find Urult the money-changer.

As we walked out of Erlian airport in daylight, it felt different from the night three months previously when we had attempted to sleep there and had our first encounter with the Chinese police. This time we looked like conventional tourists arriving by plane; as we strolled past, I smiled at the policemen. One of them frowned in a flicker of recognition.

A taxi drove us towards the town, fifteen miles away. We noticed that although it was February, there was a lot less snow around than when we were first here, which again might look strange on camera. We would just have to do our best with the filming, making use of the banks of snow that had blown into piles.

As we drove past the route we had walked and saw all the empty desert land, it was bizarre what things had stuck in our memory.

'That's where we stopped for a noodle break,' said Leon, pointing to a lay-by.

'And, that's where you went for a Mr Lax,' I said, pointing to a rock.

Alongside walking and filming, our concerns had distilled down to life's most basic necessities.

When we reached the kissing dinosaur archway above the road, we got out, and spent an hour walking around filming, with me trying to look and speak as if I was taking my first, nervous steps into China. I had never been much of an actor – I was far too shy as a child – but now my moment of Oscar nominee glory had come. Back in Erlian, we filmed ourselves walking the streets as if we had just crossed the border – we were acting everything out backwards.

The next morning, we crossed back into Mongolia. Zamiin-Uud had not changed – it was still a grubby, frozen border town – and the sense of drab dilapidation seemed even more glaring compared to the sense of progress we had seen in Chinese towns.

Our first major task was to find Molly. We had been hoping that Urult would still be sitting in his shiny car outside the train station listening to 'Coolplay', and also that he would have kept his promise to look after Molly. But when we arrived, he and his car were nowhere to be seen. We rolled our eyes. This was the last thing we needed, having come all the way back here. Leon went shopping for food supplies, and I continued with the hunt. I eventually met a jeep driver who spoke English. He said that Urult had gone to Ulaanbaatar.

This was not good news. If Urult had left, what were the chances of finding Molly? The jeep driver suggested that I meet Sasha – Urult's older brother, the big boss in town. I was led into a building, and up to a room where Sasha sat behind a desk, Don Corleone-style, with a crony by his side. Neither of us understood a word the other was saying, apart from 'Urult'. After my attempts to describe Molly with squeaking noises and sweeping hand gestures had failed, I remembered the laptop, and flicked onto a picture of Molly. Sasha's eyes lit up. He issued a quick command to the crony, who led me into a yard and pointed underneath a parked truck. I stooped down to have a look, and there, safe and sound, sat Molly. She looked overjoyed that we had come to rescue her.

Early the next morning, we hired a jeep and a driver who drove us fifteen miles north, and dropped us in the middle of the desert. Then followed a surreal thirty hours of dragging Molly hither and thither across the plains and into the hills, again pretending we were passing through for the first time. On the afternoon of the second day, we reached the top of a hill and decided to call it a day.

It would be very hard to hitchhike back to town with Molly, so we decided to leave her on top of a hill. We did, however, make a note of the surrounding hills and tracks. An adventure friend of Leon's, Charlie Walker, was planning to walk through the Gobi in a couple of months' time. Leon would send him a kind of treasure map of how to find Molly.* We flagged down a passing car back to Zamiin-Uud, crossed back into China (acquiring our new three-month visa stamp on the way), and then caught our flights, via Beijing to Xian, and another taxi back to the city of Pucheng, where we had stopped walking nine days previously.

Sitting in the *ludian* that night, I said to Leon, 'Well I think that was a great success.'

'Yes, all things considered.' Leon looked relieved.

We had discussed at length any moral qualms about the reshoot. Were we duping viewers? Only within the bounds of being creative to make a show, we felt. Code Z was not the equivalent to, say, pretending we had done something we had not in order to make our lives easier. In fact, it had made our lives a lot harder, and we were just repeating something we had already done. We had no regrets.

Leon pulled out the whisky, took his swig and handed it to me.

I passed it back and said, 'I think you definitely deserve a double swig tonight. You've done really well with this. Code Z was a daring idea, and the darned thing actually worked.'

'Thanks,' said Leon. He tipped the flask back again, and I could see that a huge weight had fallen from his shoulders.

In addition to getting the needed footage, the Code Z palaver had also made us realise how, although we were inexperienced and

* Unfortunately, by the time Charlie got there, she was gone. Hopefully she had found a good new home with the local nomads.

cavalier when we set out, we had come a long way with our filming and teamwork. This trip was proving to be a baptism of fire (and ice) for both of us, especially for Leon, as he faced the brunt of the filming pressure. He was rising well to the challenge.

40
The Warriors

Distance to home: 1,729 miles

We now had less than a week until Christine was coming to meet us; as we resumed walking towards Xian, it felt as though we had entered a new phase of the expedition. The hints of spring from before Code Z had become more pronounced. Even at night, the temperature remained above zero. By day, although the sky was a dull, hazy grey, it was warm enough to stuff our down jackets and gloves away in our rucksacks and, instead, stroll along with bare hands, wearing a mere double layer of thermal tops. Amazingly, my foot was by now feeling quite strong, and I was almost back to walking at full speed.

The land was also changing. The flat plains were starting to brim with budding orchards and freshly ploughed vegetable fields. Clusters of farmers were hard at work, bringing life back to the world. We also passed through bigger towns in the midst of rapid expansion – whole new streets of apartments were going up, and sometimes half the buildings looked less than a year old. The narrow road, meanwhile, buzzed with agricultural traffic and buses. Whenever possible, we cut along little paths beside irrigation canals.

We seemed to have fallen smoothly back into our old routine. On our second day, at lunchtime, we sat on a muddy mound and went through the familiar procedure of pouring boiling water onto our instant noodles. On roadside breaks, instant noodles were still the easiest meal. However, on this particular day, both Leon and I had a simultaneous revelation.

'Hmm,' I said, 'these noodles aren't tasting so good today.'

Leon looked up from his bowl. 'You know what, I was just thinking the same thing.'

'In fact, I hope I never see instant noodles again in my whole life.'

'Me too. Want some peanuts?'

After three solid months of noodles, we had reached our limit. If they had been a little boring before, now they had become about as appetising as mouldy bread – OK if we were starving, but otherwise more suitable for the dustbin. We had not been able to buy takeaway meals from cheap local restaurants, because they would always freeze before we had a chance to eat them. But now, takeaways would be our strategy for instant noodle avoidance.

That night we turned our head torches on and strolled into a nice field in search of a place to camp. We were quickly startled by a night watchman's flashlight shining at us and some shouting. We backed away and walked another mile before trying again. This time we were more covert, and kept our torches off. When we reached the middle of the field we pulled out our bivvy bags for the first time. These were dark green, lightweight Gore-Tex bags, which could be used instead of a tent. We had been carrying them since Datong, in the hope that we could post our tents home and use these, but it had been too cold until now. Tonight, however, was ideal. It was warmer, and we wanted to make ourselves less visible. We climbed inside the bags and lay down next to our rucksacks. None but the most conscientious of night watchmen would be able to spot us tonight.

About eight miles from where we lay down in our bivvy bags, on one spring morning thirty-eight years previously, a few local farmers had got up and gone out to dig a well. Several metres down, a farmer, Yang Zhifa, who was at the bottom of the pit, hit something solid. It seemed to be manmade, and he thought it might be some old pottery that he could sell. But, as he dug more, he discovered it was actually a statue of some kind. The local authorities were duly informed, and archaeologists arrived to take a look and have a dig for themselves.

To their astonishment, they began to unearth one statue after another: an entire army of military figures. And, more astonishing still, these were not just any old statues. Rather, they had been built as part of the tomb complex of the most famous of all Chinese Emperors, Emperor Qin – the man who had first united China into one Empire, and who had in so many ways defined its future.

Ancient historical accounts had given fantastical descriptions of Emperor Qin's tomb – a mausoleum the size of a small mountain. It was said to have had life-size replicas of Qin's palaces, and a huge replica of the Empire – with rivers of mercury to depict the waterways. It had apparently taken thirty-eight years to build, using a slave army of 700,000. However, because it had never been discovered, much modern scholarship had thought the accounts were greatly exaggerated.

But after two thousand years of lying silent and forgotten beneath the ground, the unearthed figures – now known as the Terracotta Warriors, or Terracotta Army – changed everyone's minds. For although the statues were not even mentioned in the ancient accounts (perhaps because they were seen as a small sideshow compared to the main tomb), they proved the scale of the works, and it was not long before the tomb itself was identified, about a mile away, inside a manmade hill.

In the morning, Leon and I packed up our bivvy bags; after two hours of walking, the fields around us turned to concrete. The fields that Yang Zhifa used to farm were now covered with a vast archipelago of restaurants, car parks and shops selling life-sized replicas of the warriors. We walked through the maze and joined a throng of tourists disembarking from buses and trooping towards the entrance.

'There's the big man himself,' said Leon, turning on the camera.

Overlooking the car parks stood a large statue of Emperor Qin. 'He doesn't look like the kind of guy you'd want to have a drink with,' I said.

The statue depicted a powerful man with a hard face. The historical accounts had given him a reputation for being a callous, brutal and authoritarian leader. Millions of lives were lost to his building projects – not only this tomb complex, but also the roads, canals and the early Great Wall. He was a military leader, having destroyed other kingdoms in his quest to unite the Empire. And significantly, in contrast to emperors who came after him, he was not a fan of Confucius or his emphasis on virtuous, exemplary leadership. Rather, Qin ruled by a harsh doctrine known as legalism, with a code of punishments for all who failed to show total obedience. He also did not appreciate those who disagreed with him. Most infamously, he was alleged to have had thousands of important Confucian books burnt, and 460 Confucian scholars buried alive.

We paid our entrance fee, passed through the gate, and walked towards the first and biggest of the buildings – the size of an aircraft hangar – that housed the famous warriors. I had actually visited the site before, in the middle of my bike trip. Back then I had virtually no understanding of Chinese history; without the proper context, although they were impressive, the statues did not blow my mind. But this time I knew more about China, and what this Emperor had created. His Empire was so vast that it was taking Leon and me six months to walk down through it – largely on good roads, in a time of peace and safety. And he had united and ruled this place over 2,000 years ago.

As we walked into the building, I knew what to expect, but I was still surprised. The warriors were standing exactly as they had been last time I was here, faithfully in rows. They were still guarding their Emperor, just as they had done through the many long centuries. They seemed so human, and yet enchanted, growing out of the ground like ghoulish soldiers from a Hollywood B-movie. The guidebooks were full of interesting facts. There are thought to be over 8,000 warriors in total, though only about a quarter of these have been excavated so far. The figures were not mass produced, but rather seem to have been modelled upon a real army, for they are all entirely individual. They have different ranks, armour, facial expressions, ages and lengths of beard. But what they do have in common is that they are unarmed and their hands are empty and half clenched. Their weapons were perhaps looted shortly after they were made; or, if made from wood, have rotted away over the centuries. Their faces, meanwhile, are human and intent – a little afraid, perhaps, and yet steeled for battle and their fate as foot soldiers of the Emperor.

The Terracotta Army reflected not only the power and wealth of the first Emperor, but also his obsession with his own life, and life after death. Research has shown a remarkably consistent set of beliefs about the afterlife in ancient China: one's tomb should contain items that were needed in the next life. Qin wanted an army on standby, near to the palatial tomb in which he had been buried with sacrificed concubines and servants.

After his unexpected death (quite possibly from drinking a potion that his magicians said was the elixir of life), there was a succession crisis involving dastardly eunuchs, heirs forced to commit suicide, and then revolt and civil war. The dynasty that he had founded, and hoped would last for a thousand generations, did not outlast him by even a couple of decades. And so continued the bloody relay baton of the 'Mandate of Heaven', passed on through the centuries from one severed hand to the next. What did survive him was the idea of a coherent, united China.

Although the warriors have now been liberated from the earth, they are still servants of the State, the new Communist China, displaying the nation's former glory for millions of tourists every year. We walked through the crowds, and back out past Emperor Qin's statue at the entrance. He looked down disapprovingly on us visitors who were still alive, and I looked back up at his stern face. I had read that although he was undoubtedly harsh, like the early historical sources said, it was perhaps unfair to brand him as worse than many of the other emperors. Many of them were unimaginably brutal.*

Twenty minutes after leaving the tourist zone, we reached a large park, dominated by a giant hill. Inside this hill was the Emperor's tomb; until the discovery of the Terracotta Army, it had also been lost for 2,000 years. The task of building the mountain-tomb has been compared, in terms of scale, to the pyramids. We gazed up at

---

* Many European rulers through the ages were, of course, no better. The negativity of Qin's reputation was partly due to the fact that his main chronicler, Sima Qian, was a Confucian scholar from the Han dynasty. Naturally, to further legitimise their own rule, the Han dynasty wanted to show that Qin was a bad emperor.

it wistfully – fifty metres high, and covered in trees. However, although it has been proved that it does indeed contain the Emperor's mausoleum, archaeologists have (tantalisingly, but probably wisely) still never opened it up. They say they still lack the right technology, though of course conspiracy theories abound. I, for one, hope I live to see the day when its secrets are revealed.

41
Tunnel of Doom

Distance to home: 1,679 miles

26–28 FEBRUARY

The next day we finally arrived in Xian, the ancient capital, but now something of a concrete jungle. However, it had been hard to estimate our arrival date in advance, so we had ended up arriving forty-eight hours early for Christine and our much-needed five-day break. Rather than waste precious days waiting, Leon and I decided to keep walking and two days later we would mark our spot on the map and hitchhike back. We would have a chance to explore Xian more then, and the rest days would be all the sweeter for our extra miles.

So we walked straight out of the other side of Xian, and by lunchtime found ourselves walking across another hazy plain.

'I could get used to walking on flat ground like this,' I said. 'How long until we reach the next mountains?' We knew from the Google satellite map that south from Xian, almost until the coast, we would face line after line of rugged country.

'Probably about an hour,' said Leon, scanning the iPhone map as he walked.

Out of the haze, a vast ghostly shadow on the horizon started to form into a more solid shape – the Qinling Mountains. As we got closer, we saw that the Qinling were very different to the mountains of the north. They rose up in a more angular and vertical way, because they were made from hard limestone, rather than the soft loess that was easily moulded by rain and wind. They were also far less arid – a tangle of thick, subtropical vegetation wrapped itself around the pale cliff faces and glancing peaks, and little streams cascaded down. A winding lane led us upwards, and the mountains kept rising higher until they disappeared. It felt as though we were entering the world of ancient Chinese swordsmen and flying daggers. An enormous motorway appeared, once again boring through the cliff faces, and our road started weaving along underneath it.

The Qinling were a formidable barrier to cross; positioned as they were just south of the ancient capital, they had exerted great historical and cultural influences on China. However, for now, Leon and I were not thinking about their significance, but rather how far we could get through them in the next day and a half. Although we had reached Xian early for Christine, this did not mean we were 'ahead of schedule'. The foot injury, the focus fiasco and the nine days spent on Code Z meant that it was now inevitable that our remaining three months in China would be quite gruelling. It therefore made good sense to get as far as we could before our break. And there was one obvious way for us to do this: the Zhongnanshan Tunnel.

This tunnel was not like the short motorway tunnels we had walked through thus far. Those had usually been less than half a mile long, and we could easily see the light at both ends, even when we were in the middle. The Zhongnanshan Tunnel, at 18,040 metres (over eleven miles), was the longest road tunnel in all of China, and the second longest in the world.

That we were even considering walking through it perhaps showed that our exhaustion was making us lose all sense of reason. We were aware it would be a stupid thing to do – we had even started referring to it as the 'Tunnel of Doom' – but we did not seem able to resist the temptation.

'What about the pollution inside?' said Leon.

'It's a brand-new tunnel,' I said. 'It's only been open for a year, so the fans inside will be in top working order. Fumes won't be a problem. But what about the police?'

'Maybe we could go through it in the middle of the night,' said Leon. 'Even if there are CCTV cameras, the guards will probably be asleep. The last thing they would ever expect would be a couple of crazy foreigners walking through it at 4 a.m.'

'And it's easier to get forgiveness than permission in China,' I said. I had read that somewhere and it sounded good. It seemed to sum up our approach to the police in general.

So, with our decision made, we walked into the night, because we wanted to get as close as possible to the tunnel entrance before we slept. At 9 p.m. we came upon a group of migrant workers seated around a little bonfire. They said we could sleep in the derelict house behind them, and pointed to a bare front room, without a door. There were a couple of old doors leaning against the wall, and one of the men lay the doors on the ground and indicated, with a smile, that they would make ideal mattresses for us. We thanked him and rolled out our sleeping bags on the doors.

The alarm went off, and it took me a moment to remember why I was getting up at 3 a.m., and why there was a slight sense of dread at the back of my mind. Walking through an eleven-mile Chinese road tunnel was the last thing I felt like doing now, and it suddenly seemed like an incredibly bad idea. My hands trembled a little as we packed our sleeping bags and walked back into the darkness.

We climbed up onto the open motorway that led to the tunnel, and as we walked down the hard shoulder in single file it was completely quiet. The motorway lights shone down brightly from above, and behind them I could see the shapes of the Qinling Mountains looming in and out of the night. The double-laned tunnel entrance came into sight. It was well lit, and beside it was a small checkpoint cabin and a police car. We kept walking, and saw a guard in the cabin leaning back in his chair, watching TV. He did not notice us slip past, and a moment later we were inside the Tunnel of Doom.

It quickly lived up to the name we had given it. White lights and blackened walls shot before us, dead straight, stretching into the heart of the mountain and never coming to an end, promising no escape. There were in fact two parallel tunnels, one for each direction, and we were walking, as we always did, on the side facing the oncoming traffic. There was a decent width of pavement to walk on – at least we were safe from cars. However, I could smell fumes.

At this point, I knew we should probably just cut our losses and turn back, but now that we were here, bizarrely, we felt we had no choice.

We increased our pace, and heard the first vehicle before we saw it: a thick rumbling and booming sound, echoing off the walls. A moment later, headlights appeared and the car roared past. I tried to take only shallow breaths. We were going to have to spend at least three hours in here. I looked over my shoulder. Leon had a foreboding expression on his face and, behind him, the mouth of the tunnel gradually disappeared from view. Ten minutes in, it had vanished forever. We stopped walking and looked at each other.

'Blimey, it's hot in here,' I said.

Leon puffed and agreed. We dropped our packs, and pulled off our coats and thermal tops, until we were wearing only our T-shirts. In the Gobi, I had sometimes wondered when we would first reach 'T-shirt' weather. If this counted as weather, that time had come.

'Let's just see how it goes, I guess,' said Leon.

We kept walking, marching as fast as we could and keeping an eye on the distance markings on the tunnel wall. We had done one mile, and had ten more to go. Our surroundings did not change and followed a strict regularity of features. The blackened walls of the tunnel running ahead and behind; lay-bys every 250 metres; mysterious steel doors in the walls every 1,000 metres; CCTV cameras lining the roof. There were also regular large fans, just as we had hoped. What was worrying was that two out of every three fans were not working.

A vehicle passed every ten minutes, spewing black fumes in its wake. Not surprisingly, the air thickened the further we went. After three miles we stopped for another break, this time, nervously pushing open one of the mysterious doors. Inside, there was a little passageway, leading through to the other tube of the tunnel, going in the other direction. The air was slightly better inside, and there were a couple of brooms leaning against the wall.

'Well, if the road sweepers have to work here, maybe we will survive,' Leon said.

'If it gets bad, we can always hitch a ride out,' I said, trying to reassure myself as well as Leon, and ignoring the fact that a driver at 4 a.m. in China's longest road tunnel might not be that keen to stop for two semi-conscious foreigners. Not to mention the fact that we might not be able to tell when we were reaching dangerous levels of carbon-monoxide poisoning. It flashed through my mind how horrific it would be if Christine arrived on her flight the next day and I was not there to meet her, and then she heard the news that two foreign men had been found dead in the tunnel. I pushed the thought out of my mind – we were almost halfway anyway; it was easier to just keep on moving forward.

We kept walking. The mile markers ticked past slowly:

Eight miles left.

Just keep going . . . Just keep focused, Lilwall . . .

Seven miles left.

Keep going . . . Try to speed up . . . I wonder how Leon is?

Six . . .

Why are my palms tingling? Is that a symptom of poisoning? Could we get permanent brain damage from this? What an amazingly stupid idea.

We passed more lay-bys. Halfway through, we reached a lay-by where blackened plastic plants lined the roadside, like demonic imitations from the underworld. I touched a plant, and a thick layer of soot came off on my fingers. My right foot started to hurt again because I had not had time to do any stretching, but I did not want to stop. Leon overtook me and started to gradually move ahead.

Five miles . . .

I couldn't believe we'd been in there almost two hours, and there was still over an hour to go.

Four miles . . .

We stopped for another break in a connecting passageway, but this time the air was even worse than that in the tunnel. Leon said he was starting to feel light-headed, and I told him about my tingling palms. We looked at each other and laughed nervously, and then stopped and looked serious.

'What the hell are we doing?' said Leon.

He turned on the camera, and I talked about how I thought we should be nominated for the Darwin Award this year – the prize given out to people who are so incredibly dumb that they do the human species a favour by eliminating themselves from the gene pool by getting themselves killed in stupendously stupid ways.

Back in the tunnel, we started to run.

Three miles left . . .

Not far now . . . Maybe we can make it . . . It's 7.30 a.m. . . . It must be daylight outside now.

Two miles . . .

Leon was fifty metres ahead of me, and I continued to struggle to keep up. We were like drowning men desperate for air, imprisoned men desperate for daylight. I saw another car approaching. It had flashing lights, and a moment later my heart sank as the police pulled up beside Leon. This was not just a matter of getting told off again – it would be very disappointing if, having come this far, we could not walk all the way through.

The two young policemen sat in the car, talking. We could not blame them for being flummoxed. I do not think they had been prepared for this kind of situation in police school. One of them climbed out, slowly and cautiously, as if he were about to interact with dangerous convicts. This was clearly a situation in which we should again play the 'dumb foreigner' card.

'Hello,' I said, catching up and mustering my cheeriest Mandarin. Leon lent against the tunnel wall, and tried not to look ill.

The policeman furrowed his brow. 'What are you doing?'

'We are not able to go to Hong Kong,' I said even more cheerily. The carbon monoxide had knocked out my tonal abilities.

'What?' said the policeman, his furrows deepening.

'We started in Mongolia, and have been going for three months. China is a beautiful country!' I gestured around us at the tunnel. It did not seem quite as convincing a gesture as when we were out in the mountains and valleys. Leon tried to nod, but the way he rolled his head made him look demented.

'But you cannot walk through this tunnel,' said the policeman, starting to sound exasperated.

'Really? Why not?'

The policeman started to talk about the fumes, but realising that there was no point reasoning with the insane, he said, 'You just can't.' He turned and talked to his colleague in the police car, and then turned back to us. 'You will have to come with us.'

We protested that we only had two miles to go. The police car was going in the opposite direction to us. We would be out of the tunnel quicker if we walked. The policemen, however, were insistent. No matter how many times the argument went round, they were not going to let us go. Leon and I, for the second time in two weeks, reluctantly put our rucksacks into the back of a police car, and climbed in.

Off we drove, and suddenly the miles that had been ticking down, ticked back up: three, four, five, six, seven, eight . . . Leon said his head was still throbbing, and I noticed he looked pale.

Nine, ten, eleven, twelve . . . Our police car burst out of the tunnel and back into the world of men.

Leon wound down the window and gasped.

I laughed, nervously.

Part Five

Into Southern China

一山不容二虎

Two tigers cannot share one mountain.

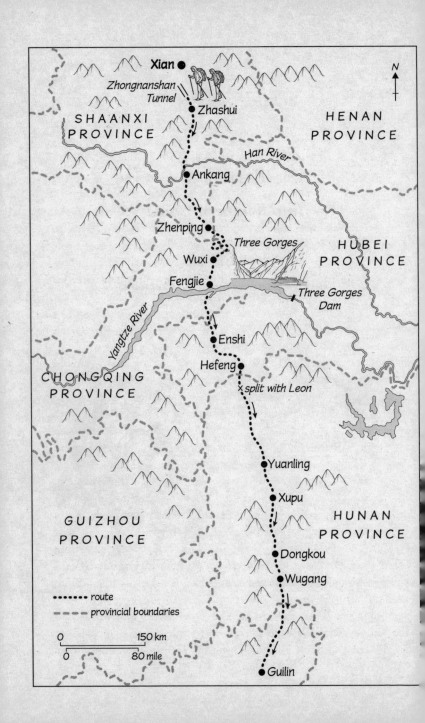

42

Proper sausages

Distance to home: 1,679 miles

29 FEBRUARY–3 MARCH

The police car sped down the motorway and all the way back to Xian. We were disappointed to have got this near to the end, only to then get caught. As we entered the urban area we were momentarily concerned that they were taking us to a police station for another interrogation. In fact they just wanted to drop us in the city and a long way from the tunnel – to make sure we did not just turn round and walk back through it again. This suited us well, because later that day Christine would arrive.

Xian, the provincial capital, was a gargantuan grid of roads, flyovers and apartment blocks. It was the provincial capital of Shaanxi, but for almost a thousand years it had been the capital of the entire Empire. At its peak, under the Tang Dynasty in the seventh to tenth centuries, it was the largest and most cosmopolitan city in the world. It had then fallen from favour and, because it was built mostly from wood, almost nothing from those times remained. There were, however, still some impressive city walls from the more recent Ming Dynasty, and a handful of temples and towers.

When we arrived in the city centre, instead of looking for a modest *binguan*, we headed straight for the luxury five-star Shangri-La hotel. This was way beyond our budget but, incredibly, when the hotel chain had heard that we were raising funds for a charity through our walk, they had kindly offered us free accommodation in two cities on our route.

Looking as if we had just walked 1,500 miles, we strolled into the serene lobby. We were astounded to receive a welcome fit for royalty from the staff in smart uniforms. They gave us fragrant tea in porcelain cups, took our smelly rucksacks and showed us to our magnificent rooms. A few hours later, Christine arrived. I had woken up that morning at 3 a.m., walked through a hellish tunnel, and been forced into a police car. And now I was relaxing in the tranquillity of the Shangri-La with my wife – it was the strangest day I'd had for a while, and part of me wondered whether I had passed out in the tunnel and was inhabiting a carbon monoxide-fuelled dream.

Better even than the Shangri-La's soft beds and sparkling bathrooms was the buffet breakfast. We were treated to a gigantic spread of bacon and sausages, mushrooms and melons, croissants, cereal and cappuccinos: surely just what a couple of tired, trans-China walkers needed in order to recover a semblance of togetherness of mind and body. On our first morning, Christine and I strolled into the dining room and saw Leon already there. He was eating his fourth plate and reading the paper, his large feet protruding from the white Shangri-La slippers.

'How's the headache?' I asked.

'Still there,' he replied, smiling dopily, putting another proper sausage in his mouth.

Having been married for only two and a half years, being apart for the past eight weeks had been quite hard on Christine and me. That we could talk on the phone regularly made things slightly easier; however, sometimes when we spoke, we were having very different days. When I was in a lonely, sad mood, she might be feeling elated and energetic, or vice versa, and this could lead to misunderstandings and arguments. We had to work hard to resolve these on the phone so they were not left hanging. Christine had already also managed to use the publicity platform of the trip to raise over £12,000 for Viva. This helped us to feel that the pain was worth it.

For much of our five days together in Xian, Christine and I happily stayed put in our five-star sanctuary. We just needed to spend time together – we could come back another time and be tourists. But we did occasionally go out to explore. One day, we visited the packed, narrow streets of the Muslim Quarter, where hippy backpackers and wealthy tour groups mingled with Chinese Muslims wearing skullcaps. The streets sizzled with kebabs, and the call to prayer rose up from the ancient mosque and echoed through the streets. Islam had come to the city down the Silk Roads from Central Asia during Xian's Tang Dynasty heyday. This had been a time when the Empire was very open, and Christians, Buddhists, Muslims and Confucians were all welcome to come and go.

All too quickly, after five days, and consuming (between Leon and me) fifty-six proper sausages, forty-five strips of bacon, twenty-one cappuccinos, fifteen bowls of cereal, twenty-two hot showers, forty hours of action movies and zero packets of instant noodles, it was time to say goodbye to our lives of luxury. And even more than the sausages, I was sad to leave Christine.

43
China's North–South Divide

Distance to home: 1,629 miles

4–7 MARCH

We were tempted to try walking the last two miles of the Tunnel of Doom, but in the end we decided against it. Leon still had a headache and we did not think that the police would be as lenient if they caught us trying to walk through it a second time. So we caught a taxi to drive us back through the tunnel. Bursting into the open air on the other side, we then doubled back for several miles up a country lane. We resumed our walk from a point roughly parallel with where we had been caught inside the mountain five days previously.

We were now in the middle of the Qinling Mountains, and the temperature was up to 10°C. We followed the lane beside the gentle, unfrozen Qianyou River. This was a tributary that led into the much larger Han River, almost 200 miles to the south. After an hour of walking, we saw the Tunnel of Doom exit, and the motorway hurtling forth and continuing down the valley. It was raised above our little road on concrete stilts.

Like little children walking through a city of skyscrapers, we gazed up again at the soaring limestone cliffs. After months of being surrounded by brown loess hills, we had still not got used to the damp, vertical terrain. As well as the peaks above us disappearing into the clouds, lower down we saw some steep goat tracks zigzagging amid the vegetation and grey crags. I wondered what wildlife might be living in the neighbouring, inaccessible valleys – I had heard that pandas and leopards still roamed wild in the Qinling. And these mountains also marked a significant change to the route that lay ahead of us. In fact, they were sometimes cited as the dividing line between the elusive notions of 'Northern' and 'Southern' China.

Northern China, where we had just been, was a dry landscape, suited to growing millet and wheat; it was also the birthplace of the Chinese civilisation. Southern China, meanwhile, was more humid, and for much of China's early history had been less populated and less powerful in the life of the nation. However, as history rumbled forwards, gradually more people migrated south, often driven by famine, invading nomads or the Yellow River pouring out sorrow. Life in the south was hard, and it took centuries of painful labour to drain the malarial swamps and build paddy fields. But gradually the entrepreneurial people, the more navigable Yangtze River and new, high-yielding varieties of rice, helped it to bloom. By the fourteenth century, the south produced a dynasty that ruled the entire Empire for nearly 300 years. It was the home of valuable and historically fateful crops such as the tea plant. In the twentieth century, it produced most of China's key leaders, including Chairman Mao and Deng Xiaoping.

On our second day in the Qinling, we stumbled upon the entrance of a C-list Chinese tourist attraction – the Zhashui caves. There were no other tourists in sight, but the two girls on the ticket desk said they could be our tour guides. We followed them through the huge entrance in the limestone cliff.

As we entered, a little path with multicoloured lights showed the way. The formations of caves, stalactites and stalagmites, protruded in every direction and, as the path weaved onwards, round corners, and up and down steep steps, we sometimes entered huge caverns, the size of churches. When we reached a point of interest, our guides would launch into a rapidly delivered rote-learned explanation, of which we barely understood a word. Gradually we worked out that the tour mostly involved pointing at what animals could be spotted in the rock formations:

'So this is a goldfish,' they said, pointing at a gnarly rock, before launching into a long, convoluted story about a man who went looking for a goldfish in these very caves (the man's image was now also borne by a rock face).

'Ah, how interesting,' nodded Leon and I, trying to see the resemblance. Leon was filming everything, and set up his tripod to get a steady zoom shot.

'That is shaped like a duck,' indicating a slightly sharper lump of rock.

'Indeed it is,' nodded Leon and I, scratching our heads.

We also came to ancient Buddhist shrines deep in the mountain, which in centuries past had been visited by members of the imperial family. The whole circuit was well over a mile long, and it was the biggest cave complex I had ever seen.

Before we left, we dug out some A4 pieces of paper from our rucksacks. These were our TV permission forms – complicated documents, written in Chinese, in which people gave permission to appear in the show. Tiberius had been asking us to get more of them signed, but we had not had much success so far, mainly because we were hesitant to show them to anyone lest the police got involved. This time, however, we asked the two tour guides if they would sign them. They both agreed and handed them back to us.

Leon, the Irishman, stopped and lifted his face to the sky with a smile. 'I've missed the rain,' he said. It was only a drizzle, but it was the first rain of the trip. Other signs of spring appeared around us too: men ploughing the fields; bulldozers digging gravel; villagers in teams building simple houses. We could also now sleep comfortably in our bivvy bags, though we did start to worry about millipedes climbing in with us.

At the same time as enjoying the spring, however, we continued to feel under pressure. First and foremost was the time pressure – of reaching Hong Kong by our late May deadline. Besides our promises to Christine and Clare, there was now another reason that we needed to make this date: the London 2012 Olympics committee had asked Leon to be a torchbearer for his home town at the start of June. In order to hit the finish date, therefore, going forward we would have to stick to a gruelling quota of twenty-five miles a day, with only one rest day a week, and two more short breaks with

Christine. However, we were still feeling tired from the cumulative exhaustion of the journey – even the days off at the Shangri-La had not served to completely refresh us. For these twin reasons of time pressure and exhaustion, Leon and I therefore decided once more to sneak onto the motorway.

At first it went fine and, as before, we made good progress. After three hours, however, the police caught us, and drove us back to where we had begun in the morning. Effectively we had to start the day again, but now walking on the slow country lane. We felt annoyed, as though we had been robbed of some miles, but the truth was we should not have been walking on the motorway! Not only did we lose time from getting caught but, more importantly, the motorway separated us from seeing and experiencing 'real China', the reason we set out on this trip in the first place. We resolved not to be tempted by motorways any more. From this point onwards, if we wanted to reduce our distances, we would have to seek out more adventurous shortcuts on shepherds' tracks.

Another ongoing pressure was from the filming side of things. Tiberius were continuing to request more sequences, shot at a very high quality. In one sense Leon and I found it hard not to resent their somewhat exacting demands, but in another it was good that they kept pushing us. We now felt quite slick in terms of setting ourselves up to film well, and enjoyed talking about potential stories to catch on camera. At the same time, the pressure was tiring us out further, and often made our lives more complicated.

On our fifth and penultimate evening in the Qinling, we reached a small town and decided that filming ourselves finding a place to stay might make a good sequence. With Leon and his camera behind me, I started our usual evening challenge.

'*Ludian zai nar?*' (Where is the guest house?) I asked each person I met in the street.

They looked surprised, asked me a few questions and did some good Chinese pointing. Gradually Leon and I homed in on a place to stay. This was typical of what happened every time we searched for a *ludian,* as was what happened next – some haggling with the hotel lady who tried to overcharge us a little. Once we had reached a reasonable price, we dropped our packs in our room, glad to have made it through another day.

Leon sat on his bed to record a video diary, and I went to the common bathroom in the corridor, musing to myself that we had done a fair job of filming the 'search for a *ludian*' sequence. I now looked forward to dinner. However, when I came out of the bathroom, I saw a troop of policemen heading for our room. I dashed over and opened the door for them, and Leon hastily put the video camera down as they entered.

The hotel manager lady was with them and everybody looked stern. She muttered a few things, and pointed at our camera, which sat guiltily on the bed beside Leon. Perhaps it had not been a wise idea to film tonight, considering we had recently had a couple of police encounters on the motorway.

After a long day, dealing with the police was the last thing we felt like doing. At first, they asked the usual questions and looked at our passports, and it seemed like another tiresome local police interrogation.

Once they had finished the usual questioning, they said, '*Zhe shi zuo shenme de?*' (What's this for?) and pointed at the video camera.

'Err, *wo xihuan* FILMING,' said Leon. '*Wo xihuan*' means 'I like'. Leon never could remember how to say filming in Mandarin. The policemen frowned.

Leon showed them some footage – the road, some villagers, the cave, nothing offensive. They also wanted to look at our GoPro sports camera, which I had unstrapped from my chest, and put on the bed. The GoPro looked like a stills camera and had no screen; as I handed it over, I pressed the record button. The policemen passed it round while, unbeknownst to them, filming themselves for us.

Just as we thought they were leaving, the policemen showed themselves to be the extra-inquisitive type, and demanded to see inside our bags. This was not good news because they contained the permission forms that would reveal we were filming for a TV show. My mind raced to find a way out of this.

'Our bags!' I huffed, lifting up my rucksack, before making a big deal of slowly emptying things out.

'Our bed!' I said, indicating that we slept on our roll mats, and making a snoring noise.

The policemen nodded.

'Our food!' I said, miming eating lots of biscuits, with a loud crunching noise, and offering them one.

The policemen smiled and said no thank you.

'Our torture ball,' massaging my leg with it, and groaning.

I handed it to the policemen, who tried it on themselves and laughed.

The main section of the bag was almost empty. I huffed and puffed some more. The policemen were now looking embarrassed.

'Our Kindle . . .'

Fortunately, before I got to the pouch containing the permission forms, the police decided that they had seen enough, and turned to leave.

As the door closed behind them, I sat down on my bed, heart still thumping.

'That was close,' said Leon.

44
Shortcuts

Distance to home: 1,419 miles

8–18 MARCH

We tumbled out of the Qinling Mountains to be greeted by the sight of the Han River. The water was blue-grey, several hundred metres wide, and full of gravel-dredging ships. But though impressive in its own right, the Han was actually only a tributary of the Yangtze, still 500 miles away. We crossed the water on a road bridge, and continued into another band of hills, now firmly on southern Chinese soil.

The first thing we noticed was that the weather was warming rapidly. The sun blazed down, the daytime temperature rose into the mid-20°Cs, and the sky filled with brigades of cumulonimbi. The colour and shape of the land had changed too. If the north was mostly brown, then the south was green. The angular mountains were shrouded in lush forests, and flattened into valleys of verdant crops – tobacco, rice and various leafy Chinese vegetables.

As well as the differences in physical geography, I had heard that the people were different too. The northerners speak in more clipped dialects, and are said to be taller, with single eyelids. The southerners speak in more lilting dialects, and are apparently shorter and darker, with double eyelids. I wondered whether I would notice any difference.

There were certainly plenty of people out and about. A cheerful salesman sold us some dough sticks from the Perspex box strapped to the back of his bicycle; a friendly drunk talked to us about his chickens; a motorbike taxi drove past, its middle-aged driver blasting trendy Chinese rap music and smiling. Most villages had a little shop with a poster of Chairman Mao on the wall. We often stopped to buy soft drinks and stock up on peanuts and biscuits. Once, while I was taking a break, a car stopped and two young men wanted a photo. I wearily stood up, and one man went round behind me to pose. Just before the snap, with no warning, he jumped on my back. I was giving him a piggy back and on the verge of collapsing as the picture was taken.

We also noticed that the doorstep life of China had begun. Families, often with a child or two on their laps, perched on plastic stools outside their doors. They watched the world go by and chatted. Two bearded foreigners clinking down the road made for a different sight, and our onlookers often called out jovial hellos. Sometimes we stopped to chat, and crowds of old and young would gather round. They pointed at our rucksacks and our beards. Once an old lady picked up my walking poles, chuckling to herself as she walked up and down the road with them.

And the conversations we had with these southerners were remarkably similar to those we had in the north:

Me: *Hello! Please could you tell me how far it is to the next town?*

Then, simultaneously, the whole group would ask:

Do you speak Mandarin?

Are you walking? Why are you walking?

Which country are you from?

A few more people joined in and all happily disagreed on how far away the next town was.

The children meanwhile stared shyly at us with bright little faces. When we said hello, they broke into wide smiles, and peeked at us from behind the adults. 'What is your name?'* a young mother encouraged her little boy to ask in English. He pulled from her grasp and ran away. Children seemed very visible and loved in these rural communities, and we rarely saw them crying.

In one village, I bought a cheap big straw sunhat to shade my head. A four-year-old girl with rosy cheeks and pigtails ran up and

---

* This was usually the sum total of the English language that most villagers spoke.

pointed her finger at us. '*Qiguai*,' (Strange) she said, before running off giggling. I looked across at Leon. He had no sunhat but was wearing a headband that made him look like a 1980s tennis player.

'She has a point,' we agreed.

One lunchtime, we stopped to eat in a little junction town. There were dozens of market stalls, and hundreds of people milled around in the sun. Many of the stalls sold vegetables, but there were also more unusual ones – a portable dental practice selling false teeth; a lady selling fried gooey snacks, but behind her stall she also ran a small, smart shoe shop. Against the shop front, a welder was at work on a metal door, sparks flying, and we noticed that his eye guard consisted of a pair of sunglasses with a big square of cardboard taped around the edges.

At a roadside restaurant we tucked into our bowls of fried noodles. A man on another table called across, asking to see some foreign money. Christine had given us more US dollars, so I showed him a ten-dollar bill.

'*Wo keyi kan yi kan?*' (Can I have a little look?) he asked. We handed him the note.

'*Duo shao qian?*' (How much?) he asked. He was flicking through a pile of banknotes, and seemed to be a buyer.

'Sixty *kwai*,' we said, giving him the approximate market rate.

The man hesitated. A crowd was now gathering. Another man chirped up and said he would buy the ten dollars. We agreed and the money exchanged hands. The first man looked disappointed, and asked if we had any more. We did, and so more money swiftly exchanged hands. The noodle chef, who, in between flipping noodles, had been watching over everybody's heads, now also barged in and also bought ten dollars. We thought we had rounded up the rate and made a slight profit, but when we checked later on, we realised we had made a slight loss. Perhaps doing shady money deals in China was not our forte.

To our fresh, amateur eyes, there were few differences in the people in the south. We did notice more women driving cars here, but there could have been many reasons for that. I once asked a small friendly crowd if they were northern or southern Chinese, and they looked at me, slightly confused, before tentatively saying southern. The concept did not seem important to them. And thus my layman's conclusion was that these southerners were not really different to the northerners. Above all, they were still just the friendly, exuberant, irrepressible, unpredictable Mainland Chinese!

The heat, though pleasant, brought a different type of exhaustion to the cold. The early hours of the morning were especially beautiful. But, as the day warmed up, we started to sweat, and soon got blisters from our damp socks and rashes from our rucksacks. It sapped our strength. The tiredness felt as if it was sinking deep into our bones and our minds. Yet, each day, we got up and did it again, walking twenty-five miles, one step at a time. Through the green hills, through the deep shady gorges. Past the farmers and villages and rivers and trees. There were many new roads being built through the mountains of southern China – tunnels blasting out of hillsides, and bridges spanning gullies. In quick succession we spotted two exceedingly dangerous-looking jobs: a man welding the outside of a high bridge without a harness, and a truck reversing to the edge of a cliff to tip its load over – with the back wheels stopping just a foot from the crumbly cliff edge.

Keen to implement our plan to find adventurous shortcuts, Leon scanned the iPhone. After spotting a good opportunity to cut a corner through some hills, we turned right at the next tobacco field and followed a track past a series of farmhouses and beehives. The path led upwards for an hour, then fizzled out. We scrambled through a bamboo forest to the summit. Unsure of where we were, we used a compass and descended through some terraced paddy fields, and after two hours stumbled back onto the road. We had saved ourselves perhaps five miles, and it had been a fun little adventure. Thus encouraged, and our hopeavism brimming, we kept a lookout for more shortcuts in the following days.

Two days later we set our sights on a longer one. Armed with a double takeaway each from a cheap restaurant, we followed the Google satellite maps onto a small path leading into the mountains. The limitation with using satellite maps, however, was that they did not show contours. It was impossible to tell how high or steep the slopes were. As we climbed, the path became gradually steeper, and less worn. And yet we were still hopeful that, despite the height we were gaining, and the prevalence of precipices rising all around us, we would still be able to get through.

'This is clearly a human track,' we told ourselves, as we ascended higher and higher.

'Other people have come here too,' we announced, whenever we saw an old beer bottle or biscuit wrapper.

'No one would climb up here, unless there was a way down the other side,' we said as darkness arrived.

We were still not even at the top, and the mountain was a lot bigger than we had thought. We camped on a little island in the middle of the stream and determined to keep going the next day. But when morning came, as we continued, the path grew smaller still, and we were soon being forced to scramble up steep rocks and waterfalls – dangerous work with our heavy packs. It was forecast to rain the next day and, if this stream flooded, it would be extremely difficult to get back down.

'That's got to be a human-made path,' I said to Leon, when we spotted another little track through the undergrowth.

'But it could be made by animals,' he said, growing more sceptical.

Eventually we made it to the top, but we had lost all human trails. We could see only the prospect of cliffs on the other side. The rain would come in the evening, and we could not risk being stuck up here and so, reluctantly, we turned back. We had climbed for more than a day to try and save a day, but had ended up where we started, a day and a half behind our already hard-pressed schedule.

We reached the road where we had started, and as I stomped down the tarmac my thoughts started to spiral. I was annoyed at Leon, and no doubt he was annoyed at me. But the fact was it had been a joint decision, and so the fault lay with both of us, though it felt easier to blame someone else. I was hot and tired. I felt frustrated that we had got ourselves into this position of being pressed for time. At moments like this, the expedition seemed a far cry from the epic walk I had envisioned.

But that was the stark reality of going on adventures. There were good days and bad days, and if we went exploring we were bound to get lost sometimes. On a long expedition there were certainly going to be plenty of long, painful days. We had to take the good with the bad. Push through the bad times, and the good times would come again. We walked past a field where in the blazing sun an aged farmer ploughed the soil with his hoe. He was not complaining and his life was far harder than mine.

'Come on, pull yourself together, Lilwall,' I muttered to myself. I increased my pace, and tried to catch up with speedy Leon who, as usual, was starting to move further and further ahead of me.

45
The Yangtze

Distance to home: 1,169 miles

19–24 MARCH

To claw back time in the schedule, for the next four days we had to temporarily abandon the shortcuts through the hills and instead hit the tarmac for twelve or fourteen hours a day. We crossed a jigsaw intersection of strangely shaped provincial boundaries – briefly through Hubei Province, into Chongqing Province, back into Hubei, and back into Chongqing. The road meandered up and down monumental valleys, forcing us to trace the indented contours along their sides for miles on end. The mountains rose in orchestras of vegetation and rock, with clouds of mist dancing around the cliff faces. We also came to see how impenetrable the slopes were on this side of the watershed, and this justified our decision to turn back when we did on the aborted shortcut. We might never have got down and, if it had rained, we could have been trapped up there for days.

But despite the treacherous terrain, there were some new-looking villages hanging off the valley sides. An old man worked the ground on an implausibly steep sloping terrace. At the bottom of the slope there was a sharp 100-metre drop down a sheer cliff. I did not think that I would dare to walk along a gradient like that, let alone tend the vegetables on it.

It started to rain, and a series of little paths led us through a maze of tangerine groves, until, through the wet haze, we caught our first glimpse of the Yangtze. It was as if the colours of the dark earthy bank had dripped into the serene, green-grey water. Downstream, two vertical cliffs hemmed the waters into a narrow channel – the start of the famous Three Gorges. We walked beside the river for a while and reached the riverside town of Fengjie. We were due a day off, and decided that – instead of sitting around resting our feet – we would catch a local ferry downstream to see the first of the gorges. We would hop off the ferry in the evening and hitchhike back to Fengjie and resume our walk from the same spot the next day.

The boat chugged away from the shore, and Leon set up the tripod on the deck. I said a few words to the camera. Even though it was our day off, we had to keep filming when the opportunity arose. Leon took some shots of the bridge as we dawdled underneath it. There was other boat traffic too: large cargo ships, almost the size one would normally expect on the sea; and red hydrofoils, speeding past, heading for Chongqing 500 miles upstream.

Our fellow passengers were mostly made up of farmers and schoolchildren, who sat below deck playing cards and chatting. But there were also a few businessmen who joined us outside, and took photos of both us and the river. We motored slowly towards the towering cliffs, and suddenly we were between them. The rocks rose sheer and confident, but actually they were a shadow of their former selves, because the river level had risen 170 metres in the past twenty years. For of course, a hundred miles downstream the infamous and record-breaking Three Gorges dam had been built – the biggest dam in the world, the height of a sixty-storey skyscraper. It had caused this entire middle section of the Yangtze Valley to fill up.

Our ferry emerged from the gorge and started to zigzag from side to side of the channel, visiting the numerous villages scattered along the steep slopes. We picked up more farmers and cows and dropped off schoolchildren, donkeys and bags of tangerines. The animals stood on the bow of the boat, and we saw that one cow had a terrible festering wound on its leg. A few minutes later, another cow slipped and almost fell into the passenger cabin.

All along the banks, a few metres above the waterline, we noticed signs on which was written '175'. This was a marker indicating how many metres above the original river level the water had risen. The signs had actually been put up when the dam was first being built, two decades ago, in order that everyone would know how high they needed to move. Of course, back then, the '175' markers were high in the hills. When the American journalist Peter Hessler was a Peace Corps teacher in the Yangtze Valley in the late 1990s, he used to go jogging in the hills, and after a long ascent would stumble upon the signs. With the river running through the valley far below, it had seemed implausible that the water could ever reach that high. But here it was, and anything below it had been submerged.

A population of well over a million people had had to be relocated. 'Forsake the small home to support the big home,' the former inhabitants were told, before being given small amounts of compensation and being forced to move. I peered over the side of the boat and imagined the countless villages, towns and cities that were down there. It occurred to Leon and me that perhaps the farmers we had seen eking out a living on the absurdly steep slopes over the past few days had actually been relocated there from their previous homes beside the old Yangtze.*

The ferry dropped us off at the town of Wushan, the original version of which was now underwater. A motorbike taxi took us to the start of the motorway, from where we hoped to hitchhike back to Fengjie. It would soon be dark and the motorbike taxi driver stayed with us to see if we got a lift.

'It's too late, and no one hitchhikes from here,' he said. 'Why don't I give you a ride to a nice hotel, and you can catch a bus tomorrow.'

We needed to start walking again early the next morning, so we told him we would take our chances. But as we stood there flapping

---

* The big benefits of the dam were that it reduced flood risks, and generated huge amounts of electricity (the equivalent of ten nuclear power stations). But aside from evicting many people from their homes, it was also controversial in many other ways. Its cost had spiralled to four times the original estimate of £5 billion; the flood waters had buried many archaeological treasures; it damaged the environment – including contributing to the probable extinction of the Yangtze dolphin. More dramatically, some scientists questioned whether such huge dams increased the chances of earthquakes, and there were even (unofficial) concerns that one day the dam would collapse.

our hands at passing vehicles,* Mr Motorbike Taxi watched us with a smirk.

A succession of SUVs passed, but did not stop for us.

'I told you,' said Mr Motorbike Taxi.

We smiled. A farmer's truck loaded with pigs drove past.

'Why don't you go with the pigs,' he said. 'Plenty of room in there.'

We grimaced. A security van from the bank passed.

'Or how about this one. I'm sure they'll let you in with their money.'

It was almost dark and we began to wonder whether he might have a point. Eventually, a car did stop. We were happy to prove Mr Motorbike Taxi wrong, and half an hour later we arrived back in Fengjie. Our little boat ride had been a fun break, but it meant that we had not had a proper rest from the previous week of hard walking.

The next morning, before we set off, we had one final piece of business to transact with the Yangtze. The sun was rising above the valley walls, and I felt nervous as Leon and I poised on the edge of the water. A crowd of workmen gathered on the road above to watch. I braced myself and jumped, and as I plunged deep into the cold, ancient waters, I felt, at least for a few seconds, all the tiredness, the aches and the stresses of the road wash away.

---

* This is the standard hitchhiking gesture in China. Peter Hessler refers to it as 'petting the dog'.

46

Meaningless penance

Distance to home: 1,069 miles

24–27 MARCH
I awake at 6 a.m. to the sound of my alarm going off and open my eyes to see that I am inside a bivvy bag. I push my face towards the small drawstring hole, and inhale the fresh morning air. As I sit up I groan from my aching back and legs, but can't help smiling at the limestone cliffs and forested hillsides that surround us. My campsite is in the middle of a terraced potato field, and everything is covered in a thin layer of frost – despite the warming daytime temperatures, it is still only March, and we are high in the mountains.

We get up fast and start packing. After four months, everything has its place in our rucksacks. In go sleeping bag, laptop, filming wires, hard drives, personal things, food and bivvy bag. We will walk in the same clothes we slept in. While packing, I pour a cup of instant coffee and now, with everything stowed away, I down the dregs and slot the thermos into a side pouch. We swing the heavy packs onto our backs and wander back onto the road.

Although our eyes are still half closed, and our clothes are damp, the morning, as always, is magical. I wonder what China has in store for us today. As if on cue, at that moment, long, loud yells echo from a small mountain beside the road. We keep walking and see a line of people on the hillside doing a blend of Tai Chi and aerobics, occasionally stopping to have an enormous shout. We follow a little path towards them; when we reach their bit of the cliff, they welcome us to join in. Even after I have taken my pack off, I can hardly balance on one foot, but I can at least add my voice to the final hearty shout as the morning's session ends.

Onwards we go, and time blurs from one day into the next. As we walk, like a couple of retired spinsters with nothing else to do all day, Leon and I yabber at each other. Sometimes we talk about practical matters, or trivia. But other times we talk about more meaningful things: personal heroes; who will be remembered a thousand years from now; famous people we have met – Leon's granddad used to be the Provost of Aberdeen so he has met Gorbachev and the Queen, I haven't really met anyone except the parents of The Edge from U2 at a Rotary Club event. We attempt to memorise Tennyson's *Ulysses*, testing each other on alternate lines, until we think we have it down well enough to wow all ears at a dinner party.

And, unsurprisingly, with no one to talk to except each other, we continue our steady descent into exhausted insanity, so much so that we sometimes make strange meaningless comments.

'From this point, that road is either going down or going up,' I say as we walk down a flat bit of road.

'That truck's come from somewhere,' says Leon, as a truck comes round the corner.

'This warmth will be nice until it's not nice,' I say as the sun rises.

We have also been inadvertently developing more and more of our own language for things – Orlandos, Jases, the Tunnel of Doom, needing to go for a Mr Lax. A word we have recently started using a lot is 'bashing' – as a replacement for walking. When we have to walk down a long tarmac road we call it tarmac-bashing; around lots of spurs, spur-bashing; up lots of switchbacks, switchback-bashing. But however much we talk about bashing things, the truth is, it is us who are getting bashed. Our feet are bashed by the enormous features of Chinese geography, our heads are bashed by the hot sun, our shoulders are bashed by the heavy rucksacks, and on top of all this we are just feeling generally very bashed by the ongoing filming pressure.

My diary entries are increasingly illegible:

14 March: 73 days to go, I am sick of this, want to cry and go home.

Showing little initiative filming.

19 March: [the *ludian* owners] think we are mad . . . hopping around like we are insane . . . groaning . . . refuse to wash . . . don't eat much

we are losing it

20 March: ridiculously tired

gross chicken

21 March: amazing – we feel regenerated the next morning – the human body!

Expect thunderstorm

Is life a competition I wonder? If so, who is the winner? The most flourishing? The person who dies with the largest bank balance?

Bodies getting beaten down, sore feet

tired, ChinesePod

horrible chicken

25 March: Leon burps like toad

26 March: Finding suppressed emotions bursting out. Sometimes anger. I prayed a lot.

Our exhaustion is also making us less enthusiastic about meeting people, and we are beginning to get seriously tired of reciting our catechism. It seems easier to talk to each other, though even that is getting ridiculous and boring. But how can we get ourselves out of this state? We are too behind schedule to take any more time off, too tired to muster new enthusiasm. We still have two months to go, and that is a long time to be slogging through a blur of sweat and pain.

What's more, although we are now working well as a team, and have developed a solid friendship, we are also getting snappy with each other. Small annoyances are intensifying, escalating; whether it is Leon getting more impatient with my slowness after a break, or a misunderstanding about the filming, or something as silly as my grievance over how, while I think I always listen to the music

Leon recommends and puts on my iPod, he never seems to listen to mine!

It is not that we dislike or do not respect each other, but that we have simply spent too much time together – we are feeling claustrophobic with each other's company. However, we are still bound together by filming needs – and the fact that we only have one iPhone to navigate with, and always have to sleep in the same small ludian *rooms, or share the same farmer's field at night, just makes it all the harder. With the twin problems of exhaustion and claustrophobia, we wonder what we can do to avoid the rest of this expedition becoming a meaningless penance.*

47
The radical solution

Distance to home: 1,044 miles

27–30 MARCH

Leon and I glared at each other.

I finally said, 'Well, you go on the road, and I'll go along the stream then.'

Leon shrugged and picked up his poles. 'Fine, I'll see you in the next town.'

For the past few minutes we had been squabbling about which route to take. I wanted to try a potential shortcut along a stream, while Leon wanted to play safe and go back to the road. We were both tired, and wanted our own way, and for the first time we decided not to agree, and instead go separate ways. Our routes intersected again after two hours.

A couple of days later, the same thing happened. This time, I wanted to take another shortcut, walking through a forest up the side of a mountain, while Leon wanted to follow the road up the switchbacks. My hopeavist tendencies were continuing to nudge ahead of Leon's. However, this time, my shortcut ended up taking longer, and Leon waited for me for half an hour at the top. Then, as we set off again, I realised that I had lost the camera's furry microphone cover. I had to climb back down into the bushes to find it, leaving Leon to wait another hour. He was fuming by the time I got back, and stormed off in a mood. Thankfully a few minutes later he stopped and we both apologised.

Out of these small incidents, a new idea began to grow that would soon have far-reaching consequences for the expedition. We decided that we needed to split up – not just for an hour or two, or even a day or two, but for several weeks. It would be just what we needed to spice things up, a total break from our routine, a breath of fresh air.

Over the past four months we had become dependent on each other – I was doing most of the speaking to the locals and presenting to the camera, while Leon was doing the majority of the map reading and filming. If we split up, we would both be forced to handle all these tasks on our own. More important, it would make this into an exciting challenge again. Together we had survived a winter in the Gobi, the steep cliffs of the Yellow River, and getting lost on jungle-clad mountains. But now, things seemed too easy. Perhaps it was strange that we wanted to make our lives harder again, but we did.

Naturally, our plan needed an appropriate name. We brainstormed for a while, and in the end came up with one that fitted the bill: 'Operation Lone Wolves'. The main reason we had set out walking together in the first place was for the filming, so our biggest new challenge was that we would have to film ourselves. We would ask Christine to bring back the spare camera when we met her in the city of Enshi the following week, and we could make the split after that. We informed Tiberius, who recognised that we needed the break from each other, and agreed to it. They just asked us to make sure that we filmed any angry words about each other before we split. We told them that the spectacular punch-up they seemed to be hoping for was not on offer, but we would have a good whinge to the camera about each other when the opportune moments arose.

We stumbled down a hillside and arrived in Enshi, a small city nestled amid vast mountains. Leon and I were virtually dead men walking, but we had made it to another pit stop. With a renewed sense of excitement about what was ahead, I dumped my pack in a *binguan*, and jumped in a taxi to pick up my wife from the airport.

It was one of the benefits of the modern age that Christine had been able to come out on cheap flights to see me several times during the walk. That, and affordable international calls, certainly made things easier. But by the time I reached Enshi, apart from her brief visits to Datong and Xian, we had been apart for four months, and we still had two to go. Time was dragging.

In many senses, the trip was harder on Christine than on me. While I was out having adventures, with more than enough things to keep me preoccupied, Christine was at home, with an empty flat. She had been making the most of it – having friends and family to stay, investing in people. And she had thrown herself into running Viva's Hong Kong office.

But sometimes it had been hard for her not to worry, especially when I was out of phone reception for a few days. In the Gobi, when she had been unable to get through for more than a week, her imagination had got the better of her.

'I was thinking that if something did happen,' she said, 'then the voicemail message would remain the same forever and I would never speak to you again.'

I felt guilty that I was causing her worry. But I was also incredibly proud of how well she had coped and pushed through the tough times. 'Walking Home From Mongolia' was a test for her too.

And so, in Enshi, with two long months still ahead, we reminded ourselves that the time would pass and then I would be home once more. And once I was home, the adventure of 'normal' life for us would restart. Hopefully, having got through the test of the walk, we would together be stronger in facing the other tests of marriage and of life that would, no doubt, come our way.

48
Heigh-ho

Distance to home: 934 miles

31 MARCH–5 APRIL

The day Leon and I parted ways, the sky broke open with our first Chinese thunderstorm. It was five days after we had left Enshi, and we had just entered Hunan Province. Thunder boomed up and down the valley, and lightning flashed, but as I walked alone through the downpour, I could not help but feel a strange sense of liberation. Leon was up ahead somewhere, yes, but now he would not be waiting for me to catch up, or standing with his tripod and preparing to film me. In fact, we hoped we would not see each other for another three and a half weeks, until we reached the city of Guilin. My mind felt clearer, and my surroundings seemed to have come alive: the mountains, bold and imposing; the valley, lush and inviting; the rain, cool and glorious.

But although I had always felt reasonably content in my own company, I also now felt more vulnerable, and strangely nervous. Not that this was a bad thing. The extra adrenaline made me feel like I was on an adventure again. I had a new spring in my step, despite the fact that my pack was actually heavier. In order to be self-sufficient, we now carried a camera and a tripod each. Some items we had been forced to split. I had kept the laptop to write articles and the basic phone, while Leon had kept the iPhone. For navigation I would have to rely on the pages torn out from the road atlas, supplemented by my best attempts to interpret Chinese pointing.

The rain eased off as I began a long climb, and I scrambled on little tracks between the switchbacks. I could now take shortcuts to my heart's content, without the risk of annoying Leon if they did not pan out. My foot was almost completely better too, and I felt fit as I walked. At the top of the hill, I set up the tripod and camera on a ledge, and climbed back down. I walked backwards and forwards in front of it a few times, and then climbed back up and packed it all back up again. The whole thing took half an hour. My appreciation of Leon's hard work increased dramatically.

As I descended, the hillsides burst into colour, with blossoms of pink, white and yellow. It was getting dark by the time I reached the valley floor. Now that I was on my own, I had been moving, and taking breaks, at a slightly more leisurely pace, and this meant that I would probably have to walk for an extra hour in the evening to cover the necessary distance. Tonight, I had my sights set on a town about five miles ahead, where I hoped to find a *ludian*. My phone beeped – a text message from Leon.

'I have reached the town. I am staying at a *ludian* on the left just as you enter. Try and find a different one.'

The potential of accidentally bumping into each other was one of the flaws in Operation Lone Wolves. This was because for the first few days at least, it was impossible to find alternative routes that did not massively increase how far we had to walk. We would therefore warn each other when there was a chance our paths might cross, and so hopefully avoid each other, even if sometimes we stayed in the very same settlement.

I marched on into the night, and after an hour saw a few buildings – the town. I kept walking, expecting it to grow into a high street. But two miles later, I saw the lights receding behind me, far across some fields. Without Leon and his iPhone, I had missed the turn-off. My Chinese road atlas map showed only simple little lines for roads, and dots for settlements. It was far too inaccurate for knowing which turn-off to take.

I tramped onwards, alone in the Chinese darkness. I was now surrounded by empty fields, and passed only the occasional farmhouse. The moon was hidden behind thick clouds. I adjusted my heavy rucksack on my shoulders, and resigned myself to bivvying in a field – not a glamorous start to my solo walk. However, having expected to reach the town, I had now run out of water. I hated going to bed thirsty, so I started looking for a farmhouse that was still awake where I could hopefully fill my bottles.

I spotted a large white-tiled bungalow with a light on in the porch. There was a bulldozer parked beside it, and three people stood outside finishing dinner. They had not seen me approaching through the dark, and I hesitated about whether to approach them. Had I been with Leon, this would have been no big deal, but I suddenly felt butterflies in my stomach.

'Stop being a wimp,' I whispered to myself. I needed some water, and what was the worst that could happen?

So I walked out of the gloom and gave my usual cheery hello and recited my catechism. I was a *Yingguoren* (a British man), I loved China, I said. I held out my water bottle and asked if they might fill it up. It was strange to hear the sound of my own voice.

At first, the three faces looked up at me, wide-eyed, as if I was an apparition. One of the men, who was topless with an impressive belly, burst into a grin.

'*Yingguoren!*' he said loudly. '*Yingguoren!*'

Everyone laughed, and suddenly I was given a stool to sit on and offered a cigarette. A motherly looking lady went inside and re-emerged with a flask of tea, and a bowl of bony meat and steaming rice. Tremendously grateful for this unexpected hot meal, I started eating and, meanwhile, more people appeared from out of the house.

'*Yingguoren!*' everyone exclaimed, staring, bewildered, at my dishevelled clothes and rucksack. It felt as if the people were looking at me slightly differently to when I was with Leon. Did it make them more protective of me (because there was only one of me), or more suspicious (because strange people tend to travel alone)? I did not know, but I decided there was no harm in asking for a place to sleep.

'Can I dumpling here?' I asked, getting my tones wrong again.

Everyone looked at me as if I were deranged. I repeated myself a few times until they understood. There were some slightly awkward looks, and another man, who seemed to be the boss, appeared. I had initially assumed this was a farmhouse, but now more and more people were appearing from inside it, and I concluded it was some kind of workers' accommodation.

The boss looked at me suspiciously. I said I would be quite happy to sleep on the concrete slab on the porch. 'It's very comfortable and dry here,' I enthused. It would certainly be better than a muddy field.

His eyes narrowed, but the crowd all shouted at him, and a moment later he uttered a reluctant yes. Everyone disappeared back inside and I started to lay out my roll mat and sleeping bag. But before I had lain down, the motherly looking lady reappeared. She seemed to be the night guard, and she beckoned me inside and said I could sleep on the floor. I gratefully dragged my things into the empty front room, and collapsed. I was sleeping in a random house in China with dozens of mysterious people living in it, but I was warm, safe and dry, and that was good enough for me.

At 5.45 a.m. I awoke to the sound of loud conversations, laughing and some heavy rain outside. Opening my eyes, I saw an army of Chinese peasants traipsing through my room, staring, chatting and lighting cigarettes.

Sitting up, I clicked the camera onto the tripod, turned it on and then lay down in my sleeping bag. I pretended to be asleep for ten seconds, before feigning waking up, rubbing my eyes and explaining where I was to the camera. Self-filming was going to require a lot of motivation. I got up properly, and followed the workers through into the kitchen. I realised that it was not raining outside at all, but rather the noise was coming from a line of sizzling woks loaded with food. I was ushered into the queue, given a big bowl of fried noodles, and then I followed the crowd outside.

About fifty people stood eating, smoking and staring at me. They beckoned me over, and I stood among them, wolfing down the greasy, delicious noodles.

'What is your work?' I said.

Everyone replied at once, but I did not understand the replies. They started trying to act out some kind of digging motion, but I was still at a loss. Eventually they said, 'Come and see.'

A few minutes later, everyone dumped their bowls in a communal washing-up tub and filed around the back of the house. They then all grabbed a shovel or pickaxe and, together, like a troop of merry dwarves, we set out marching briskly into a pine forest. There were young boys in their mid-teens, and middle-aged ladies in their forties, there were old men who looked tough and sombre, young women who looked frail yet cheerful. The lyrics of heigh-ho, heigh-ho started to drift through my head as we walked.

We arrived in a section of the forest with lots of holes in the ground. Without any orders being given, everyone split into teams of two or three, and got to work. They approached the trees, which were all about three metres tall but, rather than starting to chop them down, they began digging away at their bases. Once they had dug underneath them, they pulled the trees out of the ground, and bound their roots in huge balls of rope. They worked hard, and fast, and almost without speaking. Although I tried asking why they were doing this, I could still not figure it out. Were they transferring the trees because a road was about to built here? Or were the trees to be sold? I did not want to be in their way, and I needed to get going, so I waved goodbye to my hard-working new friends, and hit the road, alone again.

49
Tea

Distance to home: 854 miles

6–8 APRIL

The waitress slapped a small china cup on the table, and poured some hot tea into it. Virtually every restaurant in China offered free tea. I took a sip. It was my fourth day since the initial split, and I had spent the morning walking up a valley lined with neat rows of tea bushes. Standing among them were two ladies with weathered faces and jet-black hair. They had looked up at me only briefly before returning to their intense work – plucking the little tea buds and placing them in wicker baskets. Tea, of course, originally came from China, and had been the beverage of choice here for thousands of years. Yet ultimately, tea had been a mixed blessing to the Empire, for it had played a significant role in bringing China's multimillennia-long dynastic era to a tragic close.

In contrast, for most of history, tea was virtually unknown in Great Britain. But as the British East India Company began to trade more and more with China in the 1700s, they were delighted to discover a budding market in London for the exotic dry leaves. By the 1800s, tea was transported back by the shipload, and the British were completely addicted – consuming pots of the stuff for break-fast, on 'tea breaks', and at 'tea time'.

China, at this point, still knew itself as the centre of civilisation, completely self-sufficient, just as it had been for thousands of years. And what was more, under the Qing Dynasty of the seventeenth to nineteenth centuries, China was a very closed Empire, and certainly not interested in building strong mutual trade links with the strange-looking Europeans who were increasingly starting to arrive. These distant nations would be permitted the honour of being vassal states, but all trade was restricted to the port of Canton (now Guangzhou), where foreigners were sequestered to a single island and even forbidden from learning Chinese (anyone who tried to teach them could be imprisoned or executed).

The British were humiliated, yet had no choice but to buy the precious tea under these strict terms. And what made matters harder for them was that they could not find anything that they could offer to the Middle Kingdom in return. This meant that they were paying for all the tea with British silver, resulting in an enormous profit for China and a gaping trade deficit for Britain.

Gradually, however, the British realised that there was something they could sell to the Chinese people: opium. This substance was derived from the poppy plant and grew well in the new colony of India. Once the foreigners started selling it, it did not take long for drug addiction to sweep across the Chinese nation. The drug profits were then used to buy tea, which in turn was sold to thirsty Britain. For the British, this arrangement was, of course, extraordinarily profitable and ideal. For the Chinese, however, it was a disaster. It not only cost the Empire its former tea profits, but, with the proliferation of drug addicts, also wrought havoc across society. The Chinese outlawed opium, and protested to the British, but were unable to stem the trade.*

Eventually, in 1839, a highly motivated and industrious Chinese court official came down hard on the foreign drug traders. He blockaded them in Canton, until a huge stock of opium was handed over, which he then destroyed. The British were furious, and things quickly escalated into what became known as the First Opium War. At this stage in history, the British gun ships and tactics were far superior to China's, and they quickly beat the Chinese into submission and forced upon them the first of the infamous 'unequal treaties'.

This treaty forced the Chinese to cede to the British an island off the south coast, as well as grant them access to five 'treaty ports'

---

* At its height, levies from the tea trade amounted to almost 10 per cent of the British government's entire revenue.

for freer trade.* This successful outcome (for the British) also unfortunately set a terrible precedent for the other foreigners – and soon the Americans, the Japanese and other European nations also vied for treaties of their own. And so both the opium and tea trades prospered, and the foreign powers began to meddle more and more in the affairs of the Middle Kingdom.

At the same time as (and in large part because of) this foreign meddling, internal unrest now rattled the Chinese Empire. And then, as the twentieth century dawned, Japan, in particular, began to show more colonial ambitions towards its ancient rival. Having taken over Korea, the Japanese moved aggressively into China's northeast, and from there set their sights on bigger goals still. In the decades that followed, the ancient imperial system collapsed, and the Middle Kingdom tumbled into an era characterised by feuding warlords, invasion by the Japanese and, eventually, civil war.

As Sarah Rose notes in her book about China and England's tea trade: 'No one can reasonably lay the blame for this [the fall of the Empire] on tea alone, but neither can one ignore the role that foreign desire for this quintessentially Chinese commodity played in opening China up to the West, and in the country's subsequent fall from Imperial self-sufficiency.'

I had been sitting in a daze as I drank my cup of tea. Two portions of egg fried rice arrived. One of them was in a polystyrene box – a takeaway for dinner that night in case I got lost. At this village, the road heading south had run out. I was about to attempt to find a shortcut over a mountain, and down to a reservoir on the other

---

* However, reaping their vast, immoral profits from the opium and tea trade was not enough for the East India Company – they also wanted to possess the secret of tea. In the 1840s, they sent an expert botanical spy to China, Robert Fortune, who disguised himself as a Chinese official, and covertly visited the mysterious inland tea plantations, which the Chinese had hitherto managed to keep secret. Once there, he stole both the secrets of tea manufacture, and samples of the plants themselves, and thus the precious 'botanical gold' was transported to India and beyond for cultivation, and China forever lost its monopoly. The story of Robert Fortune is told in detail in Sarah Rose's book *For All the Tea in China.*

side. The thought of taking shortcuts on my own made me nervous, because I would be much more vulnerable than before. This time, however, I had a new strategy: I would gather local knowledge and find a guide.

A crowd of ten-year-old boys had started to gather around me. I chatted to them while I ate, answering my catechism, and letting them ask questions. I asked them whether there was a path over the mountain.

'Yes, there is,' everybody said, including an old lady who was watching us and smiling. This was a good start.

'Could you show me the way?' The boys had a couple of skateboards, and looked as if they were up for an adventure.

'We can,' everybody said.

'Good!' I said.

'Good!' everybody said, and we all laughed.

So we set off, me and my carefree little band of guides. One of the children skidded ahead on his skateboard, while another, the most confident, sang me a cheerful song, which I did not understand. In return I sang him 'For he is an Englishman' by Gilbert and Sullivan, which he clearly did not understand either, but we both complimented each other on our respective vocal skills.

A mud road led us to the start of a small path, at which point the boys gave me some instructions, which I vaguely understood. They then said they had to go back to the village.

'OK, thank you very much,' I said, waving a little downheartedly as they walked away. This was not going exactly according to plan, but at least I had made it to the start of the correct path. I climbed up through some terraced fields until I came to a village where everybody was out on their terraces, sowing and planting vegetables. They pointed me onwards, and I found a stone-slabbed track which, over the next two hours, led me to the summit. At the top, I saw a small Buddhist temple which, from the various offerings on display, looked as though it was still visited regularly.

'So far so good,' I said out loud to myself. 'Now to find my way back down.'

The stone slabs continued downwards for a few minutes, until I reached a large spread of wide paddy fields, filled with several inches of water.

'This looks promising,' I mumbled, as I balanced my way along a series of earthen banks leading me through them.

However, I was still high up the side of the mountain. At the edge of the fields, I reached an abrupt cliff edge. Looking out, I saw that on this side of the mountain everything was much steeper, and I was now in the midst of thick, precipitous jungle, from which sprang huge moons of limestone rock. This seemed to be the trend with Chinese mountains – one side was reasonably easy to climb up, but the other side was very hard to climb down.

I spent the next hour walking up and down the paddy fields looking for a path going down. I did find one promising track, but after a few minutes it became steeper and steeper. I had to turn round and walk back up. It would be dark in a few hours and I was starting to feel anxious. If I twisted an ankle up here, there was no Leon to go and get help.

Thankfully, after another half an hour, I found a more promising route, which had been hidden by some bushes. This led me down, down, down, until two hours later, at dusk, I arrived back on a tarmac road.

I felt very relieved, and very tired. I did not know exactly where I was. But I knew this road ran parallel with a long reservoir, which lay somewhere in the gloom below me. Somehow, the following day, I would need to find a path around the water, or a ferry across it. But first I had to find a place to sleep. There was no traffic on the road, and as I started walking along it I thought I would probably have to bivvy.

A moment later, a motorbike dragging a farm trailer appeared. It was being driven by a young man in his late teens, and he stopped beside me.

'I live a few miles further up the road,' he said. 'Why don't you come and stay?'

This was perfect. I said thank you very much and that I would be along in about an hour.

Darkness arrived, as did the pain in my feet from a hard day of getting lost in the hills. Half an hour later, Christine called. While we chatted, I sat down on the roadside and removed my boots to rub my feet. At that moment, I saw some headlights, and the man on the motorbike appeared again.

'You are getting near,' he said.

'Great,' I said.

But then the man started to talk about money. I had not thought he was going to charge me to stay, and I could not really understand. Christine was still on the other end of the phone, and in my exhaustion, I asked her if she could talk to him. I handed him the phone. They talked briefly, and he handed the phone back to me.

'Rob, are you safe?' Christine asked. An ominous question.

'Yes, I think so. Why?'

'Well, the guy is asking for 300 RMB (£30) to sleep on the floor. He does not sound very friendly.'

I made a show of picking up my poles, and got to my feet, trying to make myself look like a tough gruff crazy Englishman. 'It's fine honey, I'll just tell him I'm not interested, and sleep in a field,' I said, trying not to alarm her, before I said goodbye.

I stood shining my head torch in the young man's eyes while we negotiated.

'You will have to pay 300 RMB,' he repeated. He did seem rather aggressive suddenly.

'That's too much, I can pay 100 RMB at most.' A generous amount to sleep on someone's floor.

'No, 300 RMB.' Perhaps he did not realise I could just camp.

'Sorry, no thank you, goodbye.' I started walking off, feeling annoyed, disheartened, and a little jittery. I braced myself as the man drove his motorbike back past me, but he disappeared into the night without looking back. I let out a sigh. He had, of course, been well within his rights to ask me to pay, but it was an exorbitant amount, and he should have told me when he first gave the invitation. For a moment I felt vulnerable – out here on my own on some unknown Chinese road in the dark. Although rural China usually seemed a safe place, especially when I was with Leon, I had heard stories of cyclists getting robbed. I would be a fool to think I was immune from that.

It was 10 p.m., I had been walking for almost fifteen hours, and it was time to hide and camp. I spotted an orange grove, set out my bivvy bag underneath it and climbed inside. I used the camera tripod to drape my mosquito net over my head, and closed my eyes.

I wondered how Leon was doing? Staying in some luxurious *ludian*, no doubt. We had exchanged a few text messages. It sounded as if he too was invigorated by the renewed sense of adventure from being alone. But although we had been on separate tracks for the past few days, we were now about to converge in the city of Yuanling, where we would both be taking a day off. We hoped that we would not bump into each other.

50
KFC

Distance to home: 774 miles

kfc all clear

I read Leon's text message and left my hotel room. On our days off, Leon and I had both fallen into the bad habit of eating at Kentucky Fried Chicken, China's Western fast-food joint of choice. And now, as we were both in the same city, and there was only one KFC, we had to coordinate our movements carefully, or we would end up eating together. In order to experience the adventure of walking through China alone, we were doing our best to maintain our solitude.

The next day, I let Leon leave the city two hours before me, to give him a head start. We were stuck on the same route for the next few days, but with his increased walking speed, we hoped he would stay ahead. It was raining heavily as I set off at 9 a.m., and mid-morning my phone rang. It was Leon.

'Hi Rob, I've been hauled into the local police station about ten miles beyond the town.'

'Why? Is this a closed zone?'

'No, I think they just want to find out what we're up to. A patrol car has already seen you, and they've told me to wait here until you arrive.'

And so, an hour later, I strolled through the entrance of the police station. Leon was sitting on a hard seat, bedraggled and bored, surrounded by a few policemen. It was good to see him again. We went through the usual routines with the police for half an hour, after which they let us go.

As our common road was about to lead us into a compulsory shortcut through some big mountains, we decided it would be safer to stick together for the next couple of days.

'What I've been wondering,' I said, resuming our latest movie debate, 'is why Al Pacino is so rarely in a decent movie these days?'

'That's a very good question,' said Leon, 'I've been wondering the same thing about Robert De Niro.'

The following day, the road deteriorated into a muddy track, and the mountains around us became thickly forested. The villages were mostly built from wood, and the people all seemed to work in the logging industry. We saw wood mills beside the road, and trucks loaded with logs rumbled past regularly.

By the afternoon, there were no longer any bridges to cross the rippling streams. We had to remove our boots and socks to wade through, following the villagers in their flip-flops. The mountains loomed bigger and bigger and we knew the road would run out soon. Because the forest was dense, Leon agreed that we should search for a guide.

At one of the final houses before the road disappeared, we stopped and asked a young man if he knew anyone who could show us the way through the mountains. The man frowned at us, and stroked his chin. He seemed to be weighing us up, or rather, in the tradition of Mr Wolf the cabbie, he seemed to have understood that we were in a weak bargaining position.

He started at 300 RMB (£30), and we haggled for a while. He eventually agreed that for 200 RMB (£20) he would feed us and let us stay the night in his wooden hut and the next day someone would guide us through the mountains.

'Who?' we said.

'Him,' said Mr Wolf II, pointing to a little old man who had appeared. 'He is my father.'

The old man barely reached up to my armpits, and was wrinkled and slightly hunched. We wondered if he was fit enough for a long, mountainous trek, but we did not seem to have any choice. We shook hands with Mr Wolf II.

At that moment another small old man walked past. He was carrying a large log – so large that it could really be called a tree. He broke into a wide smile when he saw us, and put down his tree. He walked over with twinkling eyes, shaking his head. He looked as if he could not believe we were there.

'Where are you from?' he asked, smiling and with an air of wonder in his voice.

'We are *Yingguoren*,' we said in Mandarin.

'*Yingguroren!*' he replied, amazed. 'British people are foreigners!'

It seemed he had never seen a foreigner before, buried as he was in these mountains, carrying trees around on his back all day. He shook our soft hands with his leathery hand.

'Can I try and lift your tree?' asked Leon.

'Of course,' said the man. He was two feet shorter than Leon.

Leon bent over, and tried to lift up the tree, but was barely able to get it off the ground. We renamed the man 'Mr Steel' for his strength.

Mr Steel also looked at our map, and was astonished by our reading ability.

'You cannot read Chinese characters, but you can read English letters!' he exclaimed.

The next morning it was raining hard, and Mr Wolf II's father led us into the mountains. We soon renamed him 'Mr Iron' because, although he was not as tough as Mr Steel, he was still very hardy. He wore Wellington boots and a mackintosh, and plodded before us at a steady pace. We followed a series of winding paths. Sometimes the path had been washed away by landslides and we had to scramble along collapsing slopes. Other times we waded up streams, or passed through abandoned logging camps. We would never have made it through without Mr Iron. After five hours, we crested a final mountain, and he pointed us down a path into a new, much less forested valley, with a proper road running down the middle of it.

The next day Leon and I split up again, now hoping that we really would not see each other until Guilin, about two weeks away. But although we were separate again, we both had an immediate obstacle to overcome: another closed zone. This time we knew about it, because a few backpackers who had got in trouble there had mentioned it on online forums. And it seemed that this was no small closed zone, but a colossal one, perhaps a hundred miles long and wide. Rumour had it that it was the site of a monumental bunker, complete with nuclear missiles, and thousands of miles of underground tunnels.

However, all this information was quite vague and it was difficult to establish exactly where the closed zone began and ended. The task fell to hardworking, Mandarin-speaking Christine to call up all the county police stations, asking them one by one if their county was 'open' or 'closed'. Sometimes the police did not even know the answer for their own county, let alone for their neighbours'. After making many calls, she emailed Leon and me the results of her research, and we marked them on our respective maps.

As Leon and I were both determined to avoid any more lifts in police cars, we had two options for the way forward. One was to take the most direct road south, which would cut across a corner of the closed zone. The other was to follow a tiny road that veered just outside the boundaries of the zone, and would be an extra day's walk. Over the phone, Leon and I tossed a coin to decide who did which. Leon won, and chose his preferred route of sneaking through the small ten-mile section of closed zone in the middle of the night. I would go around on the longer route, using my speciality of getting lost in the mountains for a day or two, and then stumbling out on the other side.

51
Mao

Distance to home: 685 miles

14–20 APRIL

My shortcut, for once, worked well, and after two days in the hills I arrived back on a road, heading for the city of Dongkou. Ten miles out, I saw a crowd of villagers gathered in front of a display of some kind. A young man with a microphone was exhorting them about something very, very loudly. From a distance, it looked like one of the old 1960s Cultural Revolution Rallies – for the youthful and zealous Red Guards. But, as I got closer, I saw that the small crowd were not youthful, but middle-aged, and they were not zealous, but appeared somewhat weary and unenthused.

I joined the back of the crowd, and attempted to ask a man what was going on, but the microphone was so loud that it was impossible for us to hear each other. I nudged forwards, and saw a huge plastic banner covered with photos of Chairman Mao. The man with the microphone spotted me and grinned happily. He continued his exhortations with even more volume, passion and rapidity, because now there was a foreigner in his audience. I could not make out much of what he was saying, apart from the fact that he was clearly talking about how wonderful Chairman Mao was.

I squinted at the banner. It depicted the Chairman doing various amazing things: a charismatic leader on the Long March in the 1930s; a heroic soldier fighting the Japanese in the 1940s; a marvellous leader declaring the People's Republic in 1949; a strong old man swimming the Yangtze in the 1960s. He had firmly reunified the country after the civil war; he had made China a nuclear power; he had helped spread the wondrous benefits of socialism.

I pulled out my camera and, standing as far back from Mr

Microphone as I could, I asked a few bored-looking villagers what they thought of Mao.

'*Hao bu hao?*' (Was he good?) I asked. It was a dumb question, but we were in a public setting, and my Mandarin was not up to in-depth investigative journalism.

'*Hao,*' (Good) they mumbled, but with a telling lack of enthusiasm.

'*Mao cong Hunan lai,*' (Mao comes from Hunan) I said. We were still in the Chairman's own Province.

'*Dui,*' (Correct) they said, nodding, but with blank faces.

I was getting a headache from the noise. I said goodbye, and continued along the road. I wondered what the villagers really thought of Mao. Were they proud of the fact that he was from their province? About 300 miles east of here, just over 100 years ago, little Mao Zedong had been born. His village was so remote that when the Empress Dowager had died in 1908, Mao did not find out until he left the village two years later. He grew up during a time of great change in China, and by the time he reached adulthood, the Emperor had abdicated, the country was starting to fracture, and the Japanese were well established in the northeast. As a young man, he had drifted between jobs, and it had been when he was in Beijing in the 1920s, working as a librarian, that he had been recruited by the fledgling, Soviet-backed Chinese Communist Party (CCP, or 'the Party'). He was at first given only minor responsibilities, and even though he did not seem a particularly outstanding leader at the time, what he lacked in charisma he made up for in guile. Over the next two decades, he manoeuvred himself through the Party leadership, until by the end of the Long March* in 1936, he was its undisputed leader. And, most importantly, he was recognised as such by the CCP's then ardent sponsor, Joseph Stalin.

Meanwhile, in the 1930s, China had descended into full-scale war

---

* The downtrodden CCP's escape from near annihilation, via a circuitous and perilous journey around southern and central China. It stills holds a legendary status in the history of the CCP.

with the Japanese. After Japan's defeat in 1945, civil war broke out between the two main powers in China, the Communists and the Nationalists. At first, it was expected that the Nationalists would win, but with Soviet backing, and against the odds, it was Mao's Communists who prevailed. The Nationalists fled to Taiwan where they declared themselves to be the real government of China, but in exile – a situation that endures to this day.

By the time of this remarkable victory, Mao was already fifty-six years old. His real impact on China, however, had scarcely begun. Although he had managed to unite a badly fractured country, the scale of his mismanagement from this point onwards was almost unprecedented in world history. In his 'Great Leap Forward' campaign of 1959–62, he attempted to increase the nation's food production. To achieve this, among other things, he instigated a 'death to all sparrows' policy, because sparrows ate certain crops. Villagers had to dutifully make a racket all day and night to stop the birds from landing anywhere, thus causing them to fall dead from the sky. But with the top of the food chain knocked out, the result was a plague of insects that decimated crops and contributed to a mass famine that killed tens of millions of people.*

Even more infamous was his unleashing of the Cultural Revolution in the 1960s, a ploy to eliminate his political enemies. Youths became 'Red Guards' and, whipped up into hysteria, rampaged across the nation, beating up their teachers, and destroying whatever they could find that belonged to 'old China'. Millions died, uncountable historical treasures were destroyed, and as the movement veered out of control, China almost imploded.

The horrors had lasted into the 1970s, and I found it strange to imagine that they had occurred so recently. All those villagers I had just met would have been about the right age to have been Red Guards. I wondered what they made of me – a foreign devil, whom

---

* Mao was a great enthusiast for intervening in nature generally. Journalist Jonathan Watts summed up the Chairman's attitude as 'Think big, move fast, worry about the consequences later.'

they had been taught to hate when they were young?* I did not know. I had not wanted to ask.

And what had they really made of the Mao propaganda being blasted out by the enthusiastic young man? As I had walked through China over the past five months, I had on an almost daily basis spotted posters of Mao pinned up, in pride of place, in homes and shops. The portraits usually depicted the Chairman with a slightly smug half-smile, his big forehead taking centre stage, framed by his strange tufts of hair. I felt angry about what Mao had done, and that his reputation was still being guarded.

But I took some comfort from the knowledge that he was gone forever. Even into the 1990s, China was a famously drab country of morose people, extreme poverty and grey clothing. But, for all China's ongoing human rights issues, at least those darkest of times were over. There had been so little joy in those times. But today, China buzzed with life and optimism.

* During his travels through China in the 1980s, Colin Thubron had stumbled across an old pile of English-language textbooks in a school. They were left over from the times of the Cultural Revolution, and included English pages in which children were taught how to interrogate foreign POWs.

52
Solitude

Distance to home: 585 miles

21–27 APRIL

It was now late April. The temperature was pushing up to the mid-30°Cs, and the humidity was intensifying. By the end of each day my shirt was drenched in sweat, and all I needed from my *ludian* was a bucket of cold water to pour on myself. I pressed onwards, through valley after valley, over mountain after mountain. The valleys were filled with pristine paddy fields, gleaming in the sun, often with grizzled old men walking behind an ox and plough. The trio of man-ox-plough moved back and forth together, churning the smooth mud into slushy beds for the rice. Sometimes there were mechanical ploughs too – a sign that, slowly, the benefits of China's prosperity were reaching these rural communities. The mountains, meanwhile, were covered in thick bamboo forests, and I saw teams of men at work chopping them down and loading the thick poles onto trucks.

In the heat, I wore my wide-brimmed hat, and sweat dripped off my nose and stung my eyes. My left knee had been getting steadily sore from the long days. I strapped it up with a knee support, which helped – though in the sweaty conditions, blisters started to develop underneath. In less than two weeks I would reach Guilin, where Leon and I would meet up, and where Christine would be visiting me a final time. Home was still almost 600 miles' walk away. I hoped my body would hold out.

My hot, tired brain, meanwhile, was often on autopilot. I would wave and say '*nihao*' hundreds of times a day to the various people who called out to me. One day, as I walked past a house with a fiercely barking dog, I only noticed a few seconds later that I had just said a friendly '*nihao*' to the dog as well. The beard I had shorn for Code Z had regrown and, along with my big hat, made me even more of an object to be stared at than ever.

One day, as I walked through a valley of paddy fields, a moped sped past. The young man driving it, and the middle-aged lady on the back, stared at me, as usual. A moment later, I heard a sudden bang and turned to see them veering across the road. They hurtled off the verge and landed in a paddy field with a splash. I dashed across to see if they were OK. Fortunately, they were, but it looked as if the bike engine was waterlogged. The lady started shouting at the man and pointing at the road – the reason they had lost control was because they had driven into a rock in the middle of the road. And it dawned on me that they had hit the rock because they were too busy staring at me.

As I approached the end of Hunan Province, I set out on my final shortcut. This one led me past a reservoir and up some shepherds' tracks into the hills. That night, I camped on a crest of grassy meadows, at least ten miles from the nearest village, and surrounded completely by nature. I was precisely on top of the watershed that separated Hunan from Guangxi – our penultimate province. Clouds were rolling across the horizon, turning pink in the sunset, and I realised this was probably my most peaceful campsite of the trip. We had sometimes been very remote in the Gobi, and in Shanxi, but I had always had Leon with me. Now, I was completely alone. Not a single person on earth knew I was here.

It had been good to walk for several weeks without Leon. To face the tests of the road on my own. To be stretched, pushed out of my comfort zone. To encounter China by myself. The challenge had invigorated me in just the way I needed. At the same time, I was looking forward to seeing Leon again. My time alone had helped me appreciate how much we had been through as a team. I had learnt a lot from him – about filming, about perseverance, about out-of-the-box thinking. About the medical science of hopeavism and about the secret of Jason Statham's acting-career success. I had also learnt about teamwork – the need to appreciate each other's strengths, the danger of head games, the importance of apologising, and the essential role of forgiveness.

An expedition is like a furnace. Often teams go into one as friends, but before they are even halfway, they have ended up as lifelong enemies. In Leon's and my case, seemingly by providence, we had been thrown into the expedition hardly knowing each other. We were ill-prepared, out of our depth, and there was much that could have gone wrong. And indeed, much did go wrong, and we had certainly had our fair share of ups and downs. But through the trials and tests we shared and endured, a deepening friendship had developed. While I had greatly relished the solitude of the past few weeks, I was now looking forward to catching up with Leon in Guilin and hearing what he had been up to. I hoped he would make it to our meeting point, and I suspected, as usual, he would get there before me.

Part Six

The Home Straight

铁杵磨成针

Perseverance can reduce an iron rod to a sewing needle.

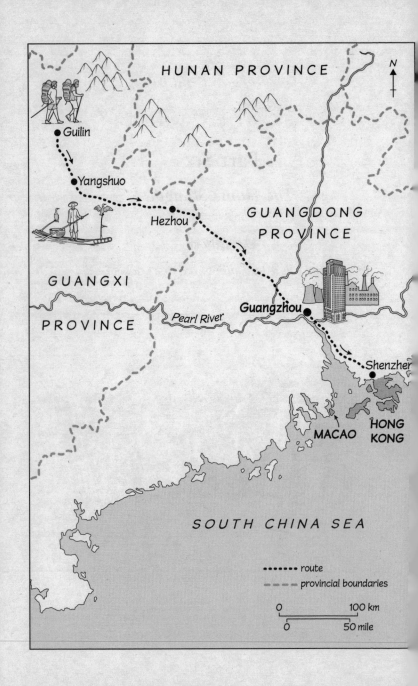

53
Two haggard wild men

Distance to home: 465 miles

28 APRIL–16 MAY

I arrived in Guilin city, and walked up through the gates of Yushan Park. Leon was standing at the top of some steps, next to a flower-bed. I raised a weary hand to wave. He saw me and raised the video camera, filming as always. I walked over and saw it was the same old Leon, though his clothes were dirtier, his beard had turned slightly ginger and his face looked sunburnt. Before we split up he had said to me, 'This expedition has made me age at an unnatural speed.' The ageing process was evidently continuing apace.

We exchanged an awkward manly hug.

'Good to see you survived,' I said. 'How was life in China without me as your fearless guide to help you along?'

'It was great!' he said. 'How was life without a tough-guy camera-man to stop you getting lost?'

'It's more fun getting lost on my own, without you complaining all the time.'

Leon pulled out the hip flask. 'Whisky?'

'Thought you'd never ask.'

We sat on the grass and had a celebratory 'we're both still in one piece' swig. Leon told me that he had made it through the closed zone in the middle of the night, and had also enjoyed being forced to speak more Mandarin.

'The most crazy thing, though, was when I was attacked by a flying squirrel,' he said.

'A squirrel!' I raised my eyebrows.

'No, not a squirrel, a flying squirrel. I saw it up on a rock face above the road. I thought it was just a normal squirrel and I started filming. Suddenly it jumped off and flew straight at my head. I had to duck to avoid being hit.'

'Wow, Leon, you're moving up in the world of intrepid TV adventurers.'

It was good to see him, like catching up with an old friend.

Our destination in Guilin was none other than the Shangri-La. The hotel had again generously invited us to stay, and the thought of constant air con, clean rooms and the enormous buffet breakfasts had often been on my mind throughout the past few sweltering weeks. After I had taken a much-needed shower, I jumped in a cab to the airport to pick up my dear Christine. This would be our final break before I got home, and the pressure of the previous months seemed to be lifting. With just four more weeks to go, we could start dreaming about living a normal life again, without our time together being limited to a few days every month or two. The four weeks would be busy for Christine – she was organising a sponsored walk for Viva whereby friends and supporters could join Leon and me for the final few miles of our long walk home. We were all excited that the end was almost in sight.

The break passed quickly but, in some ways, we were all eager to get the final stage underway. Christine flew home, and Leon and I set out walking through a mostly flat landscape of paddy fields, sprinkled with hundreds of limestone karsts. The tall bolts of limestone were draped in greenery and sprouted from the lush land like giant, camouflaged soldiers.

After three days we approached the final tourist zone of our journey: the town of Yangshuo. It was set beside a tranquil stretch of the Li River, and I had actually visited it about seven years previously. I remembered it as being full of Western tour groups and backpackers. However, this time, as we walked into the town centre, I noticed not only many new hotels and restaurants, but also that the Westerners were now far outnumbered by large Chinese tour groups.

All the way from the north of China, I had regularly seen aspects of the country's ongoing economic boom: the factories and mines;

the entire streets of new apartment blocks; the roads filling with shiny cars.* Now, here I was seeing another fruit of the swelling middle-class: tourism.†

In addition to this mass tourism that we were now witnessing, Leon and I had also occasionally encountered more independent and adventurous Chinese tourists, including some young people on long-distance cycle tours. I was glad to see that the Chinese were starting to appreciate their own country, beyond the tourist spots. I wondered whether the day might come when a proper national hiking trail would be marked out through the Middle Kingdom, going from east to west, or north to south. Perhaps a route a little like the one we had just walked, but with more trails through the mountains, and less scope for getting lost.

That night, we boarded a boat with thirty other tourists, and chugged out onto the Li River – we had signed up to see some traditional cormorant fishing. Our vessel drew up beside a wooden skiff, on which stood a grizzled, wiry man wearing a traditional Chinese straw hat. It quickly became evident that his job was not so much as a fisherman, as a man who showed us tourists how he fished. He had half a dozen cormorants on his bow, and at his command they jumped off and dived down into the water. The idea was that when a cormorant seized the fish in its ample beak, the string tied around its neck prevented it from swallowing. It had been trained, therefore, to jump back onto the skiff instead and drop its catch on the deck for the fisherman. We only spotted a couple of tiny fish being caught in this way and, after half an hour, the fisherman drew up on the land. He fed the industrious birds with his own supply of fish (bought from the market), and we all applauded.

We marched back into the countryside, knowing that we would have no more days off until we reached the industrial mega-city of

---

* In 2000 there were four million cars in China. By 2010 this had gone up twenty-fold to over eighty million, with growth expected to continue for a long time to come.
† In recent years, the Mainland Chinese, with all their new wealth, have also become the biggest single source of global tourist income.

Guangzhou on the Pearl River Estuary, about 300 miles away. So for the next two weeks we moved forward like pre-programmed robots. One foot in front of the other, left, right, left, right. Each day followed a similar pattern. We woke, we gulped down instant coffee, we walked, we ate, we collapsed. After six months, this was our way of life, our day job, our night job, our meaning and purpose. We were two haggard wild men on the loose in southern China.

The weather was now up in the mid-30°Cs, and we walked in shorts and T-shirts. We each had a pair of running shorts from a sponsor, which reminded us of the kind of shorts that middle-aged German men wear when on holiday, so we renamed them our 'Germans'. As the sun beat down my mind filled with memories of all that we had been through: the cold, harsh emptiness of the Gobi; the bleak loess mountains of Shanxi; the unstable scree slopes of the frozen Yellow River. All that seemed unreal to me now. Back then, in the cold, I had thought that I would never complain when the weather grew warmer. And now here I was in the searing, waterlogged air, dazzled by views of valley floors carpeted in thick green crops; grey karsts rising out of the land; ageing farmers, hard at work with their oxen for all hours of the day.

Back together, Leon and I enjoyed being able to relaunch our rambling conversations. When our morale dipped, we recited Tennyson's *Ulysses*, which we had memorised in Shaanxi, or got to work on a Jason Statham script we had come up with. In our exhaustion, though, sometimes our moods became irritable. Some things that had been a part of our routine for months started to seem tedious. One night, we reached a *ludian*, and Leon took the lead with haggling for a better price. His conversation with the *ludian* lady was going playfully, but slowly; as I stood watching, suddenly I lost my patience and rudely demanded a lower price. Leon shot me a look, so I shut up. I later apologised and tried to be especially polite to the *ludian* owner.

On the other hand, things that had once been a source of stress were now barely noticeable. Being questioned by the police, for example. They still stopped us occasionally and asked what we were doing. Now, when we explained we were walking to Hong Kong, they were not quite as disbelieving as before – for Hong Kong was only one province away. After a few minutes chatting, and perhaps a glance at our passports, they sent us on our way. Spread out in filing cabinets across the Middle Kingdom there were now records of us staying in random Gobi *ludians*, getting caught in a closed zone, walking through the nation's longest tunnel, strolling down motorways, filming *ludian* owners, and (on numerous occasions) simply being a bit odd and insisting on walking through China. Judging by how vast the country was, and how minor and random all our transgressions, it seemed unlikely that the paper trail we had left behind us was going to land us on a list of 'China's most wanted'. Perhaps we should never have been worried about the police finding out about the TV show in the first place.

Leon pulled the rain cover over the camera as an electric storm flashed across the sky and rain thumped down on the paddy fields. We were crossing into our final province – Guangdong. Foreigners used to call it Canton, and from this came the English name for the local dialect – Cantonese. I soon noticed shopkeepers talking in the singsong tones, and I felt as though I was entering more familiar ground. For Cantonese was spoken in Hong Kong, and it was Christine's mother tongue. Rather than counting down in months or weeks, we were starting to count down in days. My pace quickened, with the incredible thought that I really would be home soon.

54

Guests of honour

Distance to home: 165 miles

17–19 MAY

'That's five McDonald's and eight KFCs,' I said.

'No, four McDonald's and nine KFCs,' said Leon.

'Really?'

We had just spent the previous day and a half walking fifty miles through the industrial suburbs of Guangzhou city. We were finally nearing its heart, and in the space of a couple of hours we had seen more McDonald's and KFCs than we had done in the last six months. The streets were becoming more and more glitzy, with fashion shops, luxury brands and smart office blocks. Through the smog we glimpsed our first skyscrapers.

Guangzhou is the capital of Guangdong Province and one of the biggest cities in China, and in the world. It was part of a vast conurbation known as the Pearl River Delta, which stretched around the coastline for over 100 miles. A quarter of all China's goods were made in or passed through this prosperous and booming region. In fact, it had been near here that post-Mao China had first reopened itself to the world.

In 1978, two years after Mao had died, his successor, Deng Xiaoping, had declared a new approach to China's economy: 'Communism with Chinese characteristics'. He had released farmers from collectivisation, allowing them to sell their excess crops and thus having more incentive to work. He also authorised entrepreneurship, liberating the latent and extraordinary Chinese talent for doing business. Most notably, Deng had begun to implement an 'open doors policy', whereby foreign investment was permitted. And so China's huge, industrious and cheap labour force was unleashed.

The results were staggering. From this point forwards, China's growth continued at an average of over 10 per cent per year for more than thirty years. Six hundred million people had been lifted out of poverty. Hundreds of millions moved from the countryside to work in the burgeoning coastal factory cities, turning them into some of the fastest-growing settlements in world history. This meant that now, far more than any perceived north–south divide, China had a stark coastal–inland divide.*

As we drew closer to the coast and the Pearl River Delta, we looked at the map, and were daunted by the size of the urban area. It was so much larger than any city we had been through so far. We also noticed the extensive transport networks sprouting from it, like a spider's legs. To try and redistribute some of the nation's wealth, the government had been investing more and more in transport links, and encouraging the industries requiring cheap intensive labour to move inland. This made sense of the multitude of newly built road and rail links we had seen during our walk.†

We arrived at the Pearl River near to the city centre – the very stretch of water on which the British had traded their tea and opium in the 1800s. We were now heading for the American International School; we had been invited to give a talk about our experiences to its pupils. We arrived, soaking wet from a thunderstorm, but were warmly greeted by posters stuck all along the front of the school saying: 'Welcome Rob and Leon, keep walking!'

An audience of several hundred young children of many nationalities was gathered in the hall. The pupils sat cross-legged and wide-eyed as we showed photos and recounted our adventures. We

---

* A similar rich coast–poor interior divide also emerged in the nineteenth century, when the coastal areas opened up to foreign trade
† In 2000 there were 10,000 miles of roads in China. By 2009 this had increased to over 40,000 miles. By 2020, it is predicted there will be 60,000 miles – the same as in the USA. China's infrastructure development received a huge boost when, in 2008, the Chinese government injected four trillion RMB (£400 billion) into the economy. Transport projects were mentioned as one of the key beneficiaries of these funds.

described how we had dragged Molly across the Gobi, walked along the Great Wall, and got lost in the mountains. We also did an onstage demo of our now polished filming routine, whereby I pulled the camera out of Leon's rucksack and he pulled the tripod out of mine and we were ready to shoot in seconds. Next, we emptied our rucksacks to show them all the gear we were carrying. Lastly, we called for a volunteer to get inside it, and a six-year-old girl came up and bravely climbed in. As I walked around the stage, she felt unimaginably light compared to our normal load. Everyone giggled.

At the end of the talk, several dozen little hands shot up.

'What was your favourite place?' asked one girl.

'The Gobi,' said Leon.

'The Wall,' said I.

'Where did you go to the toilet?' asked a boy. More giggling.

'Behind rocks and trees,' we explained.

'Why did you do it?' said a more serious-looking child.

'To have an adventure and to explore China,' we said.

They were all good questions, and this last one in particular gave me pause for thought. Why *had* we done it? It was easy to give this short, simple answer, but sometimes when I had asked myself that question along the way, it had not seemed enough. When I could not sleep because of the cold, or I could not walk properly because of my foot, or the filming pressures were drowning our enthusiasm, or when I felt like punching Leon, or when he felt like punching me, I occasionally wondered whether the whole trip was just fuelled by vanity and ambition, or maybe just stupidity. Yet, as we now stepped back and told the story, I saw how much we had learnt, how far we had come. And, actually, the things that had gone wrong, or caused us grief along the way, were part of the adventure, the test, and were part of what had made it all worthwhile.

The American International School was not our only appointment in Guangzhou; through our little talk, the American Chamber of Commerce (AmCham) had heard about us. It happened to be their annual summer ball that weekend, so they invited us to come along as their 'guests of honour'.

The ball sounded like an elaborate affair, with tickets costing roughly the same amount of money that we would spend in a whole month of walking. Suspecting that our expedition clothes might be inappropriate for the occasion, Leon and I went shopping. We each bought ourselves the smartest shoes, trousers, shirt and tie we could afford for a total of £50. However, I ended up buying trousers to fit my usual waistline, having forgotten that I had lost some weight on the walk.

Despite our incongruent beards, we felt quite respectable as we walked into the lavish hotel in our new clothes. A jazz band was playing, hundreds of guests were milling around in black tie, and non-*baijiu* alcohol was flowing freely. Everyone was shown to their seats and, just before the entrées were served, Leon and I, the inadvertent 'guests of honour', were called up to say a couple of words. We walked slowly to the front. We had not been expecting this, and I suddenly felt like a hedgehog caught in the headlights. Before us, the banqueting room was filled with a distinguished crowd, including a number of ambassadors and consular-generals, several Chinese billionaires, and one of Barak Obama's brothers.

'This is a bit of a change to living in a Chinese field,' I said, holding the microphone in one hand, and holding up my trousers with the other.

'And the food here is certainly better than instant noodles,' declared Leon.

There was a moment of awkward silence from the room. I realised that perhaps when they invited us to be the guests of honour, the AmCham folks might have assumed we were some sort of all-American heroes. And yet, here we were, a couple of tramp-like Brits with ill-fitting trousers. But then the kind Americans and their guests all laughed and applauded politely, and Leon and I returned to our seats, relieved, and ready for a well-earned feast.

Seeing the opulence around us, it was hard not to feel strangely disconnected from the China outside the ballroom. Our walk into this immense, prosperous city over the past two days had also displayed a very different side of the nation to what we had experienced in the interior. Was this the future of China, I wondered?

In his bestseller *When China Rules the World*, Martin Jacques argues that China is all set to move beyond being a mere economic superpower. Rather, it will soon have a far-reaching cultural and political impact on the world. China's cultural power is in fact already visible – one just needs to look at how few Western restaurants there are in China compared to the vast number of Chinese restaurants in the West.

I got talking to a clean-shaven economics advisor from one of the foreign consulates. He was probably less than ten years older than me, but clearly much more intelligent. Nonetheless, I felt I might be able to impress him with my knowledge of Jacques' arguments, so I asked what he thought about the theories. To me, a layman, they seemed quite persuasive.

'Ah, it's horseshit if you ask me!' he said.

'Oh!' I said, trying not to sound too surprised. 'What are your views?'

The economist explained that in his view all the 'China's going to rule the world' theories were based on an assumption that China's strong economic growth would continue as it had been doing for the past thirty years. That, he said, was not necessarily going to happen. And besides, China faced a great number of challenges.

I had heard about some of the challenges, and had even seen some first-hand on the walk: an increasingly severe environmental crisis; growing social inequality; the subversive potential of the internet*; the enormous, precarious property bubble; rabid nationalism; the terrible 'test'-based education system; a corrupt credit system in which many loans were granted more on the basis of political connections than business merit. Perhaps the biggest problem was that a generation of spectacular growth had fuelled the Chinese people's expectations. If the economy faltered now,

---

* Chinese internet users are five times more likely to have blogs than Americans. The Chinese government is increasingly struggling to keep the expression of views under control. There are a purported 30,000 cyber-police making up the the 'Great Firewall of China'.

there would be widespread social unrest, and the authoritarian system might not be able to handle it.

But then I remembered a point made by Jacques in response: the Chinese government has just successfully overseen the biggest economic transformation in history – for 1.3 billion people. If it can do that, surely it is capable of coping with these other new challenges too.

There seemed to be so many competing views. Perhaps it was futile to try and predict the future, especially for China. Just look at the past century. Who would have guessed that Marx's radical ideology would take over the ancient Middle Kingdom? Who would have predicted that Mao could do so much harm in the last twenty years of his life? Who would have said that after almost imploding in the 1970s, China would go on to become the world's second biggest economy in just three short decades?

The Chinese people we had encountered on our walk were, without a doubt, among the most vibrant and industrious people I had ever seen. And China's size alone makes it sure to be one of the great nations of the future. But more precisely what that future holds, I would have to leave to the experts.

My conversation with the economics advisor moved onto a new subject.

'I'm about to change postings,' he told me, 'and in the interim I'm going to drive around my own country for a month.'

'Well, in that case,' I said, feeling more confident in my own area of expertise, 'you should definitely grow a beard.'

He thought for a moment and then nodded. 'You know, I've never grown a beard before, so I might just do that.'

55
Countdown

Distance to home: 80 miles

20–24 MAY

'Your Mandarin's not bad now, Rob,' said Leon, as he finished filming me chatting to a passer-by.

'Thanks.' We picked up our poles and started clinking forwards again. 'Your filming skills aren't bad either.'

'I was thinking, with your knowledge of Chinese history and language, and my filming experience, we're just about ready to go on a walking expedition across China, filming a TV show as we go.'

'That's a great idea. I reckon it would take about six months. When are you free in the coming year?'

We continued talking as we walked along a promenade that followed the Pearl River out of the city. However, Leon was being quieter than normal, and actually looked quite pale. A few days earlier, as we had entered the city, he had mentioned that he was feeling unwell. We had put it down to exhaustion. But the late night out at the AmCham Ball seemed to have made matters worse. Now he said he could feel a fever coming on. He was, however, determined to keep going, because eighty friends and supporters would be joining us for the final few miles, in just five days' time, and we could not be late for them.

We came to some steps leading down into the murky Pearl waters.

'We've done the Yellow and the Yangtze, do you want to complete the hat trick?' I said.* Leon, feeling unwell, did not, so I quickly

---

*Although small compared to the Yellow and Yangtze giants, the Pearl was the third great river of China. Other significant rivers such as the

stripped off and jumped in wearing my Germans, much to the surprise of a bunch of Chinese fishermen lining the bank. The water was beautifully cool, but it smelt bad, and I could see a lot of rubbish floating around, so I swam around for less than a minute before rejoining Leon on the promenade.

We soon left Guangzhou behind us, but this was not the end of the buildings, for industrial compounds and factories continued to crowd the roadsides. The thick, smoggy air was full of dust, and the grime stuck to our sweaty arms and faces. Industry would, in fact, envelop us all the way down to the border with Hong Kong.

As the early evening arrived, the streets filled with tens of thousands of young men and women, out for dinner after a hard day's work in their factories. They often walked in groups, chatting to each other or on their mobile phones. Some contacts from the AmCham ball had invited us to visit two factories on our way through. We were glad to have the chance to catch a glimpse into the lives of China's famous young workforce, who had changed the world.

The first factory we visited made medical accessories, such as swabs and face masks, for export to hospitals in the USA. As we were led onto the factory floor, we saw hundreds of women hard at work. Each job was highly specialised, whether cutting, or measuring, or attaching one item to another. The labourers worked incredibly fast, and barely looked up as we passed. They were paid per item they made – time was money.

Then, the day before we reached the border, we visited the factory of Dahon folding bicycles – a company that held a two-thirds market share of the folding bicycles industry. Luckily for us, Dr Hon, the mastermind behind these bikes, was also at the factory. He was having a busy day, so we were told we had only a few minutes to interview him in his office. I hoped that after my countless hours of appearing on camera, my TV-documentary interviewing skills were up to it.

Mekong, the Amur, and the Brahmaputra pass through only parts of China.

We entered the room. Dr Hon sat behind his desk, looking intelligent and dignified. I became conscious of my sweaty, unkempt appearance. We shook hands, and I sat down opposite him. I thought I should attempt to build a little rapport before I moved on to my more serious questions. I explained our long walk and how I was now almost home.

'In fact, my wife is from Hong Kong,' I said, pointing over my shoulder in the rough direction of Hong Kong.

Dr Hon frowned.

'That is your wife?' he said.

I looked over my shoulder and saw a bearded, dizzy-looking Leon holding the video camera.

'Err, no, that's not quite what I meant.'

We all laughed, and Dr Hon's remark was probably the most memorable moment of the interview.

Back outside, the sales manager, Dennis, let us take a couple of their latest bikes for a lap of the car park.

'Next trip, Leon,' I shouted, enjoying the incredible smooth spinning, 'we have got to go on folding bikes, these are amazing!'

As we hit the road, back on our weary feet again, I reflected on how different this walking trip had been from my three-year bicycle adventure. Although I had been through considerably more dangerous places when I had cycled home from Siberia, this trip had actually felt like the harder one. This was partly because I was now married and partly because of all the filming pressure. But perhaps, most of all, it was because walking was so much physically harder than riding a bike.

By pedal power, I had been able to easily cover four times the distance each day and, crucially, all the weight was carried not on my body, but on the bicycle racks. When cycling, though I often felt tired, I was never in serious pain. When I fell behind schedule, it was easy to ride a few extra hours a day to catch up without dire physical consequences.

All that said, I did not regret choosing to walk instead of cycle through China. As well as being able to sometimes go entirely off road, the walking had allowed me to encounter China at ground level, just as I had hoped.

We were now less than twenty-four hours from the China–Hong Kong border. For most of history, Hong Kong had been part of the ancient Chinese Empire, but then, in the nineteenth century, almost by accident, the tiny piece of territory had become the dominion of another Empire.

In 1841, during the build-up to the First Opium War, the British were evicted from the Portuguese trading settlement of Macao. They took their ships and set sail, heading east, looking for a suitable place to set up a new base. They came to a somewhat unpromising, mountainous island, about a mile off Mainland China. Upon landing, they were still unimpressed. There were only a couple of dozen local villages on it, and the rocky terrain was largely uncultivable. The space between the island and the mainland did, however, form a well-protected, deep-water harbour – a significant factor because the region was notorious for typhoons. And so the British stayed. In Cantonese, the name of the island meant 'fragrant harbour'. The British called it by its Cantonese name: Hong Kong.

As a result of the British victory in the First Opium War, the Chinese were forced to cede the island and a tiny area of mainland (Kowloon) to the British as a permanent possession. The colony then expanded when, in 1898, the British obtained a ninety-nine-year lease on a further piece of land, stretching twenty miles into the mainland, known as the New Territories.

History rumbled on, and during World War II, and the subsequent Chinese civil war, the territory flooded with refugees.* In the years that followed, the concentrated labour force, combined with Hong Kong's strategic location, allowed the colony to bloom. However, the end of the ninety-nine-year lease from China was approaching.

* Hong Kong was also occupied by the Japanese for several years during World War II.

In 1984 Margaret Thatcher agreed that, in 1997, Britain would hand back not only the New Territories but all of Hong Kong. The Iron Lady was a strong negotiator, and was able to include an agreement that although Hong Kong would come under the ultimate sovereignty of Beijing, it would keep its laws, its freedom of speech and its currency.*

And thus the unique notion of 'one country, two systems' was born. To most people's surprise, this arrangement has so far worked reasonably well.

On 24 May, bang on time, we arrived in the border city of Shenzhen, itself a major conurbation of over ten million people, and full of skyscrapers and crowded streets. However, Leon's health had been gradually deteriorating. 'I've never felt this bad in my whole life,' he mumbled. 'This is even worse than when I had malaria in Cambodia.'

Although he was still coherent, and keen to film everything he could, both Dr Leon and I were beginning to grow concerned. Dr Leon had originally diagnosed heat stroke, but this no longer seemed to fit. Perhaps it could be malaria (which was rare in China), or dengue fever (also mosquito-borne and far less rare). As I noticed Dr Leon starting to worry, I remembered that a sense of humour was what had got us this far. So I told him it was most likely 'girl's disease', which only afflicted girls like Leon. This was just what Dr Leon needed to hear. He turned to me and told me not to be so sure. In fact, in his expert opinion it was far more likely to be 'hero's fever.'

As we walked through Shenzhen's crowded streets, I took over the filming and navigating. Dr Leon leant hard on his poles and concentrated on not falling over. We spent our final 20 RMB on ice cream and water and, just before dark, we were stunned to see signs pointing to Hong Kong.

The signs led us to an immigration building, where we were stamped quickly out of China. We then joined the queue to enter

* For fifty years after the handover.

Hong Kong. Most people in the line were business people or commuters. I reached the front. The immigration official narrowed her eyes at my thick beard and sunburnt face, unsure whether I could be the same person as in my passport photo. I smiled back at her. I was not afraid of Hong Kong border officials. This was my home.

56
Journey's end

Distance to home: 40 miles

25–26 MAY

I open my eyes and it takes me a moment to remember that I am no longer in Mainland China. I am in Christine's uncle's flat, in the town of Sheung Shui, just across the border.*

I have only one and half day's walk through Hong Kong territory to get home. I rise, dress and pack for the penultimate time. In the living room, Leon is up and looks worse than ever.

'How are you feeling? How's the girl's disease?' I ask.

'Still pretty bad,' he says, 'but I'll make it. It'll take a lot more than hero's fever to stop me now.'

We haul on the packs with a groan. Our packs have served us well, but boy, we will be happy to get rid of them and walk like free men again. Today we must walk twenty-five miles to the Hong Kong harbour waterfront. I have told Christine I will meet her there at sunset.

We head out into Sheung Shui town, in search of the road south. We find ourselves in a different world: cars drive on the left; they do not jump the traffic lights; the pedestrian crossings make funny clicking noises; the street signs are in English as well as Chinese. The people are different too. They are still almost all Chinese, but they do not shout or smoke so much. They still watch us, but they are not staring. When we look back at them, they quickly look away. Hong Kong is a different way of being China.

We follow the main road into the open countryside. Although

---

* The previous evening, after crossing the border, we had been forced to take the metro through two miles of no man's land.

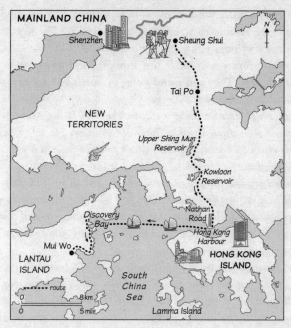

famous for its cityscape, much of Hong Kong, especially the New Territories, is green and wild, the land rugged and steep. We pass through another town and start climbing a hiking trail into the hills. On the other side of the next mountain is the start of the main Kowloon urban area, through which we must pass to reach the water.

It is hot again, 31°C. Leon continues to wilt, and says his fever is worsening. But he staggers on. Remarkably, even as we climb, he still summons the strength to film. He continues to insist on using the tripod and wireless mic to get the highest quality possible. From start to finish, this expedition has been a professional rite of passage for him, with plenty of drama and moments of despair. He has passed the test: no one can dispute that any more.

'Seeing as both your big bicycle trip, and now your big walking trip are finishing at my house,' I say, as we walk, 'maybe you should write two books and call them "Cycling to Rob's House", and "Walking to Rob's House". It would be a great brand.'

Leon is unfazed. 'What about: "If you think Rob is some kind of tough guy, then look at Leon – Parts 1 and 2"?' he says.

I smile. I will miss bantering with Leon.

After two hours we reach the summit, and meet some local mountain bikers. They smile and point us down the right track. We continue down, and see some monkeys dancing through the trees above us. I had known there were monkeys in Hong Kong and yet I had never seen them before. There are so many places to explore, even this close to home. Maybe I don't need to fly 3,000 miles with a one-way plane ticket the next time I want an adventure.

We wind around the edge of a reservoir, and along a clifftop path. Through a gap in the hills we catch a glimpse of something we have long awaited: the ocean. It is grey-blue, immense and tranquil. Super-freighters lumber back and forth, carrying raw materials into China, or manufactured products out of it.

It has been a long walk from the Gobi to reach this point. Most people in Mongolia have never seen the sea. Most people from Hong Kong have never seen the desert. The sea is quite a similar environment to the desert in some ways – monochrome, sterile, dangerous for humans, and yet somehow peaceful and enticing.

'I've missed the sea,' says Leon. He stands and smiles, in a daze. He grew up on the wild north coast of Ireland.

Around another corner, the mountains part again and we see the earth erupting into a mass of steel and concrete, ten thousand apartment blocks breaking through, standing to attention. In the distance, we can see Hong Kong Island. Dozens of skyscrapers are montaged against the mountain. Helicopters flit through the sky beneath like tiny insects.

'This is it,' we say. A long hill winds us down through a spaghetti junction of motorways, and an hour later we reach Nathan Road. This will lead us all the way to the harbour.

It is now 5 o'clock on Friday afternoon. Hong Kong is always in a hurry, and we are about to walk down its busiest road, at peak time, wearing enormous rucksacks. We are instantly swept up in a deluge of frantic shoppers, dating couples, stressed-out employees, laughing teenagers and gruff tradesmen. The shop fronts are brightly lit with displays of delectable foods, sleek outfits and futuristic electronics. Sizzling street restaurants cram into the alleyways beneath bulky tower blocks. The further we go, the thicker the crowd becomes. It is every man and every woman for themselves. People do not even notice us, for this is a city that has seen it all.

At 6.30 p.m. the sun is setting, and we are only halfway down Nathan Road. Three more miles to go. That will take us at least an hour, maybe two in these streets. I send Christine a text apologising. I can't believe she is only a few miles away now.

A mile before the water we meet some of the Tiberius team, who have come to help film the end. It is good to see them. At times, it has been a strained relationship during our months on the road. Now, a smile and a handshake remind us they are on our side.

As we continue down the road, trying not to bash anyone, or be bashed, we cannot help but notice it is a beautiful night. Gentle clouds drift across the sky, illuminated by the city lights. The air is unusually clear. Finally, we approach the Star Ferry Clock Tower, which started ticking back in 1921. We climb some steps onto the viewing platform, which overlooks the waterfront. It is crowded with tourists taking photos. Hong Kong's epic skyline towers all around us, and the water is rippling with the reflection of a million lights.

I wander forwards, followed by Leon and the Tiberius team filming. I am supposed to meet Christine on this platform, but how will I find her? I panic.

Then I see her. Sitting, waiting, looking beautiful, tender. What has she been through to get to this point? The waiting and the worrying. I must never take her for granted.

I walk towards her, and she sees me and my unwieldly rucksack through the crowd.

'Hi honey,' I say.

'Oh no, cameras!' she says, seeing Leon and the Tiberius team behind me.

And then, finally, she is in my arms again.

*

The next morning, I wake up with Christine in a hotel on the waterfront. I am still not home. That is today's task.

My old friend Tobi has offered us a lift on his junk across to the island where I live. Christine catches a fast ferry ahead of us to help all the sponsored walkers to gather.

Leon and I sit out on the deck as the junk churns its way across the sea. The water is thick with cargo ships. The sky is grey. Leon looks ill, but steeled to make it to the end.

The junk draws into the small pier at Discovery Bay, where the sponsored walk will begin. I see a crowd gathered, all in white T-shirts proclaiming: 'Walking Home From Mongolia in support of Viva'. I stand on the edge of the boat and wave. There is a cheer from the shore, and a hundred arms wave back.

'Do you want to swim ashore?' I say to Leon.

'Sorry, I feel too rough, you go for it.'

'OK, well done Leon, we're almost there.'

I leave my rucksack on the deck, jump and am suddenly underwater. I rise to the surface and start to swim, though also realising that I have jumped too soon. I am still over a hundred metres from the shore. It will take me five minutes to reach land. The crowd cheers again and laughs.

I laugh too and start to paddle slowly. This will be my last moment of solitude before the end. I look up and make out familiar, smiling faces on the shore. I think of the multitude of faces I have met on my path to get here:

Sahana the throat grabber,

Uruult the money-changer,

Mr Cheerful the train signaller,

Gaoyu the hospitable student,

Chinese Li the Mao singer,

Mr Wolf the taxi driver,

Mr Steel the tree carrier.

Faces I will most probably never see again. They had all looked after me well.

I reach the shore finally, and grab a piece of rope trailing down to the rocks. As I climb, the rope snaps and I fall back into the sea.

More laughing and cheering from the friends above. I scramble up the rocks instead, and I am on dry land again, dripping wet, being hugged and greeted. Leon arrives off the junk.

For the final walk, our happy group of home-bound walkers form a procession stretching along the waterfront, the children running ahead at the front. People ask me how it was. It is difficult to answer. So much has happened. So much learnt. So much to be thankful for.

'What's next?' someone asks.

It's a good question. I wonder how it will be settling into 'home' again.

We pass along the clifftops and reach a viewing point. From here, I can see down to my own village. With Christine at my side, we descend a long staircase and reach the end of the waterfront. Leon joins us.

We stroll onto the beach, and drop our packs for the last time.

'Ready for a swim now?' I say.

'Ready,' says Leon.

We sprint down across the sand, into the water and dive in. A moment later, half the sponsored walkers are running in too.

We have made it.

We will all have a celebratory dinner together that night on the waterfront. Before that, I need a shower. Christine and I slip away from the crowds and walk down the little village paths hand in hand.

Soon after, we turn a familiar corner and there is our flat. I turn the key.

We are home again – together. At long last. Home.

Epilogue

A few days after our return, Leon flew back to the UK, arriving just in time to carry the Olympic torch through his hometown in Northern Ireland. He wore the compulsory white baggy torchbearer uniform. We joked that in the photos, with his ragged beard and sickly demeanour, he looked as though he had just escaped from some kind of madhouse. In the weeks that followed he continued to feel unwell, but after the Hospital for Tropical Diseases had tested him negative for malaria, dengue fever and brain problems, they concluded that it was simply a virus that his exhausted body would take a month or two to fight off. Thankfully, he was soon back to normal.

A few months later I was back in London to see my family, and Leon came round to my parents' house. He had forgotten to bring the whisky, but he had brought his Germans, so we went for a run. It was surreal moving at such speed along a flat, murky English canal, after walking for six months through the deserts and mountains of China.

'Would you prefer to run fifty miles a day without a pack, or walk twenty-five miles a day with one?' I asked as we ran.

'Run, definitely,' said Leon. I agreed. We started talking about potential running expeditions. It was easy to dream up exciting trips from the comfort of home.

Leon was in fact about to embark on a new expedition. My old friend Al had recruited him to walk across the Empty Quarter on the Arabian Peninsular. They designed and built a trailer considerably bigger than Molly, and loaded it up with the two essentials for desert survival: water and instant noodles. They set off from Oman, and six weeks later arrived in Dubai, dusty but smiling.*

* Leon's latest adventures and shenanigans can be discovered at www.leonmccarron.com

In the middle of walking through China, when everything seemed to be going wrong, Leon and I had sometimes joked that we were filming 'the worst TV show ever made'. Indeed, we had made some serious mistakes that had nearly undone us. In part, this was due to our overly cavalier attitude when we set off, inexperienced as we were in the ways of the TV world. But if we had not been so cavalier, perhaps we would never have set off in the first place.

Back in Hong Kong, Tiberius waded through the 240 hours of footage that we had shot, going the extra mile to produce a TV programme that did an impressive job of capturing the wildness, the people and, at times, the hilarity of the journey. Some episodes paid a lot of attention to our more clownish moments, which I found rather embarrassing. But I decided that being able to laugh at my own bumbling silliness was probably no bad thing. The magic of television also made my Mandarin abilities look quite good!* The show premiered on the National Geographic Adventure Channel across Australia and Asia during the final stages of writing this book. A photo of Leon dancing in the Gobi whiteout made the front page of the TV section in the *South China Morning Post*.

Back in my settled life, I started working for Viva again, and writing this book. I went running in the Hong Kong hills to keep up my fitness. The metatarsal on my right foot continued to ache, especially when I forgot to stretch my calves. Perhaps I really had walked across China on a fractured foot, though I suspect it has now healed too much for anything to show up on X-ray.

I have also wondered if I have another big expedition in me. It is a question I am often asked. What's next? Will I again fling myself far from home, and set off on a long journey to try and get back again? After his Arabia trek, Leon emailed me about a new idea

---

* Less than one minute of 'Code Z' footage was used in the final show – mainly to depict a few wide montage shots of walking through the desert. But we were still glad to have gone on that little side trip to help ensure the show was made in the first place, and to give Tiberius more to work with.

– a world record he wants to break, no less. We have scheduled a call to discuss this more next month.

Then, the other day, as I sat writing, I thought I heard a soft whisper:

'I've got adventures enough for you here, Rob.'

Indeed there are adventures here. The adventure of working for a charity that I passionately believe in, and find it a great privilege to be a part of. The adventure of deepening my friendship and marriage with Christine.

Sometimes, on the walk, I pondered on the Tennyson poem that Leon and I had been memorising – about Ulysses, who spent so long on his Odyssey, trying to get home to Ithaca. And I knew Joseph Campbell's theory about the hero's journey: that in many of the world's greatest stories, a somewhat reluctant protagonist finds himself or herself dispatched far from home, having to go through all sorts of ordeals to get back again. Like Dorothy trying to get back from Oz, Frodo and Sam wanting to get home to the Shire, Luke Skywalker trying to figure out his destiny.*

And all this made me wonder what 'home' actually meant. For many people, 'home' is where they grew up. I once asked a group of teenagers what they thought, and one of them replied, 'It's where my stuff is.' During the walk, I had many temporary homes: on desert plains, in *ludians*, as a guest in other people's homes. And, of course, before me constantly was the ultimate goal of my flat – the place where I lived. But was that really my home?

And then recently, I listened to a group of wise people debating what 'human flourishing' was supposed to look like. One of their conclusions was that human flourishing is what happens when we know ourselves to be unconditionally loved. And it seems to me that the place where we are unconditionally loved, and hence can flourish, is home.

I am blessed to have grown up in such a home.

---

* Or more recently, the character of Tony Mendez in the film *Argo*, who goes to Iran to bring his fellow Americans home, and ends up rediscovering his own home in the process.

Epilogue

I belong to a faith, at the heart of which is the claim that I am completely loved and which also calls me to live courageously as a pilgrim. On this pilgrimage of life there will be times when I fall down. But instead of giving up or becoming bitter, I must get up and keep walking and reject the view that life is all about winning. Rather, I must keep a soft heart which, despite the tests and trials, is learning to love.

And I am blessed to have found Christine, someone who is committed to loving me. We are pilgrims together. Yet all the time, when I am with her, I am home.

> Fount of mercy, call back the one who flees from you.
> Draw towards you the one who attempts to escape.
> Lift up the one who has fallen.
> Support the one who is standing.
> Guide the one who is on a journey.

THOMAS AQUINAS

Acknowledgements

There are many people to thank, both from the expedition itself, and from the writing of the book.

First, the expedition.

Thank you to the countless hospitable people of Mongolia and China, who looked after us and helped us on our way as we walked. Some of you are mentioned; most of you are not. I hope my attempts to depict your exuberance and kindness do you justice. A special thanks to Gaoyu and the Li family for hosting us on that cold Chinese New Year's Eve in Hequ. Also, Enoch and Tim for putting us up on our way through Beijing during Code Z.

Thank you to those new friends we made in Ulaanbaatar who showed us round before we caught the train to Sainshand. Especially Uuree Sangi, Trish Neufeld, Kyle Gunther, Sharon Goldhawk and Marti Lambert.

Thank you to Ripley Davenport for giving us Molly Brown.

Thank you to the brilliant sponsors of the expedition who helped to make the whole thing possible*:

Berghaus – for saving the day by stepping in at the last minute, and providing all the warm clothing and accessories;

Kobold – for an excellent expedition watch;

Osprey Packs – for the rucksacks;

Mountain Hardwear – for the warm sleeping bags;

Hilleberg – for the sturdy tents and bivoanoraks;

ECCO Shoes Oxford – for the three pairs of comfortable Yak skin boots each;

Aquapac – for helpful waterproof bags;

* For a specific kit list, please see the expedition website www.walking-homefrommongolia.com

Acknowledgements

Casio – for stepping into the breach at the last minute with point and shoot stills cameras;

ChinesePod.com – for the brilliant podcast lessons which were such a fun way to learn Mandarin on the road;

Karina Moreton from Panoramic Journeys – for so helpfully sorting us accommodation and giving us a tour of Ulaanbaatar;

Sports Performance, in particular Doug Horne and Aaron Smith – for providing physio and podiatry sessions, and expert advice during the expedition. If I need physio or podiatry in Hong Kong, I know who to go to.

Giovanni Tomaselli for helping to source GoPro cameras at the last minute.

Tobi Doeringer for generous support and giving us a junk ride on the final day. Ward Platt, Sun Young Moon, Mark Francis and Stephen Hunter for the TV opportunity. Luxson for the innovative Punkt app.

Kalun Lau for designing the 'Walking Home From Mongolia' 'brand', Mark Nam for rescuing us with a great website after ours crashed, Josh Boyle for bringing heavy gear out for us from the US, Ashu Kher for the indispensable iPhone, and Chris Niem for donating an iPod shuffle to Leon. Dr Aric Hui for medical advice during the trip – definitely more credible than Dr Leon!

Friends who have sent messages of encouragement and prayed for us while we walked. Christine's good friend, Sarah, for watching *Ugly Betty* and playing Scrabble with her during those winter months. The eighty-plus friends and supporters who came on the last few miles and helped us raise the grand total of over £63,000 for Viva's work with children at risk.

Thank you to the Tiberius Team – Cohen Leung, Kate Kun, Nicholas Shay, Philip Yang and Elain Yu for your dedicated and extraordinary hard work. And thank you to Charmaine and Duncan Jepson for pushing this forward and, at the end of the day, pulling it off. We certainly had our ups and downs, but I am glad we made it through. Thank you for persevering, and making such a fine and entertaining show from the footage.

Jeanette Wang (*South China Morning Post*), Esther Au Yong and

Olivia Lim (Silverkris online), and Jill Alphonso (my paper) for commissioning articles to be written during the expedition.

Todd Miller, Colin Brown and Steven Ballantye for invaluable advice.

Al Humphreys – for great advice and regular reminders not to take ourselves too seriously. And for brutal feedback on the early drafts of the book.

Clare Symons – for letting your crazy other half come on a walk for six months.

Thank you to Leon McCarron for coming on the mad old trip in the first place, and for putting up with my foibles, irritability and annoyances. I think you got a lot more than you bargained for, but you did well!

Second, the book.

A number of friends took time out of busy schedules to read and give extremely helpful comments on parts of or all of the manuscript. Thank you to: Sarah Cheng, Andrew Gardener, Pam Golafshar, LaDonna Hall, Ian Huen, Alastair Humphreys, Queenie Lau, Leon McCarron, Kate McGeown, Anneli Matheson, Mary Ann Mhina, Will Ng, Jacinta Read, John Snelgrove, Martin Thomas, Nury Vittachi, and my sister Rosanna Brodie.

Gus Seebaran, for inviting me to the Creative Writers' forum in Oxford all those years ago.

Everyone at Viva. For prayers, encouragement, and being such great people to work with. Thanks especially to Martin Thomas for patience and support as I took time off work to get this finished, and to Justine Demmer and Chris Niem for your understanding that I was busy writing.

Tim Steward, for your generous and brilliant work on the atmospheric sketches which start each section of the book.

My parents-in-law, TW and Mazi Susie, for your encouragement and prayers, and for feeding me delicious meals, ice cream and chocolate when I was writing the book in your flat.

Joanna Davey, my editor at Hodder. For commissioning the book, patience after uncountable missed deadlines, brilliant work with honing the text, and some good, bold decisions on what we needed to cut.

Acknowledgements

My parents, for your feedback on the book, and even more for your amazing patience with – and generous encouragement of – your unconventional son.

And most of all, to my darling fellow-pilgrim Christine. We discovered a hidden gift during this book – you have an amazing talent for seeing through my forest of words, and grasping the story that I am trying to tell. Thank you for the countless times you read through the manuscript, and your many brilliant suggestions. And thank you for loving me so well.

Sources

The following books were the background reading to the expedition and the book.

Jung Chang, *Wild Swans*, HarperPress, 2012

Jung Chang and Jon Halliday, *Mao, The Unknown Story*, Vintage, 2007

Leslie T. Chang, *Factory Girls*, Picador, 2010

Frank Ching, *Ancestors*, Rider, 2009

Frank Dakota, *Mao's Great Famine*, Bloomsbury Paperbacks, 2011

Jonathan Fenby, *The Penguin History of Modern China*, Penguin, 2009

George Friedman, *The Next 100 Years*, Anchor Books, 2010

Valerie Hansen, *The Open Empire*, W. W. Norton & Co., 2000

Peter Hessler, *River Town*, John Murray, 2002

Peter Hessler, *Oracle Bones*, John Murray, 2007

Peter Hessler, *Country Driving*, Harper Perennial, 2011

Martin Jacques, *When China Rules the World*, Penguin Books, 2012

John Keay, *China: A History*, HarperPress, 2009

Michael Khon, *Lama of the Gobi*, Blacksmith Books, 2009

Henry Kissinger, *On China*, Penguin, 2012

Chai Ling, *A Heart For Freedom*, Tyndale House, 2011

John Man, *Gobi: Tracking the Desert*, Wiedenfeld & Nicholson, 1998

John Man, *Genghis Khan*, Bantam, 2005

John Man, *The Terracotta Army*, Bantam, 2008

John Man, *The Great Wall*, Bantam, 2009

Rana Mitter, *Modern China: A Very Short Introduction*, OUP, 2008

Bill Purves, *China on the Lam*, Asia 2000 Limited, 2002

J. M. Roberts, *The New Penguin History of the World*, Penguin, 2007

Sarah Rose, *For All the Tea in China*, Arrow Books, 2010

Sources

Colin Thubron, *Behind the Wall*, Atlantic Monthly Press, 1988

Jonathan Watts, *When a Billion Chinese Jump*, Faber and Faber, 2011

Jack Weatherford, *Genghis Khan and the Making of the Modern World*, Broadway Books, 2005

Specific sources quoted

Chapter 2:   *Genetics study about Genghis' offspring:*
John Man, *Genghis Khan*, Bantam, 2005. p. 15.

Chapter 10:   *Wisdom on choosing an expedition partner:*
http://www.bbc.co.uk/news/magazine-21878839.

Chapter 14:   *Like discovering a new room:*
Colin Thubron, *Behind the Wall*, Atlantic Monthly Press, 1988, p. 1.

Chapter 15:   *For a modified version of Dr Brown's talk:*
http://bit.ly/15eetsM.

Chapter 18:   *More on the controversy surrounding the Green Wall of China:*
http://www.theepochtimes.com/n2/china-news/desertification-in-china-20291.html.

Chapter 21:   *On seeing the Great Wall from space:*
http://www.journalofoptometry.org/en/is-it-really-possible-to/articulo/13188744/.

Chapter 25:   *For more information and statistics relating to number of coal mines and coal consumption in China, see:*
Watts, Jonathan, *When a Billion Chinese Jump*, Faber and Faber, 2011. Chapter 10; and http://www.worldcoal.org/resourcesfrequently-asked-questions/.

Chapter 45:   *For the cost of building the dam, and its social impact:*
Watts, Jonathan, *When a Billion Chinese Jump*, Faber and Faber, 2011, p. 64.

Chapter 45:   *Mao's attitude to intervening in nature:*
ibid. p. 70.

Chapter 49:   *For the role of tea in the eventual fall of the dynastic rule in China:*

Rose, Sarah, *For All the Tea in China*, Arrow Books, 2010, p. 255.

Chapter 53:   *For more on Chinese tourists spending abroad:*
http://www.bbc.co.uk/news/
world-asia-china-22573572.

Chapter 53:   *For number of cars in China:*
http://www.guardian.co.uk/world/2012/dec/14/
china-worlds-biggest-new-car-market.

Chapter 54:   *For miles of road in China:*
ibid.

Chapter 54:   *On Chinese internet users are five times as likely to have blogs as Americans:*
http://www.businessinsider.com/15-facts-about-china-
that-will-blow-your-mind-2010-
2?op=1#ixzz2Vnkmk5tO.

Chapter 54:   *Statistics relating to China's boom:*
http://www.worldbank.org/en/country/china/
overview.

Chapter 54:   *On Pearl River District and moving jobs inland:*
http://www.asiabusinesscouncil.org/docs/
PRDBriefing.pdf.

A *note about the charity*
I raised funds for: Viva

I think Viva is an amazing charity. Their work has helped moti-
vate me to cycle around the world and walk across countries. It's
because Viva is all about life – about inspiring lasting change in
children's lives through the power of collective action. They know
that the best possible way of bringing that lasting change to tens
of thousands of vulnerable children across our world is by walking
and working together.

As Archbishop Desmond Tutu said about Viva's strategic work:
'Just imagine what the impact would be if everyone demonstrated
a little genuine compassion for our suffering children . . . sadly
much of the work for children is not sufficiently supported and
takes place in isolation, disconnected and uncoordinated. Viva points
toward how much more we can do together. I urge you to get involved
and make a difference.'

The next time you run a marathon, climb a mountain, or take on
some other challenge, why not consider helping vulnerable children
at the same time. Find out how you can get involved in this and
other ways at www.viva.org.

About *Cycling Home From Siberia*

Cycling Home From Siberia

Before he walked home from Mongolia, Rob Lilwall spent three years cycling home (to London) from Siberia. He rode through twenty-eight countries, including Papua New Guinea, Afghanistan and Iran. Along the way he was robbed at gunpoint, chased by thugs with machetes, and camped at −40°C. It was in the middle of this journey that, quite unexpectedly, he met Christine.

Lilwall's critically acclaimed first book tells the story of his first major expedition.

'I'm not sure Rob Lilwall knows it, but he has penned a two-wheeled classic. I wanted to rise up singing and strap on my bicycle clips.' *The Guardian*

'Lilwall's story is a remarkable one . . . enhanced by the fact that he has a writer's skill for conveying a sense of place.' *The Sunday Telegraph*

'This book is a rite-of-passage adventure full of thrills, excitement and endurance tests . . . If you're a cyclist – and even if you're not – go for this book.' *The Irish Times*

Walking Home From Mongolia TV Series

To watch the series that Rob and Leon made, order the DVD from: www.roblilwall.com

CYCLING HOME FROM SIBERIA

I

Over Mordor

Siberia . . . impends through the darkness as the ultimate
unearthly abroad. The place from which you will not return
COLIN THUBRON

We had been flying east all night and I awoke to notice that it was
already daylight outside the plane. Looking out of the window onto
the empty landscape below, the dark shades of brown and green
reassured me that, although it was mid-September, it had not yet
started snowing in Siberia. I could see no sign of human life and
the view rolled away in an otherworldly blend of mountains, streams
and forests to an endless horizon. I shook my head and it brought
to mind Tolkien's gloom-filled Mordor.

My neighbour woke up and smiled at me sleepily.

'Good morning, Robert!' he said, pronouncing my name in a
slow, Russian accent.

Sergei was a Muscovite salesman of my age who was flying to
the outer limits of civilisation in order to sell safety clothing to the
local mining industries. We had met the night before when we
boarded the plane in Moscow. His English was almost as poor as
my Russian, but with the help of a dictionary I had managed to
explain to him that I was flying to the far-eastern Siberian city of
Magadan with only a one-way ticket because it was my intention
to return home to England by bicycle.

'But, Robert,' he had reasoned with me, 'there is no road from
Magadan; you cannot ride a bicycle.'

I explained that I had reason to believe that there was a road,
though not many people used it these days.

'Alone?' he asked, pointing at me.

'No, I will be riding with a friend.'

'One?'

'Yes, just one friend,' I nodded, hoping that my friend, Al, would arrive, as planned, in three days' time.

Sergei still looked unconvinced and pointed outside:

'*Holodna, Zeema?*'

Holodna was a word that I would grow accustomed to hearing over the next few months. It meant simply 'cold'. *Zeema* meant 'winter'. I had to agree with Sergei that, although the weather did not look too bad right now, the infamous weather of Siberia would not stay away for much longer. The road that we would have to follow, the only road that existed, would take us past the coldest inhabited place in the world.

I tried to bolster my case by explaining to Sergei with hand gestures towards my arms and legs that I had lots of very warm clothes, though I left out the fact that, because the trip was self-funded and without sponsorship, I was on a tight budget. Most of my clothes and equipment had been bought at slashed prices on eBay. In reality, I was not at all sure if they would be up to the job. This was especially the case for my enormous Royal Mail over-trousers which I had bought for £10. They were several sizes too big and probably more suitable for the mid-morning drizzle of London than the long, hard winter of Siberia.

Of even greater concern was the tent. It had been given to us by a kind lady who had taken an interest in the expedition after seeing our website, though we had never actually met her. We had not yet tried putting it up, but it was free, so it seemed like the ideal option at the time. Furthermore, we would have neither a satellite phone nor a global positioning system (GPS) and, in fact, no back-up whatsoever. I also did not admit to Sergei that the coldest temperature I had experienced prior to this was during a camping weekend in Scotland, nor that my main fitness training had been in the form of badminton matches against a colleague after work. Because I was not entirely sure why we were setting off at the start of winter (other than it was when we were ready to start), I just told Sergei that the winter would be an exciting and beautiful time of year to see Siberia.

'How long?' he gestured a bicycling motion.

'One year,' I said confidently. In fact, though I did not know it at the time, the ride would take several times longer than this and for the vast majority of it I would be on my own.

We dropped below the cloud level and, as the land rose to meet us, the broad, dark shapes converged as distinct mountains. They were shrouded in sparse, green forest. I felt a twinge of claustrophobia as we landed on the runway.

Inside the small, grey, terminal building the young lady at the immigration counter stamped me through, but did not return my smile. I collected my bicycle and bags and loaded them onto a 1970s-style bus outside. The gruff driver revved the engine, lit a cigarette and drove out onto the road. I was excited that I would soon be arriving in the city from where I would begin riding, but I was also daunted. Magadan did not have a good reputation with the Russians. Half a century beforehand they had nicknamed it 'The Gateway to Hell'.

An invitation from the publisher

Join us at www.hodder.co.uk, or follow us
on Twitter @hodderbooks to be a part of
our community of people who love the very
best in books and reading.

Whether you want to discover more about a book
or an author, watch trailers and interviews, have the
chance to win early limited editions, or simply browse
our expert readers' selection of the very best books,
we think you'll find what you're looking for.

And if you don't, that's the place to tell us what's missing.

We love what we do, and we'd love you to be a part of it.

www.hodder.co.uk

@hodderbooks

HodderBooks

HodderBooks